Hitler

✠

Hitler

Ian Kershaw

An imprint of **Pearson Education**

Harlow, England · London · New York · Reading, Massachusetts · San Francisco
Toronto · Don Mills, Ontario · Sydney · Tokyo · Singapore · Hong Kong · Seoul
Taipei · Cape Town · Madrid · Mexico City · Amsterdam · Munich · Paris · Milan

PEARSON EDUCATION LIMITED

Head Office:
Edinburgh Gate
Harlow CM20 2JE
Tel: +44 (0)1279 623623
Fax: +44 (0)1279 431059

London Office:
128 Long Acre
London WC2E 9AN
Tel: +44 (0)20 7447 2000
Fax: +44 (0)20 7240 5771

Website: www.history-minds.com

First published in 1991
Second edition 2001

ISBN 0 582 47280 6

British Library Cataloguing in Publication Data
A CIP catalogue record for this book can be obtained from the British Library

10 9 8 7 6 5 4 3 2 1

Set in 10.5/14pt Celeste by Graphicraft Limited, Hong Kong
Produced by Pearson Education Asia Pte Ltd.
Printed and bound in Great Britain by Biddles Ltd, *www.biddles.co.uk*

The Publishers' policy is to use paper manufactured from sustainable forests.

In memory of Martin Broszat and Tim Mason

Contents

✠

Preface to the 2001 edition

✠

When, in the later 1980s, I agreed to write this contribution to what was then a newly established series of 'Profiles in Power', I had no notion that the hateful figure of Adolf Hitler would occupy so much of my waking hours for over a decade to come. (Contrary to the presumption behind the question frequently put to me, I never dreamt about him!) I had begun the initial preface to this book with the plain statement that 'this is not a biography of Hitler'. But I had immediately followed this with the comment that 'there is certainly room for a new full-scale biographical study'. After I had initially declined the invitation to write such a study, it was, in fact, the preparatory work for this short volume that convinced me that I should undertake the daunting task of writing a new biography of the most destructively influential figure of the twentieth century. Had I fully realised what I was taking on, I might have had second thoughts. As it was, the research for and writing of that biography was to take up the whole of the 1990s.

The prior writing of the 'Profiles' book was, however, of great benefit to me in conceptualising my approach to the subsequent two-volume biography.[1] Though the 'Profiles' book was overtly non-biographical, and concentrated explicitly on explaining, as I put it, 'the nature and mechanics, the character and exercise, of Hitler's dictatorial power', the interpretation which I later advanced over a much wider canvas in the biography was already prefigured here in this short work. Its essence, as explained in the Introduction, was to see Hitler as a 'charismatic leader' (in the technical usage of this term, derived from the German sociologist Max Weber).[2] As the Introduction further indicates, this was linked to the notion of 'working towards the Führer', a phrase I took from a routine speech by a Nazi functionary in 1934, implying that in a variety of ways, consciously or often subconsciously, the dynamism of the regime was pushed on by countless individuals 'second-guessing' or interpreting Hitler's presumed intentions without the need for any direct orders from the Dictator.

Taken together, these two concepts enabled me to portray Hitler as a social product, not a demonic figure. I was able to depict him as the product of a society at a particular conjuncture – a society gripped by an extraordinary and comprehensive crisis of values, an overwhelming cultural as well as political, social and economic crisis. A figure such as Hitler would have been unthinkable as Chancellor of Germany before 1914. Even though the ideas he came to embody were all in existence and gaining some ground on the political Right in the quarter of a century prior to 1914, it took the searing experience of the war, culminating in the trauma of defeat and revolution, to create the circumstances that made Hitler possible. In the fourteen years that followed, he gradually emerged as the mouthpiece of the nationalist masses. *What* he said was not original. But *how* he said it was unique. He could emotionally stir his audiences in unparalleled fashion. He was able to rouse, excite and move them with his national revivalist rhetoric in a style that no other politician, even with a similar message, was able to match. The 'nobody of Vienna' became gradually transformed into the 'Führer of the Coming Germany', the 'representative individual' of the nationalist Right,[3] embodying the fears, phobias, hatreds and prejudices, but also the hopes, ideals and illusions of rapidly widening sections of the German population. In the terminal crisis of a failed and despised democracy, Hitler offered what over 13 million Germans now saw as the hope of national salvation.

I was anxious not to underestimate Hitler's personal contribution both to his rise to power and to his exercise of that power. I was keen not to underplay the significance of his unique demagogic skills, his political instinct for the weakness of his opponents, his characteristic readiness to risk the bold forward move where others hesitated, his ability to play off rivals against each other, and, of course, his inflexible and powerful ideological tenets. But I also wanted nevertheless to emphasise the forces that allowed that power to expand to the point where it became absolute, to the point where Hitler himself could single-handedly determine – even for dictators something quite extraordinary – the condemnation of his own country to total defeat, ruin and destruction.

The concept of 'charismatic rule' enabled me, in other words, to show how Hitler 'became possible', how an individual who would have remained a piece of life's flotsam and jetsam but for the devastating impact of the First World War on German society and on himself, could come to have such an impact on a modern, sophisticated state. Together with the notion of 'working towards the Führer', it helped to show how this (for its time) advanced state could subject itself ever further to the ideology of national salvation embodied in the secular 'redeemer' figure of Hitler. The interlinked concepts allowed me to illustrate how, having become possible, Hitler could 'conquer' Germany, how his power could become absolute, could erode governmental structures and free itself from all constraints. Finally, they aided me in indicating how, once his power had become absolute, the society that had produced Hitler was no longer able to break with him. As the bonds of 'charismatic authority' largely dissolved under the growing succession of military calamities, unending destruction, and the mounting catalogue of human misery, the German people who had tied themselves to Hitler became super-numeraries in the eyes of a Dictator now determined to go down in flames rather than seek any political way out of the looming catastrophe, condemning his own country to complete ruination in the process.

Since it was first published in 1991, this short book, like the later full-scale two-volume biography, has been well received in this country and in translated versions abroad. One of my intentions in writing it had been to try to transcend what had become a somewhat sterile debate among specialists of Nazi Germany about agency and structure, polarised into what came to be dubbed the 'intentionalist' and 'structuralist' (or 'functionalist') schools of thought.[4] It is gratifying to find much agreement that my usage of the concepts of 'charismatic rule' and 'working towards the Führer' have proved useful to this end, and even more so in helping to understand more fully the extraordinary story of how Hitler could emerge from total obscurity to gain such popularity within Germany, unleash a new World War, and instigate the most terrible genocide yet known to mankind. The kind reception of my work has encouraged me to think that my approach to the phenomenon of Hitler is therefore a fruitful one. So I have not felt the need to introduce any substantial changes to the text for this new edition. In a few places, nevertheless, I have made minor amendments to incorporate the results of research published since the first appearance of the work. I have appended a brief survey of some recent developments in research on Hitler and also added a new select bibliography, incorporating, in particular, publications of special relevance or importance since the book first appeared.

Ian Kershaw
Manchester/Sheffield, June 2001

Notes and references

1. Ian Kershaw, *Hitler, 1889-1936: Hubris*, London, 1998; *Hitler, 1936-1945: Nemesis*, London, 2000.

2. See Max Weber, *Economy and Society*, ed. Guenther Roth and Claus Wittich, Berkeley/ Los Angeles, 1978, pp. 241–54, 266–71, 1111–57.

3. J. P. Stern, *Hitler. The Führer and the People*, London, 1975, pp. 9–22, esp. p. 12.

4. These terms are explained in the Introduction, and are fully examined in Ian Kershaw, *The Nazi Dictatorship. Problems and Perspectives of Interpretation*, 4th edn, London, 2000, esp. chs. 4–6.

Acknowledgements

✠

The publishers would like to express their gratitude to Peter Newark for permission to reproduce all the photographs and illustrations which appear throughout this work. These images were supplied by the following collections: Peter Newark's Pictures, Peter Newark's Historical Pictures and Peter Newark's Military Pictures.

✠

Hitler's power: an enigma

As the subject of a power profile, Hitler is by any stretch of the imagination a remarkable case. For the first thirty years of his life he was a nobody. In the remaining twenty-six years of his existence he came to leave an indelible mark on history as the dictator of Germany and instigator of a genocidal war which marked the steepest descent in civilised values known in modern times, ending with his own country and much of Europe in ruins.

Born into lower-middle-class respectability in the small Austrian border town of Braunau am Inn in 1889, Adolf Hitler's early life offered not a single hint of the figure who was to make the world hold its breath. It seemed rather to point to a future of insignificance and mediocrity.

The sixteen-year-old Hitler left his secondary school without sorrow. His years there had been unhappy ones, and his performance had ranged from poor to barely satisfactory. He failed in 1907 – a serious blow to his pride – and again the following year to gain admission to the Academy of Graphic Arts in Vienna. For the next five years or so he lived the existence of a social drop-out in the imperial capital. He was a loner with few friends and acquaintances, a fringe character convinced of his own artistic talents and embittered at a bourgeois society which had rejected them. He fled to Munich in 1913 to escape service in the Austrian army, for which he was in 1914 in any case deemed 'too weak' and unfit to serve.[1] A few months later, a well-known picture shows him as one

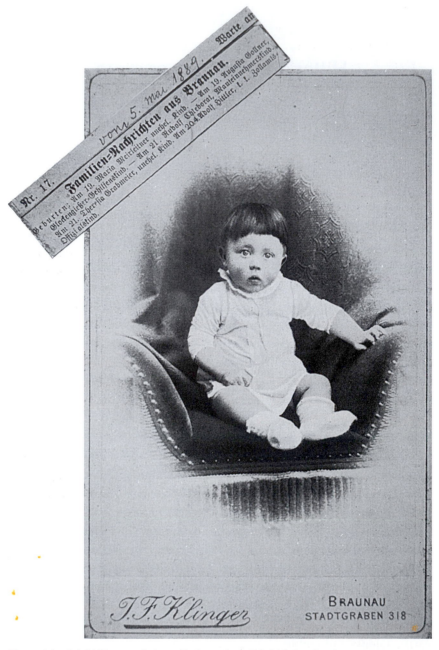

Figure I.1   Adolf Hitler as a baby, with the notice of his birth in a local newspaper.

excited face in the exultant crowd gathered in the Odeonsplatz in Munich on 2 August 1914, the day following the German declaration of war against Russia.[2]

Hitler hastened to volunteer for service in the Bavarian army. As a lance-corporal in an infantry regiment, he was distinguished twice for bravery – once with the Iron Cross First Class – and considered unfit for promotion on the grounds that he lacked leadership qualities.[3] His comrades regarded him as something of an odd-ball – quirky and introverted, brooding over Schopenhauer[4] while they talked of home and girlfriends. There was nothing to suggest he was a man going places. Whatever strong views he already held and occasionally expressed, including the need to break the 'inner internationalism' after the war,[5] few took any notice.

The war, wrote Hitler a few years later, was the 'most unforgettable' and 'greatest time' of his life.[6] In the 1940s, cooped up in his East Prussian field headquarters, the reminiscences of his lance-corporal days at the front flooded back – by then, no doubt, a substitute for the failures of the warlord. Unquestionably, the war was a crucial formative period for Hitler, an experience immeasurably strengthening the already existing amalgam of deeply ingrained prejudices and burning obsessions which fired his unpersonable personality. For one who had 'found himself' in war, news of the German defeat and revolution – received while Hitler was in a Pomeranian military hospital blinded from mustard gas – was a stunning blow. He was temporarily traumatised and unhinged. The hatred which had been welling within now burst ferociously into the open.

On release from hospital, Hitler worked for the army in routine political surveillance of extremist groups in Munich, which brought him into contact with the infant German Workers' Party, which had just been formed as one of many such sectarian extreme nationalist–racist groups. Joining what was soon to become the Nazi Party now took him into the active beerhall politics of Munich. As those around him, and Hitler himself, came to recognise an unusual talent for articulating the most vulgar populist prejudices and resentments in the most demagogically appealing fashion, the self-awareness and self-confidence of the political agitator began to take shape. It was the start of his emergence from anonymity.

Still, nothing at this date presaged his later meteoric rise. He had no political experience, no position of note, no access to the corridors of power. Yet the remaining years of his life saw Hitler attract public

Figure I.2 Hitler, aged 10, (centre, top row) in a photograph of his school-class in Leonding, 1899.

attention as a beerhall agitator; recover from ignominy after the notorious failed putsch to score a propaganda triumph in his trial, and rebuild his fractured Party after his period of imprisonment; emerge during the Depression as the head of a huge political army and a serious contender for Germany's highest office of state; establish dictatorial control within an astonishingly short time over a highly developed, elaborate and sophisticated apparatus of government; preside over an economic and military recovery which took aback supporters and opponents alike; tear up the post-war settlement of Europe and upturn world diplomacy; become the object of boundless adulation from the majority of his own people and of great admiration – and even greater detestation – from others; lead Germany, Europe and ultimately all the major world powers into a war of unprecedented destruction; hold most of the continent under his sway for four years; inspire the most terrible genocide yet experienced by mankind; and ultimately engulf his country in total military defeat and occupation, committing suicide with his land in rubble and the arch-enemy at his very door.

How could such a figure even for a few short years (if, for his adversaries, a seemingly endless period of darkness) come to direct the fortunes of one of the most economically developed and culturally advanced nations of the world? How could Hitler become for a while the most powerful man in Europe? Class, breeding, education, background all told against him. He was not even a German citizen (until citizenship was granted to him in 1932). He did not come from the sort of family which traditionally produced Germany's leaders. He did not emerge from within the usual power elites. He was a rank outsider. Deep-seated ideological phobias and an unusual demagogic talent to rouse the base instincts of the masses, coupled with some bizarre personal mannerisms, were for a long time all he seemed to have to offer. Yet within fifteen years of his emergence from total obscurity, he had supplanted the pillar of the old order, Field Marshal Hindenburg, as head of state; and within two decades of beginning his 'political career', the former lance-corporal was dispensing orders to aristocratic German generals in a second major European conflagration, soon to develop into a world war, of which he, more than any other single person, has claim to be regarded as the main author.

Hitler's power raises a number of highly complex problems. The question 'how was Hitler possible?' preoccupied contemporary opponents of Nazism and has obsessed historians ever since. Further difficult issues, beyond that of how Hitler attained power, relate to the character, extent and exercise of his power. Many contemporaries from all parts of the political spectrum, both inside and outside Germany, felt certain in 1933 that Hitler's power would be a short-lived phenomenon – that he was equipped for rabble-rousing but not for ruling, and that he would be ousted and sidelined by the traditional power groups once the immediate crisis had been overcome. That proved, of course, a fateful miscalculation. But it raises the problem of how Hitler, having become Chancellor, was able to consolidate and extend his power, and this consideration in turn provokes questions about the bases of his power, the shifts in strength which took place among the powerful groups in Germany supporting him, how such shifts affected the scope and exercise of his own power, and the effect of the peculiar form of political authority represented by Hitler upon the existing structures of government and administration. Analysis of these issues ought to allow us to assess in what relationship Hitler's power stood to the impersonal 'social forces' which shaped and conditioned it, what degree of autonomy Hitler possessed in the individual exercise of power, and the relationship of that personalised power to Germany's path into the abyss during the Second World War.

In their attempts to tackle such questions, historians have always had to face up to the difficult task of balancing the relative importance of 'personality' and impersonal 'structures' and forces in the process of historical development. Though this problem is general to the interpretation of all historical periods, it has led to particularly acute divisions in the analysis of Nazi Germany. The emphasis which historians have placed upon 'personality' or 'impersonal determinants' has characterised the whole nature of their interpretations of Hitler.[7]

At one extreme, Marxist–Leninist interpretations, produced by contemporaries in the inter-war Comintern and upheld until recently in particular by East German historians, conventionally attributed little weight to the role of personality in history. Consequently, such historians minimised the importance to be attached to the personal role of Hitler, and denied the existence of any significant practice of autonomous individualised power. Whatever power Hitler exercised, according to such an interpretation, was no more than the power of the most extreme imperialistic groups of German finance capital. These groups had 'reared' Hitler for power, paving the way for him to act as their popular mouthpiece and 'agent' in destroying the might of organised labour and providing a framework for the recovery of capitalism from its unprecedented crisis, and for the expansion which would secure the hegemony of German capitalism in Europe and ultimately the world. The 'real' rulers of Germany, according to such a scenario, were the leaders of 'big business'. Their interests – those of large-scale capitalist enterprise – shaped Nazi policy. Having installed Hitler as dictator at their behest, they continued to determine the contours within which he could act. Hitler's personal power, in such an interpretation, was a chimera. As an independent variable, it did not exist.

Such an interpretation carried little conviction among western historians. Though East German writing did much to reveal the complicity of 'big business' in Nazi rule, its inadequacies lay both in exaggerating the manipulative capacities of industrial leaders and in neglecting the problem of how, in specific circumstances, a personalistic form of rule can develop a relatively extensive independence from economic interests, ultimately subordinating them to non-economic ideological priorities.

Where a 'liberal' historiography has dominated, the role of personality has generally been accredited with far greater independent importance than is acceptable in Marxist analysis of whatever sort. Whereas historians of the German Democratic Republic produced not a single biography of Hitler, fascination with the person of the German dictator among non-Marxist writers began in his lifetime, when the first biographies were published, and shows no sign of coming to an end. The details of Hitler's life have been exhaustively researched, the component parts of his ideological 'mind-set' meticulously examined, and even his 'psychohistory' speculatively uncovered. Despite a plethora of studies, however, interpretative problems remain which, in some ways, are the obverse of those provided by Marxist–Leninist writing.

In the early post-war years, the explanation of Nazism and its baleful consequences was at times so exclusively personified in Hitler that it could seem as if an entire nation's otherwise healthy evolution had been hijacked by the diabolical influence of a single man. Former Armaments Minister Albert Speer, for example, spoke soon after the war of Hitler as a 'demonic figure', 'one of those inexplicable historical phenomena which emerge at rare intervals among mankind', whose 'person determined the fate of the nation'.[8] Such a demonisation of Hitler has long since given way to a more sophisticated understanding of his place in modern German history. But even the best biographies have seemed at times in danger of elevating Hitler's personal power to a level where the history of Germany between 1933 and 1945 becomes reduced to little more than an expression of the dictator's will. The Third Reich, in such a perspective, can appear to be merely old-fashioned personal tyranny in modern dress.

Figure I.3   Hitler in a jubilant crowd in Odeonsplatz, Munich, 2 August 1914, the day after Germany had declared war on Russia.

The contrast of the biographical approach, at the one extreme, with the impersonalistic Marxist-Leninist approach, at the other extreme, could scarcely be more stark. Whereas in East German historiography Hitler figured as little more than a cypher of capitalist interests, the leading West German biography of Hitler[9] practically ignores capitalist interests, which are implicitly if not explicitly seen as wholly subordinated to his political and ideological dictates. Hitler's power, in these polarised interpretations, was, it seems, either a wholly negligible element, or so supreme a factor that the whole Nazi phenomenon can be summarily depicted as 'Hitlerism'.

The alleged personalisation of Nazism through an excessive concern with Hitler's ideological intentions and motive has, in fact, continued to be a central focus of debate among historians of the Third Reich. From a non-dogmatic, and non-Leninist, Marxist position it has been candidly admitted that 'we do not yet have even the makings of a marxist account of the personal power of the fascist leader in the inter-war years'.[10] Debate about Hitler's role, and about the nature and extent of his personal power, has largely, therefore, been the province of non-Marxist scholars.

Approaches are now commonly regarded as falling into two main categories, which have come to be dubbed – not altogether satisfactorily – 'intentionalist' and 'structuralist' (or 'functionalist'). In the 'intentionalist' clutch of interpretations, Hitler's supreme power as 'master in the Third Reich'[11] is taken for granted, and the history of Nazism in power is seen as the history of the programmed and consequential implementation of Hitler's ideological intentions. As one leading exponent put it, 'it was indeed Hitler's *Weltanschauung* and nothing else that mattered in the end'.[12] In such an interpretation, Hitler is conceived as a classical embodiment of power in a totalitarian state.

The contrasting approach has, on the other hand, highlighted the conditioning of political decisions by 'structural' constraints, such as economic limitations on freedom of manoeuvre, or by the specific 'functioning' of key components of Nazi rule, as in Hitler's inbuilt need to avoid any action which might threaten his standing and prestige. Hitler's ideology has been seen less as a 'programme' consistently implemented than as a loose framework for action which only gradually stumbled into the shape of realisable objectives. These considerations have led to emphasis being placed upon the unclear processes of decision-making in a chaotic system of rule. Hitler's scope for action, the degree of his personal autonomy from constraining factors, and the extent to which he actively intervened in shaping policy have, consequently, been called

while some argue that he knew what the people wanted, he

seriously into question. In this light, Hitler has been depicted as 'unwilling to take decisions, frequently uncertain, exclusively concerned with upholding his prestige and personal authority, influenced in the strongest fashion by his current entourage'. Far from being a leader of unrestrained personal power, it has been suggested, Hitler might be better regarded as 'in some respects a weak dictator'.[13] *Hitler wasn't that great.*

In heuristic terms, the polarisation of the debate has often served a useful purpose. At times, however, it has appeared sterile. At any event, it seems time to move on. We can begin by accepting unequivocally the unique place of Hitler in the course of German history between 1933 and 1945. Would a terroristic police state under Himmler and the SS have been erected without Hitler as head of government? Would Germany have been engaged in general war by the end of the 1930s under a different form of authoritarian regime? Would discrimination against Jews have culminated in genocide under a different head of state? In each case, it seems highly improbable. Hitler, one can then suggest at the outset, was crucial to these developments. But in historical explanation *both* the intentions of the leading actors *and* the external conditions which promote or negate those intentions are centrally important. The motives, aims and intentions of powerful political leaders are indeed of vital significance. But they are not 'free-floating'. They have to operate for the most part in circumstances which extend beyond the control and manipulation of any single historical personage, however great the political power possessed by that individual.

The chapters which follow start from the premiss that Hitler's personal power was indeed real, not a phantasm. But they interpret the extent and expression of that power in large measure as the product of the collaboration and tolerance, miscalculations and weakness of others in positions of power and influence. And they suggest that the progressive extension of Hitler's power, which reached the point where its exclusively destructive potential became all-consuming and wholly antagonistic to the preservation of rational political authority, was mainly the consequence of the concessions and capitulations which others were prepared to make. Examination of Hitler's power cannot, then, begin and end with Hitler. The actions of others, and the conditions shaping those actions, are also vitally important.

A prominent Nazi declared in 1934 that in the Third Reich it was 'the duty of everybody to try to work towards the Führer along the lines he would wish'.[14] Fanatical followers of Hitler took this literally. But many of the less committed were by their actions also wittingly or unwittingly, subjectively or objectively, 'working towards the Führer' in promoting the circumstances in which his power became unconstrained and his vague or 'utopian' ideological imperatives found implementation as government practice. The exercise of Hitler's power, this suggests, was heavily conditioned by his *symbolic* power as Führer. The readiness to accept a level of personalised power quite extraordinary in modern state systems and to 'work towards' the person wielding such power lies, therefore, at the root of our enquiry.

'Power' can be abstractly defined as 'the probability that one actor within a social relationship will be in a position to carry out his own will despite resistance'.[15] The complex organism of the modern state contains a whole series of interlinked, but relatively autonomous, power bases. Apart from the domain of political power (in a narrow sense) residing in the bureaucratic, executive, judicial and administrative apparatus of the state itself, partially autonomous spheres of military power, economic power and ideological power may – all or each of them – uphold or undermine the current form of political domination.[16] 'Domination' (or 'rule') is 'the probability that a command will receive prompt and automatic obedience in stereotyped forms, on the part of a given group of persons'.[17]

As defined here, 'power' is a relative, not absolute, concept. The mastery gained by one person or group is at the expense of the loss of power of another person or group. This does not, of course, rule out the possibility – even likelihood – that two or more persons or groups could extend their own power, at least temporarily, at the cost of a third party. In the case of the Third Reich, this could be taken to indicate that not only Hitler and the Nazi Party, but also the traditional power elites – able through the entente with Nazism to refurbish in some measure their own power base – profited from the loss of power of democratic institutions.

With the progressive destruction of any 'rational' structures for the distribution of power, the further consolidation of one element of power at the expense of others is likely. In the Third Reich, the initial 'power cartel' comprising both Nazi factions and groupings of the non-Nazi traditional national-conservative elites engaged during the following years in ceaseless internal power struggles, from which certain radical factions emerged as the strongest. Their success usually owed much to their direct dependence upon Hitler's patronage. But, conversely, Hitler's own power position was greatly strengthened by the success of those elements in the 'power cartel' of the Third Reich which owed most to him and were the most radical executive agents of policy directly related to his ideological

11

Figure I.4   Hitler (front left) with comrades from the 16th Bavarian Reserve Infantry Regiment.

imperatives. A distributive notion of power can, in other words, help in conceptualising the process by which Hitler's power *gradually* became absolute at the expense of other elements in the power equation in Nazi Germany.

A key to an understanding of the gradual expansion of Hitler's power can be found in another concept of Max Weber: that of 'charismatic rule'. This concept, as it will be deployed (derived and in some cases amended from Max Weber) in the chapters to follow, makes use of 'charisma' in a specific technical sense which is not equatable with the loose application of the term, for instance, to democratic politicians or other figures in the public eye possessed of a striking or attractive personality. In contrast to domination resting on the 'traditional authority' of hereditary rulers, or the impersonal bureaucracy of 'legal authority' which characterises most modern political systems, 'charismatic authority' is founded upon the perceptions – by a 'following' of believers – of heroism, greatness, and a 'mission' in a proclaimed 'leader'. Unlike the other two forms of domination, 'charismatic rule' is inherently unstable. It tends to arise in crisis conditions, and is subject to collapse on two major counts: either through failure to live up to expectations, or by becoming 'routinised' into a system capable of reproducing itself only through the elimination, subordination or subsumption of the 'charismatic' essence.[18]

Though Max Weber was writing before Hitler appeared on the political scene, his concept of 'charismatic rule' has implications for both the sources and the exercise of Hitler's power. It is valuable in comprehending the character of Hitler's power base within the Nazi Movement and the corrosive impact of that power when superimposed upon a contradictory form of domination – the legal, bureaucratic framework of the German state apparatus.

From a Marxist perspective, it has been claimed that the notion of 'charismatic rule' is difficult to reconcile with the existence of a modern capitalist state.[19] Indeed, it does seem that the exercise of 'charismatic domination' stands in contradiction to the forms of regulated government necessary for the *reproduction* of capitalism. However, the emergence of 'charismatic' claims to power, and the nature and function of the 'charismatic' expression of power, can without difficulty be grasped within capitalist state systems *in crisis.* Here, Max Weber's insights – though he was for the most part drawing upon examples of 'charismatic authority' far removed from the political systems of the twentieth century – have relevance to the peculiar characteristics of fascist forms of leadership, and of the unstable power base of the fascist-style state.

In the modern capitalist state system, political power usually rests upon the occupation of a particular office, and the function which that office serves. It is, basically, *impersonal* power. The bureaucratic, impersonal exercise of power residing upon a basis of equally impersonal legal norms is the core of what Max Weber outlined as the 'legal—rational' framework of domination. In the context, however, of a socio-economic crisis of the scale of that afflicting Germany in the early 1930s which, enveloping a political system never from the outset fully accepted by important sections of German society, rapidly developed into a *crisis of the state itself*, this very impersonal basis of the functional exercise of power could come under frontal attack and be decried by those who felt that they had suffered most through it. The consequence was the violent lurch, in the terminal crisis of the Weimar Republic, to a widespread (if far from all-pervasive) readiness to accept an entirely different system of government based upon the exercise of *personal* power associated with *personal* responsibility.[20] Such a putative system can be described by the concept of 'charismatic domination'.

It seems clear that this form of rule in a modern state system could only be the product of the most severe crisis conditions imaginable, and that it could not supplant a modern bureaucracy but had to be superimposed upon it. It is also difficult to imagine how it could create a lasting structure for the perpetuation of personalised domination. Its transience, as an attempted crisis solution ultimately doomed to failure, cannot, however, mask the fact that in the circumstances such as Germany offered in the early 1930s it could develop as a force of extraordinary and consuming potency, and establish itself as an agent of unusually dynamic corrosive and destructive capability.

The concept of 'charismatic domination' says nothing in itself about the *content* of a specific 'claim' to leadership and the reasons for the acceptance of such a claim. These vary according to circumstances, background and the particular form of 'political culture'. A psychological factor of some general importance to the prevalence of fascist-style 'charismatic' forms of leadership claim in the 1920s and 1930s was the relatively recent collapse of monarchies accompanied, however, in some sections of society, by the remnants of a quasi-religious hankering after a 'god-given' form of supreme authority, which could now be clothed in new, more populist, garb. In addition, the traumatic impact of war and its accompanying hypertrophied militaristic and chauvinistic values provided a general condition in which 'heroic' leadership claims could find a hearing.

The specific features of the German variant of 'charismatic domination' – those distinguishing it, for example, from the Duce cult under Mussolini, or from the personality cults surrounding Stalin and other leaders in the differently structured communist systems – derive from the interaction of the all-embracing crisis experienced in Germany after the First World War (and particularly in the early 1930s) with particular traits of German political culture. A 'national' history often seen as a lengthy prehistory of belatedly and partially attained national unity, shaped largely by wars (triumphant or disastrous) on 'German' soil, and heavily featuring discontinuities, disunity and division, left a proneness – particularly but not solely in bourgeois circles – to a heroicisation of politics. The pantheon of German national heroes, apart from cultural giants such as Goethe or Beethoven, was more or less exclusively populated by figures, mythical or mythologised, who had won famous victories furthering the ultimate ideal of a united German Reich.[21]

Heroic images of Frederick the Great or Bismarck stood out in even sharper relief given the disappointments of the reign of Kaiser Wilhelm II, the trauma of defeat in war, revolution and conquest of the state by the hated socialists, the 'national disgrace' of Versailles, the spectacle of a once-powerful nation wracked by inflation then depression, and the perception of Weimar democracy as a system ridden by division and party-political squabbling. By the 1920s, before Hitler came to prominence, a longing for a new great leader – sometimes envisaged as the embodiment of warrior, high-priest and statesman – was a commonplace on the German Right. Such a leader, it was imagined, would rid Germany of its divisions, restoring the Reich – a term which itself had acquired mystical connotations – to unity and greatness.

By the early 1930s and the onset of the crisis which provided for a wider currency for such ideas, a claimant touting the 'heroic' qualities which 'charismatic' leadership demands, and backed by an organisation bearing all the hallmarks of a 'charismatic community', was on hand.

The 'charismatic community' comprised in the first instance those closest to Hitler – the immediate 'following' among the Nazi leadership elite – who formed the initial agency of transmission of the personality cult surrounding him. Their relationship with Hitler was not determined by any impersonal, formal office which he held as Party leader, but by bonds of personal loyalty of an archaic, quasi-feudal kind, deriving from their recognition of his 'mission' and his 'achievements', and reciprocated by Hitler because of his own high level of dependence upon his most trusted 'paladins'.

Figure I.5 Hitler (second from right, back row) recovering from a leg wound during convalescence at Beelitz, near Berlin, in October 1916. His medical tag is attached.

Outside the narrow group of Nazi leaders, the main bearers of Hitler's 'charisma' were the activists of the Movement, the chief carriers and purveyors of the message of his 'great deeds'. Further crucial bearers and exploiters of Hitler's 'charisma' were the leaders and functionaries of those organisations – the most important of which was the SS – which owed their own existence and expansion of power to their close attachment to the Führer. Beyond them was the mass of 'Hitler believers' in the population at large, whose adulation provided Hitler with a platform of popularity which greatly strengthened his position of power. Even the reluctant admirers, the lukewarm who nevertheless saw no alternative, and the opportunists ready to shout 'Heil Hitler' louder than anyone if it was to their own advantage to do so, objectively contributed to the enhancement of the 'charismatic' Führer cult.

A power profile of Hitler must explore the attainment, consolidation and expansion of 'charismatic power', its twin bases in repression and acclamation, and its expression and impact when it had reached its peak of relative autonomy and absolutism. Our enquiry must also incorporate the concessions made to 'charismatic rule' by those non-Nazi elites who had little belief in it but were, for their own reasons, prepared to embrace it or at least tolerate it, until their own power ambitions were swallowed up, overrun or bypassed by it. It will, finally, have to examine the destructive force of 'charismatic' power – the way it eroded all 'rational' structures and patterns of government and administration, culminating in the ultimate 'running amok'[22] of the 'charismatic community' once the power base was collapsing.

The underlying thread to our enquiry into the establishment, magnification and dissolution of Hitler's power lies in the inbuilt corrosive impact of 'charismatic rule' upon the 'rational–legal' basis of political authority – the destructive influence of arbitrary personalised power upon impersonal, regulated forms of domination.

Our examination of the process by which such an unlikely figure as Hitler could come to wield such extraordinary personalised power has to begin by considering how 'charismatic' qualities became attached to him. A key point was unquestionably the perceived appropriateness of his personal attributes to the demands of the situation; the matching of his promise of salvation to the expectations of solution to the crisis. We have to start, therefore, by looking at the very promise of salvation itself. How did Hitler perceive his 'mission', and why did his early little band of devotees see in him the answer to Germany's needs?

17

Notes and references

1. Werner Maser, *Hitlers Briefe und Notizen*, Düsseldorf, 2nd edn, 1988, p. 42.

2. Maser, *Briefe*, p. 59. The demonstration in Munich is usually dated to 1 August. For the correct dating to 2 August, see A. Joachimstaler, *Korrektur einer Biographie. Adolf Hitler 1908–1920*, Munich, 1989, p. 100.

3. Fritz Wiedemann, *Der Mann, der Feldherr werden wollte*, Velbert/Kettwig, 1964, p. 26.

4. Hans Frank, *Im Angesicht des Galgens*, Munich/Gräfelfing, 1953, p. 46.

5. Maser, *Briefe*, pp. 100–1.

6. MK, p. 179.

7. For an excellent survey of historiography on Hitler, see Gerhard Schreiber, *Hitler. Interpretationen 1923–1983*, Darmstadt, 1984.

8. Cited in H. R. Trevor-Roper, *The Last Days of Hitler*, 3rd edn, London, 1962, p. 46.

9. Joachim C. Fest, *Hitler. Eine Biographie*, Frankfurt am Main/Berlin, 1973.

10. Tim Mason, 'Open Questions on Nazism', in Raphael Samuel (ed.), *People's History and Socialist Theory*, London, 1981, p. 205. Since the fall of the Berlin Wall, such a biography has been attempted by two historians from the former German Democratic Republic, Kurt Pätzold and Manfred Weißbecker, *Adolf Hitler. Eine politische Biographie*, Leipzig, 1995.

11. Norman Rich, *Hitler's War Aims*, 2 vols, London, 1973--4, vol. 1, p. 11.

12. Karl Dietrich Bracher, 'The role of Hitler: perspectives of interpretation', in Walter Laqueur (ed.), *Fascism. A Reader's Guide*, Harmondsworth, 1979, p. 201.

13. Hans Mommsen, 'Nationalsozialismus', in C. D. Hernig (ed.), *Sowjetsystem und demokratische Gesellschaft. Eine vergleichende Enzyklopädie*, 7 vols, Freiburg/Basel/Vienna, 1966–72, vol. 4, column 702.

14. '. . . die Pflicht eines jeden, zu versuchen, im Sinne des Führers ihm entgegen zu arbeiten.' Niedersächsisches Staatsarchiv, Oldenburg, Best. 131 Nr 303, f. 131v, speech of Werner Willikens, State Secretary in the Ministry of Food, 21 Feb. 1934; transl. N&P, ii, 207.

15. Max Weber, *Economy and Society*, ed. Guenther Roth and Claus Wittich, Berkeley/Los Angeles, 1978, p. 53.

16. See Michael Mann, *The Sources of Social Power*, vol. 1, Cambridge, 1986, ch. 1.

17. Weber, p. 53.

18. See Weber, pp. 241–6.

19. Mason, 'Open questions', p. 207.

20. See André Gorz, *Farewell to the Working Class*, London, 1982, pp. 58–9, 62–3.

21. See Norbert Elias, *Studien über die Deutschen*, Frankfurt am Main, 1989, pp. 425, 412–52.

22. The phrase is that of Hans Mommsen, 'Hitlers Stellung im nationalsozialistischen Herrschaftssystem', in Gerhard Hirschfeld and Lothar Kettenacker (eds.), *Der Führerstaat: Mythos und Realität*, Stuttgart, 1981, p. 70.

✠

Chapter 1

Power of the 'Idea'

Hitler's personality should not be overrated as a factor in his power. Nor, however, should it be ignored. Its greatest impact was upon the circle of the earliest, most fanatically devoted followers, his most committed 'inner circle' of disciples. Looking for a cause and a leader before they 'found' Nazism and Hitler, they formed the core of the 'charismatic community' which saw greatness in Hitler.

The 'charisma' in Hitler's own personality, so influential among his close followers, was rooted in the power which flowed – for those already open to it – from his 'idea', his political credo, together with the remarkable ability he showed from the moment he entered active politics to sway the masses. In this chapter, therefore, we examine the emergence of the 'conviction politician', and the response to the personality and ideas of Hitler of his early followers who became some of the most important personages in the Third Reich.

In physical appearance, Hitler was unprepossessing.[1] He was of medium height and fair complexion. His head seemed to dominate the whole of his body. His high forehead was concealed by the drooping forelock. The centre-point of his face seemed to be his trimmed moustache. He never looked smartly dressed. His teeth were poor and in later years the deterioration in his formerly good eyesight eventually necessitated him wearing reading glasses (though he was anxious not to be seen in public in them). His slightly protruding eyes and unblinking gaze were his most striking feature.

Hitler's personal habits were repetitive, conservative, but at the same time rather quirky. He held as far as possible to fixed daily routines, was near teetotal and (from the early 1930s onwards) vegetarian, did not smoke or drink coffee, and had a fetish for cleanliness which saw him washing with abnormal frequency. He needed little sleep, read avidly and widely (though unsystematically), and possessed an extraordinary memory for factual detail. He monopolised conversation with opinion-ated views on a wide range of subjects. On anything connected with history, art and architecture, he considered himself particularly expert. He was also especially interested in medicine and biology. His reliance upon his self-learning went hand in hand with an utter contempt for 'intellectuals' dependent upon a formal education. There is no doubt, however, that, though his knowledge was half-baked, one-sided and dogmatically inflexible, he was intelligent and sharp-witted.

Though, even in his regular entourage, Hitler remained in human terms distant and unapproachable, he could show great consideration in trivial matters, such as what to give his secretaries as birthday presents. He liked the company of women, and was invariably courteous and gracious towards them, especially if they were beautiful. He could make those around him laugh with a cutting humour and a talent for mimicry. And he had a strong sense of loyalty towards those of his comrades who had endured sacrifices to support him from the early days.

These personal characteristics would have been insufficient to single out Hitler for attention had they existed in isolation from his political world view and his ability to sway an audience by the force of his public speaking. Seen in purely personal terms, detached from his political philosophy, Hitler was indeed a mediocrity. But his political creed and the conviction with which he expressed it transformed him into a personality of quite extraordinary dynamism.

It was for long thought after the collapse of the Third Reich that Hitler's message consisted of no more than the empty phrases of the power-thirsty demagogue, that the man behind the message was as devoid of genuine ideas as were the classical tyrants of old. It is now universally recognised, however, that behind the vague missionary appeal lay a set of interrelated ideas – however repulsive and irrational – which congealed by the mid 1920s into a cohesive ideology. While Hitler's fixed ideas, which remained unchanged in essentials down to his death in 1945, could not individually or in themselves go far towards explaining his mass appeal, or the growth of the NSDAP, they did amount to a personal driving-force of unusual strength. They provided Hitler with the all-encompassing world view which gave him the opportunity exclusivist ideologies offer of ordering every idea within his own comprehensive philosophy and of ruling out as absolutely untenable any alternative proposals. They gave him, too, the 'missionary' zeal of the leader who appears to combine the vision with the certainty that his path is the right one – in fact, the only one which can be taken.

Though he was often indecisive about precise political actions, Hitler never wavered about the certainty of his ideas. To those in his proximity, who shared his general prejudices, the strength and certainty of conviction, extending beyond that of the average bigot or crank into a grandiose and irrevocable formula for a glorious future, was a major factor in establishing his personal supremacy. The simplicity of his dualistic world-view of a Manichean struggle between good and evil in which everything was reduced to absolutes – all or nothing – was matched by the fanatical ferocity and unyielding tenacity with which his views were upheld. Such 'attributes' made him a notable figure in the circles of the *völkisch* Right in which he mixed in the early 1920s. And the fact that his public appearances rapidly made him the leading propaganda exponent of such views and opened up contacts to leading circles of Munich's moneyed bourgeoisie made him indispensable and assured him of the support of others on the extreme Right.

The essence of Hitler's personal world-view comprised a belief in history as racial struggle, radical antisemitism, a conviction that Germany's future could be secured only through conquest of *Lebensraum* ('living space') at the expense of Russia, and the uniting of all these strands in the notion of a life-or-death fight to the finish with Marxism – most concretely embodied in the 'Jewish Bolshevism' of the Soviet Union. These interlocking ideas were significant not only in the sense that they were held to with extraordinary tenacity for over twenty years, but above all in that the ideological aims arising from them came to be put into actual practice during the Second World War. We have to take them seriously, therefore, in an evaluation of Hitler's power. Before proceeding further we need to look at their formation, development and content.

Exactly when, how and why Hitler's fanatically held ideas took their hold on him is far from clear. But the gradual forging of the various strands of his thinking into a composite ideology was completed by the time of the writing of *Mein Kampf* in 1924–5, and scarcely wavered thereafter. An important formative period was his time in Linz in 1905–6 after leaving school and especially in Vienna from 1907 to 1913. The experience of war and, quite traumatically, of Germany's defeat was a second,

21

even more vital influence upon Hitler. Finally, the years 1920 to 1924 saw some crucial modifications to his ideas, under the impact, not least, of the Russian civil war.

Hitler's deepest hatred was of the Jews. The roots and causes of his visceral antisemitism have been much discussed but can still not be established with absolute certainty. Some theories are outrightly fanciful. The notion that Hitler's anti-Jewish paranoia can be attributable to the fact that he himself was of part-Jewish descent is without foundation.[2] That he feared or believed that his father's father had been Jewish is more plausible, but cannot be proved.[3] Even more speculative is the attempt to link Hitler's pathological hatred of Jews to his hysterical trauma while suffering from mustard gas poisoning at the end of the First World War, which he allegedly associated with the death of his mother in 1907 following a gas anaesthetic delivered by a Jewish doctor.[4] Apart from the fact that Hitler had been grateful enough to the doctor at the time to give him one of his water-colour paintings as a present,[5] this theory presumes that Hitler was not antisemitic during his Vienna days.

In fact, we remain in the dark about why Hitler became a manic antisemite. Psychological explanations revolving around sexual fantasies and a persecution complex bear differing degrees of plausibility but ultimately amount to no more than guesswork. All that can with some certainty be presumed is that Hitler's personal frustrations at the discrepancy between his own self-esteem and his drop-out existence as a failed artist and social outsider found a focus in an ever stronger negative image which provided both explanation for his own failure and also 'proof' that history was ultimately on his side.[6]

Hitler's own story, retailed in *Mein Kampf*, tells of his conversion to antisemitism after encountering a kaftan-garbed figure with black hair locks in the streets of Vienna.[7] This was almost certainly a dramatisation. Hitler was already reading pan-German anti-Semitic newspapers in his Linz days and was even then an admirer of the Austrian antisemite and pan-German leader Georg von Schönerer.[8] But there seems no reason to doubt that whatever views he already had on Jews were inordinately strengthened while he was in Vienna. At this time he became greatly impressed by the vehemently antisemitic demagogue Karl Lueger, the mayor of the city, whom he later described, in a rare show of admiration for others, as 'the greatest German mayor of all times'.[9] Though the 'Kaftan Jew' story is almost certainly a fabrication, it is hard to imagine that Hitler's exposure to the poisonous antisemitic atmosphere of Vienna and the stridently anti-Jewish literature he soaked up at the time did not serve to confirm and sharpen his embryonic prejudice. According to his own account, from this time onwards 'wherever I went, I began to see Jews, and the more I saw, the more sharply they became distinguished in my eyes from the rest of humanity'.[10] It seems unlikely that Hitler's 'conversion' to antisemitism was as rapid or complete as he claimed in his own, later account in *Mein Kampf*. But the seeds were sown in Vienna.

The Vienna years were also a formative period in the development of other aspects of Hitler's world-view. According to his own account – plausible in its general tone if not accurate in detail – his own 'drifting' existence among the Viennese underprivileged meant that he tasted the crass social injustices of bourgeois society at first hand, and plunged him thereby into contemplation of the 'social question'. His encounters with Viennese social democracy led to a violent rejection of its class-based, anti-nationalist doctrine. His detestation of the Habsburg monarchy was part of his already pronounced, fanatical German hypernationalism which he had soaked up since his attachment to the Schönerer movement in his Linz days.[11] Once his 'recognition' of the Jew as the 'culprit' for all these ills took its place as the dominant ingredient, the essentials of an ideology based on burning revulsion towards existing society coupled with a utopian vision of a future order to be created by the strong and ruthless authority of an ethnically German national state began to slot into place. A core element – the social Darwinistic view of history as a struggle between individual races with victory going to the strongest, fittest and most ruthless – seems to have occupied its place at the centre of this world-view by 1914–18 at the latest.[12] His hysterical reaction, while lying blinded in the Pasewalk hospital, at the news of the triumph of the forces he hated with all the fibre of his being appears to have led to an intensification of his already fixed dualistic world-view – above all, his conviction that guilt for the catastrophe which had befallen him and all he believed in lay at the door of the ubiquitous Jew.[13]

Hitler had apparently earlier discussed with one of his comrades at the front whether after the war he would become an architect or a politician.[14] While in the military hospital, he claimed, he took the decision to become a politician.[15] In reality, the 'decision' to involve himself in active politics came less self-consciously and more indirectly. Still in the army, he returned to a Munich scarcely recognisable from the city he had left in 1914. Political conditions were in turmoil. After the revolution, government had been headed by a left-wing socialist, Kurt Eisner, a Jew. The assassination of Eisner in February 1919 by a young right-wing aristocrat led to political chaos and a republic of Soldiers' and Workers' Councils –

Figure 1.1 A poster announcing Hitler's speech on 'Germany's Future and Our Movement' at the refoundation of the Nazi Party in the Bürgerbräukeller in Munich, 27 February 1925.

several of whose leaders were Jewish – being proclaimed in April; and this in turn was within weeks bloodily overthrown by forces of the paramilitary Right.

Hitler refrained from any active involvement. But from his army barracks, he observed what was taking place and read widely in right-wing tracts, which presumably confirmed his own diagnosis of events. During the late spring and summer he attended army indoctrination courses. These introduced him to deeper consideration of the workings of international finance capital – a topic on which he was influenced by the ideas of Gottfried Feder, the economic 'guru' of the early Nazi Party. He also attended lectures and seminars on German history, socialism in theory and practice, the economic situation and the peace conditions, Russia under Bolshevik rule, price policy, and the question of Bavaria and Reich unity. He became noted for his impassioned and opinionated views.

Hitler's own awareness of the impact he had as a speaker in such circles constituted his own first step into active politics. And when he himself was assigned to work in the army 'educational unit', he was singled out as 'a born popular speaker who through his fanaticism and populist style positively compelled his audience to take note and share his views'.[16] 'All at once,' noted Hitler, 'I was offered an opportunity of speaking before a larger audience; and the thing that I had always presumed from pure feeling without knowing it was now corroborated: I could "speak".'[17] It was above all in autumn 1919, as Hitler came into contact with the newly formed German Workers' Party and began to realise what an impact he could have on an audience, that his way into politics – though only on the beerhall fringes – opened up.

At the time that Hitler began to make his mark as a populist demagogue in the Munich beerhalls, his political views – though held and expressed with extraordinary fanaticism – remained the conventional fare of the extreme Right. There was nothing to distinguish them from those of the pan-Germans or of other vehemently racist–nationalist groups which abounded in Munich at that time. Agitation against the Versailles Treaty dominated his early speeches. He demanded – as did all pan-Germans – the return of the lost colonies, and the uniting of Germany and Austria. France and Britain, not Russia, were seen as the main enemies of Germany. And the Jews were attacked above all as the agents of finance capital. Hitler himself claimed that his world-view had already been decisively built before the war. But vital steps towards the completed ideology still remained to be taken in the early 1920s. In particular, his ideas on the direction of Germany's future foreign policy, on the Jews, and not least on his own future leadership role, underwent significant modification between his entry into politics and the writing of *Mein Kampf.*

Apart from his own voracious – if unsystematic and one-sided –reading, which included influential social–Darwinist and geopolitical tracts, a crucial part in amending Hitler's thinking in these years was played by the Bavarian poet Dietrich Eckart, and by the Baltic Germans Max Erwin von Scheubner-Richter and Alfred Rosenberg. Eckart contributed his own philosophy of struggle to overcome 'soulless Jewishness' as the prerequisite of a genuine revolution – in contrast to the 'false' revolution of 1918 – which would bring forth new leaders and true socialism. Rosenberg and Scheubner-Richter were even more influential in focusing Hitler's mind on the 'Jewishness' of Russian Bolshevism. Both had experienced the Russian Revolution, both were extreme antisemites, and both were in touch with violently anti-Bolshevik circles. In the early ideology of the Nazi Party, neither Russia nor Bolshevism had figured prominently. But now, Rosenberg acquainted Hitler with the ideas of a 'Jewish world conspiracy' contained in the forged 'Protocols of the Elders of Zion'. And the two Balts played a decisive role in cementing in Hitler's mind the notion of the Jewish essence of Bolshevism. This provided the keystone to the edifice of Hitler's ideology. By the time we reach *Mein Kampf*, the extirpation of 'Jewish Bolshevism' has become synonymous with the destruction of the Soviet Union in the German quest for 'living space'.

The shifts in Hitler's world-view between 1919 and 1924 can be followed in his speeches and writings over this period. Under the influence of Rosenberg and Scheubner-Richter, the relationship of antisemitism and anti-Marxism in Hitler's thinking underwent a transformation during these years. Though both strands of thought had already long been present in his mind – with antisemitism dominant – they became systematically conjoined only in this period through the catalytic image of Bolshevik Russia.

Before the fusion with anti-Marxism, Hitler's vicious antisemitism had, in his public speeches, initially focused more intensively upon anti-capitalism. His first noted public comments on the 'Jewish Question' occurred in August 1919 in the context of a 'lecture' on capitalism, while he was employed by the Reichswehr to provide political indoctrination for 'unreliable' soldiers returning from captivity.[18] It was also in this capacity that his superior officer asked him, a few weeks later, to reply to an enquiry on the 'Jewish problem'. In his letter, the earliest surviving text of his statement on the subject, Hitler spoke of the Jews as a race, not a religious group, and of the need to combat them by rational means, not simply on the basis of emotion. This would necessitate the removal of their legal rights and ultimately the 'removal of the Jews altogether'.[19] Jewish power was seen as the power of money, 'the gleam of gold'. Marxism was not mentioned, though Hitler regarded the Jews as the driving force behind the revolution and social democracy. While the exclusion of legal rights for Jews was prominently expressed in the Nazi Party programme of February 1920, again there was explicit mention neither of Marxism nor of Bolshevism.

The heavy concentration upon Jewish finance capital in Hitler's early speeches was linked to his allegations of the responsibility of the Jews for the war, the defeat and the millions of German dead. So fundamental was this point to his thinking that later, in a notorious passage in *Mein Kampf*, he claimed that the lives of a million Germans killed at the front could have been saved if 'twelve to fifteen thousand of these Hebrew corrupters of the people had been held under poison gas'.[20] The fury at 'Jewish' war financiers dominated many of his early speeches. There were repeated intense attacks upon usurers, profiteers, racketeers and parasites. Over and again he demanded hanging for Jewish racketeers.[21] Genuine socialism for him, stated Hitler, meant to be an antisemite.[22] Under Feder's influence, he distinguished between essentially healthy industrial capital and flourishing 'Jewish finance capital', which constituted the real evil. Once 'Jewish Bolshevism' had been incorporated into this thinking, international capital was seen as working hand in hand with the 'international element in Soviet Russia' against German national interests.[23]

In speech after speech Hitler denounced the Jews in the most vicious terms. He rejected, as he had done in his letter of September 1919, emotional 'pogrom' antisemitism as the answer to the problem, but said Germans should be prepared to enter a pact with the devil if necessary in order to extirpate the evil of Jewry.[24] He demanded the basic solution: 'removal of the Jews from our people'.[25] He spoke of the prevention of the 'Jewish undermining of our people' by internment in concentration camps.[26] His language, violent in the extreme, became coloured with biological terminology suggestive of the eradication of germs. He proclaimed in August 1920:

> Don't think that you can combat an illness without killing its causative organ, without destroying the bacillus, and don't think that you can combat racial tuberculosis without seeing to it that the people is freed from the causative organ of racial tuberculosis. The impact of Jewry will

never pass away, and the poisoning of the people will not end, as long as the causal agent, the Jew, is not removed from our midst.[27]

In a speech to the SA in February 1922, Hitler stated that in his view only the 'single, total and exclusive' concern with the 'Jewish Question' mattered, and a few months later summed up the entire Party programme in the one point that no Jew could be a people's comrade.[28] But a change of emphasis had taken place in his expressions of antisemitism. Under the influence of events in Russia, Hitler's main target switched from the Jews as the exponents of international finance capital – not that he ever forgot or ignored this element of his antisemitism – to the Jews as the power behind Marxism, and explicitly behind Marxism's practical political manifestation in Soviet Bolshevism. Either way, as the controller of international capital or as the controller of Bolshevik Marxism, the 'Jewish world conspiracy' presented Hitler with the image of an indomitable foe. But compared with his dismissal of effete bourgeois democracy, Marxism in its Bolshevik manifestation amounted to a *Weltanschauung* which, in all its ruthless brutality, he could comprehend as a formidable force. It offered him a vision of the future which, in his eyes, only the racial struggle under Germany's leadership could prevent.

By the time of his trial for high treason in spring 1924, following the failed putsch attempt on 8–9 November 1923 when, in the Bürgerbräukeller in Munich, he had proclaimed a national revolution in the hope of overthrowing the Reich government, Hitler was telling the court that what he wanted to be was the breaker of Marxism, and asserting that the Nazi Movement knew only one enemy, the mortal enemy of Marxism.[29] The Jews were not mentioned. When the change in tone was noted by the 'Jewish' press and Hitler was asked about it, he replied in typical fashion that he had indeed changed his stance: while working on *Mein Kampf*, he had realised that he had hitherto been too mild, and that the 'Jewish Question' was not of concern solely for the German people, but for all peoples, 'for Juda is the world plague'.[30] The struggle would not be victorious, therefore, until the international power of Jewry was completely annihilated.

The connection in Hitler's mind between Bolshevism and Jewry is the crucial additive responsible for the change in intonation. It was in spring and early summer 1920 that he first came to comment on a number of occasions on the catastrophic effect of Bolshevism in Russia and on Russia being destroyed by the Jews. By July 1920 he was explicitly combining the images of Bolshevism, Marxism and Soviet Russia in the picture of the brutal rule of the Jews, for which social democracy was allegedly paving the way in Germany.[31]

The theme of Bolshevik Russia preoccupied Hitler on numerous occasions during the following months. By June 1922 he was envisaging a struggle of two ideologies, the idealistic and the materialistic, representing the mission of the German people in the struggle against Bolshevism with the forces of good united against the mortal enemy of the Jew. The state was merely the means to the end of upholding the race.[32] And by autumn 1922 his conception of the absolutely pivotal relationship of antisemitism and anti-Bolshevism had reached the point of development which was to dominate his political mission to the end. In October he wrote of a fight for life and death between two *Weltanschauungen* which were incapable of coexistence. In this struggle there could only be victors and the annihilated. The example of Russia had shown what this meant. 'A victory of the Marxist idea signifies the complete extermination of the opponents. . . . The Bolshevisation of Germany . . . means the annihilation of the entire Christian-western culture altogether.' The aim of the Nazi Party could, therefore, be simply stated: 'Annihilation and extermination of the Marxist *Weltanschauung*'.[33]

Hitler's changing awareness of the significance of Bolshevik Russia for his racial philosophy had obvious implications for his foreign-policy thinking. It is, therefore, of note that it was precisely around the time, about 1922, when he was coming to conceive of his mission as a life-or-death struggle with 'Jewish Bolshevism' that a shift took place in his concept of Germany's future foreign policy, from a traditional pan-German concern with colonialism to the notion of a continental expansionism at the expense of Russia. Under the influence of the success of 'Jewish Bolshevism' in the civil war in Russia and the threat of Bolshevisation in Germany, the fusion of antisemitism and anti-Bolshevism in Hitler's mind into an obsessive determination to destroy 'Jewish Bolshevism' was a far more powerful determinant than conventional diplomatic considerations in the reordering of foreign policy goals.

In his early speeches, Hitler conveyed little of any future intentions in foreign policy. He repeatedly berated the failures in the post-Bismarck era to ensure peace with Russia instead of siding with Austria-Hungary, and spoke of the inevitably hostile stance of Britain and France. His main target was, of course, the foreign policy of Weimar governments, which he scourged at every opportunity. He remained down to 1922 essentially anti-western in his thinking, though without a clear concept of a future

Figure 1.2 Hitler's 'assault squad' (Stoßtrupp Hitler) in 1923, the year of the Beerhall Putsch.

alliance strategy. His attitude towards Russia was ignorant and ambival-
ent. He continued to harbour a dualistic view – positive towards the
'national' people of Russia, negative towards the 'Jewish–Bolshevik' rulers
– and to favour an alliance with a non-Bolshevik Russia against Britain.
By late 1922 he was increasingly aware of the essential division of interest between France and Britain. But above all, he was rethinking future
policy towards Russia.

By December 1922 the foreign policy goals which were outlined in
Mein Kampf, and which remained at the heart of Hitler's thinking to the
end, were formulated. In a confidential discussion at that time, he turned
his back on the old policy of commercial and colonial rivalry with Britain
in the interest of winning over Britain for support in a continental policy
against Russia.

> Germany would have to adapt herself [he stated] to a purely continental
> policy avoiding harm to English interests. The destruction of Russia
> with the help of England would have to be attempted. Russia would
> give Germany sufficient land for German settlers and a wide field of
> activity for German industry. Then England would not interrupt us in our
> reckoning with France.[34]

Two years before the writing of *Mein Kampf,* therefore, Hitler's personalised world-view was to all intents and purposes complete. The struggle to
destroy the power of international Jewry, the struggle to annihilate
Marxism, and the struggle to obtain 'living space' for Germany at the
expense of Russia amounted in effect to three forms of expression of the
same integral thought. And this was embedded in, and took its justification from, an understanding of history which, turning Karl Marx's belief
in the centrality of socio-economic motive forces on its head, dogmatically
held to a view of historical development as the unfolding of a constant
struggle between races – ethnic, biological peoples. Hitler wrote:

> All great cultures of the past perished only because the originally
> created race died out from blood poisoning. . . . Blood mixture and the
> resultant drop in the racial level is the sole cause of the dying out of old
> cultures. . . . All occurrences in world history are only the expression of
> the races' instinct of self-preservation, in the good or bad sense.[35]

Though for Hitler the Jewish race was the antithesis of the highest racial
entity, the Aryan, the instinct of self-preservation was greater than
in other peoples, enabling the Jew to thrive 'as a parasite in the body of
other nations and states'.[36] Ultimate Jewish dominance would come about

through the undermining and destruction of other pure races. The next stage after control of liberal democracy is 'in the organised mass of Marxism', which 'allows him [i.e. the Jew] to subjugate and govern the peoples with a dictatorial and brutal fist'.[37] The culmination is the 'fanatical savagery' and 'inhuman tortures' of 'Jewish Bolshevism'. 'The end is not only the end of the freedom of the peoples oppressed by the Jew, but also the end of this parasite upon the nations. After the death of his victim, the vampire sooner or later dies too'.[38] But before this stage the cataclysmic showdown with the rejuvenated racial force of the German nation would destroy Jewry for ever.

The linkage of this definitive turning-point in world history to German foreign policy is left to one of the last chapters of *Mein Kampf*. The land necessary to support Germany as a world power was to come from Russia. There, 'Jewish Bolshevism' had destroyed and replaced the former Germanic ruling strata. But, 'as a ferment of decomposition', the Jew had weakened the Russian empire which was now 'ripe for collapse'. 'And the end of Jewish rule in Russia will also be the end of Russia as a state.'[39] The mission of the Nazi Movement was to prepare the German people for this task. The rebuilding of the German people to a level of strength capable of accomplishing the destruction of 'Jewish Bolshevism' was the task of a 'Germanic state of the German nation'.[40] The state itself was but the means to attaining this end.[41] But this could be achieved only under leadership of genius attuned to the task. While in prison in the Landsberg fortress in 1924, serving a five-year sentence for high treason from which he was released within nine months, Hitler came to see himself as that great leader for whom the German people was waiting.

Ideas of heroic, quasi-messianic leadership in a new Reich were commonplace on the extreme Right in Germany in the early 1920s. Initially, Hitler had seen his own role solely as that of the propagandist – the 'drummer boy' for the great leader who would arise. The example of Mussolini's success in Italy in 1922 was a stirring one for Hitler. In 1922 and 1923 he spoke more frequently about the importance of personality and heroic leadership, responsible to the people but demanding their unconditional obedience for the historic mission he would carry out. As late as May 1923 Hitler stated that he was still only preparing the path, to give the coming dictator a people ready for him.[42] Two months later, he commented that salvation could be found only in the value of personality, and that as leader of the NSDAP he saw his task 'in accepting responsibility'.[43] By the time of his trial in 1924, in which he turned the putsch fiasco into a personal triumph, his conception of his own role was emerging into the fully-fledged heroic leadership self-image which took shape only after his return to politics in 1925 following his short imprisonment.

By the mid 1920s, then, Hitler had developed a rounded philosophy which offered him a complete view of the world, its ills, and how to overcome them. Its substance never changed down to his death. When, in the 1940s, Hitler's ideas on all subjects under the sun were expounded at length to his cronies in his dinner-table monologues, the self-same underlying tenets of his world-view which he had developed in the early 1920s were still dominant. In his last recorded monologue before his suicide, Hitler remained, as ever, preoccupied by the showdown with the 'Jewish–Bolshevik' threat. His belief was unchanged that 'in a world which is becoming more and more perverted through the Jewish virus, a people which has remained immune to the virus must in the long run emerge supreme'. And he asserted that 'from this point of view, National Socialism can justly claim the eternal gratitude of the people for having eliminated the Jew from Germany and Central Europe'.[44] Hitler's last words to the German people, in his political testament written on the day before his death, adjured its leaders and their followers 'to scrupulous observance of the laws of race and to merciless opposition to the universal poisoner of all peoples, international Jewry'.[45]

Hitler saw himself as that rarest of combinations, the 'programmatist' (or 'theoretician') and 'politician' – the executor of the 'idea'.[46] He spoke of the work of the combined 'programmatist' and 'politician' as a struggle 'for aims which only the fewest comprehend'.[47] The 'doctrine' was, then, not simply a matter of passive understanding. His world-view provided an internal dynamic. Hitler spoke repeatedly of his 'mission'; he increasingly saw the hand of 'Providence' in his work; in *Mein Kampf* he invoked God's support for his struggle against the Jew.[48] He saw himself engaged in the preparation of a crusade. When the showdown with 'Jewish Bolshevism' eventually became reality with the invasion of the Soviet Union in June 1941, it was for Hitler – and not for him alone – the culmination of this 'crusading' idea.

Hitler's quasi-messianic commitment to an 'idea', a faith which brooked no alternatives, gave him a strength of will-power which in his presence was difficult to resist. The dogmatism of the autodidact who, since his youth, had read voraciously but unsystematically, reinforcing his prejudices rather than subjecting them to searching critique, provided him with an inbuilt dominance over those who met him. His extraordinary memory for detail both impressed those in his presence and also deflated attempts to challenge him. The reduction of all situations to black

33

Figure 1.3 Hitler in December 1924 on release from Landsberg, where he had been in prison for his part in the failed Putsch.

and white alternatives, one of which could be utterly ridiculed, and the rhetorical force of expression in which complex matters were dismissed contemptuously or simplified along the lines of incontrovertible 'basic truths', also meant face-to-face opposition stood scant chance of success.

The certainty of his own faith reinforced the more fainthearted or doubters among Hitler's following, while those who could not share it, were cynical, or rejected it never had a chance of access to the inner sanctum of power. In any case, Hitler stuck with his circle of 'true believers' – his loyal followers, his 'own sort'.

It was the combination of 'prophet' and propagandist which gave Hitler from the early 1920s the advantage over all other potential contenders for leadership in the top elite of the Nazi Party. Other leading Nazis lacked the combination of his demagogical brilliance, his mobilising capability, and the unity and all-encompassing 'explanatory force' of his ideological vision.

Compared with Hitler's talent for vulgar simplification and mass appeal, the ideological preoccupations of early Party 'thinkers' such as Gottfried Feder or Alfred Rosenberg, who were more concerned with the intricacies of ideas than their political effectiveness or organisational potential, were opaque and limited. Feder soon faded into relative insignificance. Rosenberg's leadership weaknesses were blatantly revealed when he was left in charge of Party affairs while Hitler was in prison in 1924.

Of other early leading Nazis, Rudolf Hess was introverted, lacked demagogic talent, and saw himself from the earliest days as a mere disciple of Hitler. Julius Streicher was no more than a vulgar racist demagogue of limited intelligence, incapable of extending his obsessive hatred of Jews into a full-scale ideology. Hermann Göring was a man of action rather than ideas, and after an early spell in charge of the SA left the scene altogether for four years following the putsch disaster, remaining thereafter aloof from Party offices. Ernst Röhm was a military turned paramilitary man, an able organiser but lacking in both ideological vision and rhetorical talent. Gregor Strasser also had organisational skills, but had limited ability to whip up the fervour of the masses. His brother, Otto, was typical of a number of leading early figures in the Movement who became estranged from Hitler through their attempts to detach an abstract 'idea' of Nazism from its embodiment in the Party leader. Joseph Goebbels was an acolyte rather than a high priest, functioning largely as his master's voice. Heinrich Himmler was a good administrator but, possessed of a cold, inhuman and cranky personality, was devoid of popular appeal. Hans Frank, the Party's chief legal expert, was a weak, vacillating character, emotional and subservient. The differing emphases in ideas and personal ambitions, rivalries and deep animosities of these and other prominent figures in the Movement ruled out each of them as potential claimants for the Party leadership and were reconciled only in the imprecise but incontrovertible future vision embodied in the person of the increasingly eulogised supreme leader, Hitler.

Already in 1922–23, the beginnings of a personality cult around Hitler had become visible. Other prominent figures in the still small Nazi Movement were speaking in public of Hitler in adulatory, 'heroic' terms as Germany's Mussolini, a leader for whom millions were yearning, and the only man who could restore Germany's greatness. Then his assumption of full responsibility for the putsch of November 1923 transformed it from a farcical failure into a publicity triumph for the radical Right, earning Hitler outright pre-eminence in *völkisch* circles. His enforced confinement in Landsberg in 1924 was thereafter turned to optimal effect. Accompanied by two dozen or so members of his bodyguard, with Rudolf Hess acting as his secretary, and being visited frequently by many other followers, Hitler made Landsberg into a Nazi 'think tank'. While writing *Mein Kampf*, he lectured the other inmates each morning on his ideas. Internment became the scene of a Nazi seminar, as his ideas were then discussed at length.

In the inner circle, Hitler's reputation as the 'programmatist' of the Nazi idea was enhanced. One of those present, a non-Bavarian local leader who had been something of a sceptic, was highly impressed by a talk in which Hitler had held forth at length about the distinction between 'programmatists' and 'politicians'. He wrote of his growing certainty as Hitler for the first time spoke of major foreign-policy considerations:

> It is my rock solid conviction that Hitler will not move one iota from his National Socialist thinking. . . . And if it nonetheless sometimes looks as if that is the case, then it is only for the sake of more important goals. For he combines in himself the programmatist and the politician. He knows his goal, but also sees the ways to do it. My stay here has strengthened what I still doubted in Göttingen: the faith in Hitler's political instinct.[49]

Growing belief in Hitler as Germany's coming leader, a secular faith in a political messiah, gripped many of those in his immediate surroundings who came into regular, repeated and lengthy contact with him from at least this time onwards. Though there were those, such as the Strasser brothers, who by no means succumbed to the developing personality cult, they became forced on to the defensive. The inner circle of believers was established. The basis of the 'charismatic community' was laid.

Rudolf Hess, from the earliest times a most fanatical and subservient devotee, spoke of 'the power of personality' radiating 'something that puts those around him under its spell and spreads in ever-widening circles.'[50] It was only during the Landsberg time, he wrote, that he fully grasped the 'mighty significance' of this personality.[51] Alfred Rosenberg admitted while imprisoned in Nuremberg after the war his admiration of Hitler from the earliest days, seeing in him the 'creator' of the Nazi Party and its political philosophy, a leader with 'a firm intellectual basis but at the same time a constantly increasing maturity in dealing with numerous problems', possessed of 'a great belief in his people and his mission', 'creative drive' and a 'will like iron'.[52] Hans Frank recalled feeling, the first time he heard Hitler speak, in January 1920, that he alone was capable of saving Germany.[53] On entering the SA in 1923, he was 'positively spellbound' by Hitler's personality. And when Hitler personally appealed to him in 1929 to give up plans to withdraw to a career in legal scholarship, Frank agreed to embark upon 'the new, strong, radiantly refulgent path in Adolf Hitler's world'.[54] Joseph Goebbels asked after reading *Mein Kampf*: 'Who is this man? half plebeian, half god! Truly Christ, or only St John?' He saw him as a genius, wanted him as a friend, and wrote in his diary on 19 April 1926: 'Adolf Hitler, I love you.'[55] Baldur von Schirach, later the Hitler Youth leader, recalled his fascination at the sound of Hitler's voice when first hearing him speak in public in 1925. It captivated him and convinced him that Hitler was 'the coming saviour of Germany'.[56] For Göring, later proud of his title 'most faithful paladin of the Führer', full surrender came only on returning to the Party in 1928 after several years abroad following the failed putsch. But his submission thereafter was profoundly subservient. In later years he was at times almost physically ill before audiences with Hitler. He claimed that Hitler had become his conscience. He saw in him 'the rare union . . . between the most acute logical thinker and truly profound philosopher and the iron man of action'.[57]

These top-ranking Nazi leaders all saw Hitler at close quarters, and were in direct and regular contact with him. They all joined the Nazi Movement when it was in the political wilderness, long before it came close to gaining power. Though career and material advantages came their way, political opportunism can scarcely be seen as the prime motive behind their commitment to the Nazi cause. The personalisation of their faith and loyalty in Hitler was crucial, and, as the above selected evidence shows, was vividly present in a period before the institutionalised Führer cult had become widely established. Indeed, they themselves were among both the earliest victims and the chief exponents of the 'Hitler myth'.

Central to this core of the 'charismatic community' was the power of Hitler's personality. And dominant within this personality was the single-mindedness of the zealot, the ardent conviction of the self-styled prophet, the ideological self–certainty of the missionary. To the closest members of his retinue, his proclaimed unity in his own person of the 'programmatist' and 'politician' gave him unchallengeable status as both the embodiment of the 'idea' and its organising genius.

In practical matters and day-to-day decisions, Hitler was often any-thing but self-certain. And in the urgent matter of building up the Party in the politically barren years of the mid and late 1920s, the details of the arcanum of Hitler's personalised ideology were not important. Indeed, the very flexibility of the individual ideas within an overall interlocking framework was massively advantageous. Even among his close depend-ants, one specific angle of ideology was often more important than another, and circumstances necessitated placing the emphasis on some parts more than others. But what was crucial was the belief that the 'future belongs to us', that one day Hitler's 'vision' – whatever interpreta-tion was placed upon it – would become reality. This was the power of Hitler's idea.

Notes and references

1. The following description relies upon Percy Schramm's introduction (esp. pp. 29–34) to Henry Picker, *Hitlers Tischgespräche im Führerhauptquartier*, 2nd edn, Stuttgart-Degerloch, 1963, and on Picker's own comments in the 3rd edn of 1976, p. 25.

2. See Werner Maser, *Adolf Hitler. Legende, Mythos, Wirklichkeit*, 3rd edn, Munich, 1976, pp. 16–38, 265.

3. See Fest, pp. 31–2.

4. By Rudolf Binion, *Hitler among the Germans*, New York, 1976. See the pertinent comments of William Carr, *Hitler. A Study in Personality and Politics*, London, 1978, pp. 124–5, 148.

5. Maser, *Hitler*, p. 97.

6. See Fest, *Hitler*, p. 65.

7. MK, p. 59.

8. Maser, *Hitler*, p. 251.

9. MK, 59; trans. MK Watt, p. 51.

10. MK, 60; trans. MK Watt, p. 52.

11. MK, ch. 2.

12. Maser, *Hitler*, p. 166.

13. MK, pp. 221–5.

14. Maser, *Hitler*, p. 149.

15. MK, p. 225.

16. Cit. Maser, *Hitler*, p. 165.

17. MK, p. 235; trans. MK Watt, p. 196.

18. JK, Doc. 60.

19. JK, Doc. 61.

20. MK, P. 772; trans. MK Watt, p. 620.

21. JK, e.g. Docs 87, 109, 138–9, p. 215, no. 184.

22. JK, p. 200.

23. JK, p. 337.

24. JK, pp. 119–20, and pp. 128, 184 for the rejection of 'emotional antisemitism'.

25. JK, p. 201.

26. JK, p. 238.

27. JK, pp. 176–7.

28. JK, Docs 357, 421.

29. JK, pp. 1210, 1226, 1232.

30. JK, Doc. 654, p. 1242.

31. JK, Docs 96, 106, 121.

32. JK, p. 646.

33. JK, pp. 703–4.

34. JK, Doc. 452; trans. Geoffrey Stoakes, *Hitler and the Quest for World Dominion*, Leamington Spa, 1987, p. 137.

35. MK, pp. 316, 324; trans. MK Watt, pp. 262, 269.

36. MK, p. 334.

37. MK, p. 357; trans. MK Watt, p. 295.

38. MK, p. 358; trans. MK Watt, p. 296.

39. MK, p. 743; trans. MK Watt, p. 598.

40. MK, p. 362.

41. MK, pp. 431–4.

42. JK, p. 924.

43. JK, p. 946.

44. François Genoud (ed.), *The Testament of Adolf Hitler*, London, 1961, pp. 103–5.

45. Maser, *Briefe*, pp. 374–5; trans. *Nazi Conspiracy and Aggression*, 11 vols, Washington, 1946–7, vi, 263.

46. MK, pp. 229–32.

47. MK, p. 232.

48. MK, p. 70.

49. Cit. Albrecht Tyrell, *Vom 'Trommler' zum 'Führer'*, Munich, 1975, p. 170.

50. Cit. Joachim C. Fest, *The Face of the Third Reich*, Harmondsworth, 1972, p. 288.

51. Albrecht Tyrell (ed.), *Führer befiehl . . . Selbstzeugnisse aus der 'Kampfzeit' der NSDAP. Dokumentation und Analyse*, Düsseldorf, 1969, pp. 84–5.

52. Alfred Rosenberg, *Letzte Aufzeichnungen*, Göttingen, 1955, pp. 86, 316–17, 342.

53. Frank, pp. 39–42.

54. Cit. Fest, *Face*, p. 321.

55. Helmut Heiber (ed.), *Das Tagebuch von Joseph Goebbels 1925/26*, Stuttgart, 1960, pp. 34, 72, 74.

56. Baldur von Schirach, *Ich glaubte an Hitler*, Hamburg, 1967, pp. 18–22.

57. Cit. Fest, *Face*, p. 118.

✠

Chapter 2

Getting power

In examining how the power of the German state came to be placed at Hitler's disposal, three developments have to be distinguished. The first is how Hitler came to acquire undisputed power in the Nazi Party, which by the late 1920s had incorporated and unified the disparate strands of the *völkisch* Right and had come to adopt as its organisational ethos the leadership principle, deriving from Hitler's perceived historical mission to save Germany. The second is how Hitler was able in the early 1930s to extend his appeal way beyond previous levels of support for the extreme radical *völkisch* Right to more than a third of the voting population, providing him with the claim to power that he alone could 'deliver' the masses. And the third is how non-Nazi elite groups, with distinctly sober views on 'charismatic' missionary claims, but with influence on those wielding power in Weimar Germany, came to take an interest in Hitler, and how the power-brokers themselves, when he looked anything but assured of a triumphant future, became prepared to hoist him into the Chancellor's seat. In these three developments, the personal role played by Hitler is greatly overshadowed by matters and events beyond his control.

The question of how such an unlikely candidate was able to come to power has been posed ever since Hitler was appointed Reich Chancellor on 30 January 1933, and has been answered in many different ways. The Nazis' own answer was the one Hitler himself never tired of providing in his incantation of the 'Party story', which prefaced – at inordinate length – many of his major speeches throughout the Third Reich. According to this version, the rise of Nazism from its humble beginnings to the 'seizure of power' had been accomplished solely through the 'triumph of the will'. Incessant struggle – this period was always referred to as 'the time of struggle' – against the odds but backed by the fanatical belief of a massively expanding host of followers in a righteous cause had eventually overcome adversity, defeated powerful enemies, and brought about national unity to save Germany from destruction through Bolshevism.

Such a heroic Party legend had purely propaganda value. There was nothing inevitable about Hitler's triumph in January 1933. Five years earlier, the Nazi Party had been a fringe irritant in German politics, but no more. The 1928 election had brought it only 2.6 per cent of the popular vote and twelve seats in the Reichstag. External events – the Young Plan to adjust German reparations payments, the Wall Street Crash, and Brüning's entirely unnecessary decision to have an election in summer 1930 – put the Nazis on the political map. Though democracy had by that date an unpromising future, a Nazi dictatorship seemed far less likely than some other form of authoritarian rule, such as a military dictatorship or even a reversion to a Bismarckian style of government, possibly under a restored monarchy. In bringing Hitler to power, chance events and conservative miscalculation played a larger role than any actions of the Nazi leader himself.

The movement

✠

Authoritarian movements, as their inter-war and post-war history shows, are from their nature particularly prone to splits, factionalism and inner-party power struggles. The early development of the Nazi Party indicates that it was no exception. As the German Workers' Party, it began life in 1919 as only one of more than seventy foundations of extreme right-wing political sects. Sharing an essentially similar *völkisch* ideology based upon a radical brand of racist nationalism, these sprang up within a year of the end of the First World War and flourished in a stridently counter-revolutionary atmosphere, particularly prevalent in Bavaria.

Rifts about tactics and strategy, disputes over points of ideology, and clashes of personality were part and parcel of the myriad strands of the *völkisch* movement from the very beginning. Within the infant Nazi Party, Hitler himself provoked the first power struggle, in 1921, which resulted in the establishment of his constitutional position as Party leader. After the failure of the Beer Hall Putsch in late 1923, the temporary front of unity reached on the extreme Right collapsed and the Nazi Party itself split into a number of rival groups. Rabid factionalism continued after the refoundation of the Party in 1925, and posed a potentially dangerous challenge to Hitler's pre-eminence, which was headed off with some difficulty in early 1926.

Even after 1930, at a time when Hitler's leadership had been consolidated and the Nazi Movement was going from strength to strength, there were a number of occasions on which the NSDAP was threatened by rebellion from its paramilitary wing, the SA, and it survived the secession of prominent members, notably Otto Strasser in 1930 and, above all, his brother Gregor Strasser, the second most powerful man in the Party, at the end of 1932. Moreover, the Party membership was itself remarkably volatile, with an extremely high turnover of members. The history of the Nazi Party down to 1933 shows plainly that it was a most unstable movement comprising extremely diverse factions and interests, with strong centrifugal and disintegrative tendencies.

'Leadership' was, then, in itself no guarantee of internal unity. But there is every reason to imagine that without the enhancement of Hitler's supreme authority in the Movement, elevated by the unusually strong personality cult which became attached to him, the Party would have been torn apart by factionalism. As it was, Hitler remained the Party's chief asset – its populist magnet and chief vote-winner. With him, most leading Nazis recognised, stood or fell the chances of attaining power. This persuaded factionalists to accept the need for at least an outward show of unity. And it encouraged those at the centre of the Party to work actively to build up and accept the Führer cult, extolling Hitler as beyond criticism, the font of ideological orthodoxy, and the focus of unquestioning obedience. This was done, from the mid 1920s onwards, not only by those, like Hess, who were genuine Hitler-worshippers, but also by leading figures like Gregor Strasser, prepared, despite reservations about Hitler, to collaborate in the instrumentalisation of the Führer cult. Once established, by the later 1920s, then bolstered by the electoral successes of 1930–32, the Führer cult developed its own relative autonomy, cushioning Hitler's own position by weakening at the outset oppositional attempts, and tying the Party more and more to his 'all or bust' strategy to gain power.

Central to the whole development of Hitler's power base within the Nazi Movement, and of the character and dynamic of the Nazi organisation before 1933, was, then, the leadership cult. 'Charismatic' authority was made into the very organisational base of the Movement itself. This made Hitler's relationship to his Party different from that of any other contemporary party leader. And it provided him with an aura of 'greatness' on which his claim to exclusive loyalty as the embodiment of a messianic mission to build a 'new Germany' was extended from the inner circle to a wider body of the faithful, a greatly enlarged 'charismatic community'. It gave him the legitimacy within the Party which enabled him to counteract the otherwise endemic and disintegratory factionalism which characterised the Movement.

As we have noted, it was as a propagandist, an agitator and an unusually talented demagogue that Hitler first won attention. Within the space of only a few months, he became the star speaker of the infant National Socialist German Workers' Party (which had changed its name from German Workers' Party in February 1920). It was Hitler who announced the Party's programme, which he had partly drafted and edited, on 24 February 1920. During 1920 he spoke more than thirty times before audiences of some several hundred to over two thousand persons. With Hitler as the 'front man', the Party membership reached 2,000 by late 1920 and 3,300 by August 1921[1] – a sharp rise since he himself had joined as the fifty-fifth member in September 1919.[2] Though most of those attracted by Hitler's rantings were from Munich's lower middle classes, some well-heeled and influential figures in the city's social and political circles also showed an interest in the stir he was making.

Through Ernst Röhm, later the SA chief, who had been a member of the German Workers' Party since 1919, Hitler gained important contacts in radical Right officer and paramilitary circles. Hitler's former commanding officer in the Reichswehr 'education' unit, Hauptmann Karl Mayr, saw to it that the army paid for 3,000 brochures on the Versailles treaty which the Party distributed in 1920, commenting in a letter to the exiled right-wing putschist, Wolfgang Kapp, in September 1920 that he had high hopes of Hitler and his Movement.[3] And Dietrich Eckart, one of Hitler's 'intellectual' mentors, was also valuable in fund-raising and links to wealthy patrons in the *völkisch* camp. It was Eckart's financial sureties, together with a contribution of 60,000 marks from a Reichswehr fund, engineered by Röhm and Mayr, which enabled the Party to purchase its own newspaper, the *Völkischer Beobachter*, at the beginning of 1921. It can be claimed with some justification, therefore, that these three – Röhm, Eckart and Mayr – were the 'midwives of Hitler's political career'.[4]

By 1921 Hitler greatly overshadowed the Party's first leader (and co-founder) Anton Drexler. A clash was unavoidable, and was prompted by moves to amalgamate with rival branches of the *völkisch* movement. Hitler rejected such notions out of hand. He no doubt feared that a merger would weaken his own hold over the Party and undermine the task he already envisaged for himself – fortified by the impact of his demagogy – as the propagandist 'drummer' of the nationalist Right. When Drexler entered into moves to bring about a merger during his absence, Hitler resigned in rage from the Party, causing a major crisis resolved only when Eckart negotiated the return of the 'prima donna' speaker under conditions which gave him absolute power within the Movement.

Everything indicates that Hitler's actions in the crisis arose from a heated, spontaneous reaction to circumstances he could not control, rather than from a premeditated strategy to acquire dictatorial power. But his indispensability as a propagandist meant that his inflexibility and refusal to contemplate compromise were turned into an advantage which greatly strengthened his own position within the Party.

The Party continued to expand rapidly. By the end of 1922 there were around 20,000 and by the time of the Putsch about 55,000 members, mainly in Bavaria and of predominantly petty-bourgeois background. From 1921 the Party also had its own paramilitary organisation, the *Sturmabteilung* (SA). Even so, down to the Putsch the Nazi Movement remained far from the largest component in the ensemble of 'patriotic' extreme-right Bavarian paramilitary organisations. The continued growth of the Party was in good measure still attributable to Hitler's talent as an agitator and scourge of the Weimar system, as Ruhr occupation, hyper-inflation and governmental instability seemed to point to democracy's imminent overthrow.

To those already predisposed to the appeal of the message, Hitler's speeches were electrifying. One of his early admirers, Kurt Lüdecke, recalling his reactions on hearing Hitler speak in 1922, wrote of his critical faculties being swept away, of being held 'under a hypnotic spell by the sheer force of his conviction', of 'the intense will of the man, the passion of his sincerity' which 'seemed to flow from him into me', and of an experience he could liken only to that of a religious conversion.[5] Such accounts of Hitler's speeches are not uncommon. But although, in the conditions of Bavaria in the early 1920s, Hitler's demagoguery continued to draw crowds from the *völkisch* clientele, without external support and

Figure 2.1 Hitler at a Nazi rally in 1930.

influential contacts he would have remained no more than a beerhall rabble-rouser.

Early well-to-do converts such as Lüdecke and Putzi Hanfstaengl, a Harvard graduate and scion of a well-regarded family of Munich art dealers, helped to provide an entrée into the salon respectability of Munich's upper bourgeoisie. The publishers Julius Lehmann (already long a Party sympathiser) and Hugo Bruckmann, and the piano manufacturer Carl Bechstein were among those offering patronage to the somewhat unlikely guest at their salon soirées. General Ludendorff, the most prestigious figure on the extreme Right, also used his influence to recommend Hitler in social circles which would otherwise have been closed to him.

Even more important was the protection Hitler and his Movement received from the Bavarian authorities. The Nazis were able to utilise the nationalist sympathies of the Bavarian police, judiciary and army leadership in a state which saw itself as a bastion of the patriotic Right against rampant socialism in Prussia, Saxony, Thuringia and elsewhere. And as the connection with Ludendorff and with the other paramilitary organisations in Bavaria expanded, with Röhm playing an important brokerage role, the Nazi Movement was able to profit from the financial contributions flowing to the 'patriotic' Right in its fight against the 'red peril'. In addition, Röhm's access to munitions collected by the Reichswehr from dissolved counter-revolutionary home guard units was vital in enabling him to supply the SA with arms, vehicles and other equipment in 1923. It was Röhm, too, who in September 1923 engineered Hitler's leadership of the *Deutscher Kampfbund* – the merged triad of NSDAP, *Bund Oberland* and *Reichsflagge* which formed the most radical and aggressive of the paramilitary organisations in Bavaria.

Without the patronage, protection and support of the Munich bourgeoisie and political and military authorities, Hitler's passage into a position of prominence in the Bavarian radical Right could scarcely have been made. And though this phase in the Party's history culminated in the débâcle of the Bürgerbräukeller in November 1923, Hitler's upstaging of Ludendorff during his trial in February and March 1924 meant that he had now claim to be regarded as the new figurehead of the *völkisch* movement – even if it seemed, at this juncture, to be a movement with the best of its future behind it. It was fitting that the clincher to his predominance came from yet another virtuoso piece of agitation before his sympathetic judges in Munich.

The disintegration of the banned Nazi Movement during Hitler's imprisonment confirmed the indispensability of his leadership. And the splintered Nazi groups, whatever their differences, shared a veneration of the jailed former leader. Moreover, his performance at the trial had boosted Hitler's reputation among adherents of the radical Right outside Bavaria. Though the factional in-fighting was to continue with notable bitterness and enmity for a year or more after his release from prison and the refoundation of the Party in February 1925, Hitler's position had become greatly strengthened through his own enhanced status and through the post-putsch collapse of the Movement. When a crisis blew up by February 1926 over Party aims and strategy, he was sufficiently powerful through his control of the key Munich nerve-centre of the Party to be able to head it off.

The crisis arose partly over personality clashes dating back to the bitter in-fighting of the post-putsch Party split and the unpopularity of some of the dominant forces in the Party in its Bavarian heartlands, notably the then propaganda chief Hermann Esser and Julius Streicher, the Nazi boss in Nuremberg. But more significantly, the crisis was provoked by the disenchantment expressed by some leading Party members in northern and western Germany (most prominently Gregor Strasser, who had joined a northern faction at the break-up of the old Party in 1924) at the vagueness of the Party's 1920 programme, the neglect of its 'socialist' claims in the Munich intonation of policy, and at the political strategy which had been adopted. Questions of whether to participate in elections, following Hitler's post-putsch strategy of winning power through the ballot-box, not insurrection, whether to support a left-wing referendum to expropriate the property of the former royal houses, and whether future foreign policy lay in siding with Russia against the west or in conquering it for German 'living space' were all issues in the dispute. But the decisive factor, which forced Hitler to act, was the demand for a new Party programme. The adoption of a new programme would have meant not only the continuing negotiability of Party 'doctrine', but – and this point was crucial – an acceptance that the leader himself was bound by the Party programme. Hitler's power within the Party, deriving not from the programme but from the embodiment of the 'idea' in his 'mission', would have been fundamentally undermined. The 'charismatic' essence of the Party would have been replaced by a paper programme.

Until early 1926, Hitler had been inactive. His characteristic indolence with regard to day-to-day administration had left the Party's management wholly in the hands of others, allowing him time to concentrate on writing the second volume of *Mein Kampf*. He kept aloof from the looming crisis. The actions of the northern Party leaders, who by this time had formed themselves, with Hitler's express permission, into a 'working group', did not amount to a rebellion against Hitler himself. But by early 1926 it was plain that the crisis did amount to a challenge to the basis of his authority as leader.

As usual, Hitler acted only when compelled to do so. At a conference of Party leaders called for 14 February 1926 in Bamberg, his speech ended the prospects of the reform 'faction' (which, in any case, had been divided within itself from the beginning). He reasserted the Party's mission to smash 'Jewish Bolshevism' (a point which had not appeared in the 1920 programme), with Italy and Britain as Germany's natural allies, rather than work towards an entente with Russia, and he rejected the expropriation of the princes.[6] Most crucially, however, he identified himself utterly with the existing Party programme. The 1920 programme, he proclaimed, 'was the foundation of our religion, our ideology', and to tamper with it would amount to 'treason to those who died believing in our Idea'.[7] Rejection of the programme, it was made plain, amounted to rejection of Hitler, the 'idea', and the memory of the Party's 'martyrs' of the 1923 Putsch.

The appeal to loyalty was triumphant. The 'opposition', which had never as such rejected Hitler or the 'idea' but had arisen from the very vagueness of the 'idea' itself, evaporated. Central Party organisation was tightened. The northern leaders accepted defeat and came back into the fold. Goebbels, dismayed after the Bamberg meeting, was invited to Munich, lionised, and subjected to the Hitler charm treatment. He capitulated. 'Hitler is great,' he wrote in his diary. 'He shakes us all warmly by the hand. Let bygones be bygones! . . . I bow to the greater man, the political genius.'[8] Shortly afterwards, in May 1926, the first Party congress since the Putsch, held in Weimar, provided a public show of loyalty to Hitler in person, and declared the 1920 programme immutable. The crisis was over. Notions of inner-party democracy were banished. All power over decisions relating to ideological and organisational matters, it was accepted, resided in the person of Hitler. The way to the fully fledged 'Führer Party' was paved.

All of this seemed at the time of little relevance within the overall context of German politics. Democracy had come through its baptism by fire in the post-war crisis. Three years after the hyper-inflation of 1923, the currency was stable, the economy picking up, the 'golden years' of Weimar culture were in full swing, the political scene was more settled

Figure 2.2 Hitler in 1931 in conversation with two of the most important figures in the Nazi Movement, Hermann Göring (left) and Ernst Röhm, head of the Stormtroopers (centre).

than at any time since 1918, and the extreme Right were reduced to a tiny rump of electoral support. The future looked promising. And without the onset of the world economic crisis from 1929 it might have remained so.

Precisely this period when the Nazi Party was in the political wilderness in the later 1920s, however, saw the creation of the organisational framework which enabled the NSDAP to exploit the subsequent Depression crisis far more effectively than the multifarious radical Right movements had handled the inflation crisis of 1922–23. A number of lingering *völkisch* movements gave up their autonomy and were swallowed up by the Nazi Movement. Though its voter potential before 1929 was puny, the activist base of the NSDAP was greatly strengthened, so that when the crisis broke, the Party had over 100,000 members.

And in this period, the Führer cult attached to Hitler became fully institutionalised within the Movement and established the base of the transmission of the cult in the early 1930s to a wider electorate. A significant outward symbol of Hitler's supremacy was the introduction of the 'Heil Hitler' greeting as a compulsory form of address among Party members. Gregor Strasser, the most prominent figure in the 1925–26 'reform' group, now placed himself openly behind the Hitler idolatry, writing in a Party publication of 'an utter devotion to the idea of National Socialism' being combined with 'a deep love of the person of our leader who is the shining hero of the new freedom-fighters'.[9] Goebbels, whose belief in Hitler had for a short time been shaken in 1926, was now effusive in his repeated elaboration of the Führer cult in his newspaper, *Der Angriff*.

What Hitler had striven for was reality: the Party's programme was now wholly subsumed within his own person. This 'programme' did not, however, amount to a number of clearly defined political objectives neatly laid out in a Party manifesto. Nor, except indirectly, did the 'programme' which was cementing the still innately fractious Party together mean the considered acceptance of every aspect of the personalised ideology of Hitler, as expounded in *Mein Kampf*.

Hitler himself had never believed that the homogeneity of the Movement could be sustained through a hard and fast programme. What was required was an unconditional act of faith in a number of loosely defined but rigidly inflexible tenets of doctrine embodied in the person of Hitler: the world as a struggle between weak and strong races, selection of the fittest, the need to make Germany powerful again, get rid of the Jews, strive for 'living space'. Divisive points were played down wherever possible. Hitler combined the fixity of basic points of dogma with maximum pragmatism in political manoeuvring, keeping wherever possible out of internal disputes. And he retained his distance from the more socially radical forces within the Movement which were more likely to alienate rather than win over the support needed to attain the goal which was the prerequisite for all else: control over the power of the state.

Partly through their own conviction of Hitler's greatness and belief in his 'mission', partly through recognition that their own careerist ambitions depended on Hitler, and partly though acceptance of a degree of dominance of the supreme leader because this excluded all alternative candidates for leadership, the second-rank Nazi bosses – divided among themselves – outdid each other in devotion to the Führer and avowals of faith and loyalty. Personality clashes and disputes over strategy were unavoidable – all the more so as long as political success was evasive. But they invariably ended in a show of loyalty and subservience to Hitler.

A bitter dispute between Goebbels and Gregor Strasser in 1927, for example, brought a public demonstration of unity 'bolstered by the common belief in a lofty, holy mission and by the feeling of loyalty binding them to the common idea and also to the common leader in the person of Adolf Hitler'. The two premisses of the 'coming victory in ideal unity' for Party members were described as 'the authority of the idea and the authority of the Führer', which had 'become one in the person of Adolf Hitler'.[10]

Beneath the apparent unity of the Party, conflict – and sometimes rebellion – continued down to the end of 1932. But Hitler's position was by now far stronger than it had been at the time of the factional dispute of 1925–26. When Otto Strasser challenged his authority in 1930 by positing once again the supremacy of the 'idea' over the 'leader', he was forced out of the Party without repercussions. When trouble brewed in the SA in 1930 and serious revolt broke out in spring 1931, Hitler triumphed through appeals to loyalty to his own person. Finally, in the most serious crisis of all, in December 1932, when the second most powerful man in the Party, Gregor Strasser, resigned following a fundamental split over strategy, he took no one with him, no factional break-off or challenge to Hitler's position ensued, and the appeal to personal loyalty proved once more triumphant. After a meeting where Hitler denounced Strasser, 'those present' – the senior Gauleiter – 'once more sealed their old bond with him with a handshake'.[11] In the following weeks, declarations of loyalty showered in from all parts of Germany.

The strength of Hitler's position within the Party dates back in the main to the 'wilderness' years of 1925–28. By the time Nazism's electoral

Plate 1 Members of the right-wing Freikorps armed with a flamethrower and supported by an armoured car during the Communist-led 'Spartacus rising' in Berlin in 1919.

Plate 2 Adolf Hitler in 1921.

Plate 3 Hitler's rise to power: the abortive Munich Putsch, 9 November 1923. Hitler stands between General Ludendorff and captain Ernst Röhm just before their trial.

Plate 4   Hitler reviews the parade of SA Brown Shirts at the Party Rally in Nuremberg in 1927.

Plate 5 Adolf Hitler wearing lederhosen (leather shorts), *c*. 1927.

Plate 6 Hitler at a Nazi Rally in Dortmund, 1933.

Plate 7 A truck load of Hitler Youth carry the slogan 'Führer command, we will obey! All say yes!'. Berlin, 1934.

Plate 8   Adolf Hitler in 1933.

surge began in autumn 1929, the nature of the NSDAP as a 'Führer Party', with idea and organisation inseparable from its leader, was firmly established. Not for nothing was it generally known as 'the Hitler Movement'. Hitler's authority within the NSDAP was absolute. The bonds of the wider 'charismatic community', the chief transmission belt of the 'Führer cult' to wider sectors of the electorate who were as yet by no means convinced Hitler supporters, had been forged.

The masses

The mass appeal of a 'charismatic' leader has only an indirect relation to that leader's actual personality and character attributes. Perceptions are more important than reality. Few of the thirteen million Germans who voted for Hitler by 1932 had met him. The Hitler they had heard about, read about in the press, or seen at election meetings and mass rallies matched an image created and embellished by propaganda. The 'marketing' of the image was vital. But so was the initial predisposition to accept such an image. Most Nazi supporters were probably at least half-converted before they ever encountered Hitler in the flesh or otherwise succumbed to his 'charisma'. Probably for the majority of those coming to vote Nazi (in the absence of opinion polls, we can never know for certain), prosaic 'bread and butter' issues, local concerns, rational considerations of self-interest, or even essentially negative feelings that Hitler could do no worse than the rest and might as well be given a chance, predominated over ideological fervour and impassioned commitment to a 'missionary idea'. In villages and small towns especially, it was often the case that people followed the example of pillars of the community – local worthies and respected members of social clubs and associations – in finding their way to support the Nazis. After 1929–30, the panoply of interest groups which operated within the Nazi Movement – affiliated organisations to tap the interest of practically every section of society from youth and women, through blue-collar workers, to farmers, traders, students, doctors, lawyers, civil servants, teachers and university lecturers – related the umbrella 'idea' of Nazism to more specific group and material concerns. It was for a whole variety of self-interested reasons, therefore, and not simply or even mainly through Hitler, that people found Nazism an attractive proposition. Nevertheless, once exposed to Nazism, all potential supporters inevitably also became exposed to Hitler's 'charismatic' image.

Not only that, but the Hitler cult, as the embodiment of the whole amalgam of disparate strands of the Nazi 'idea', served as an independent drawing card of the first importance in the variety of motivating causes attracting people to Nazism. In a sample of the main ideological themes preoccupying rank-and-file Nazi members – impressionistically significant, despite the fact that it can make no claim to be statistically representative – the Hitler cult alone predominated in almost a fifth (18.1 per cent) of the 739 cases.[12]

As we have seen, even in the upper echelons of the Party, the 'idea' contained many of its virtues in its very vagueness – the fanatical devotion to a utopian vision of a distant future rather than to specific points of a laid-out programme of action. Hitler was more able than anyone sharing similar views to excite in those who encountered him – and were in some way predisposed to the message – a vision of a heroic future for a regenerated German nation arising from the ashes of the total destruction of the old order. Hitler inspired the millions attracted to him by the conviction that he and he alone, backed by his Party, could end the current misery and lead Germany to new greatness. The vision of the future held the promise of great benefits for all – as long as they were 'racially fit' – while those enemies of the people who had hitherto held them in thrall would be not only banished, but completely extirpated.

For general appeal, variations on this broad central twin theme of national regeneration and elimination of the enemies of the nation sufficed. 'Enemies of the nation' for most Nazi supporters in the early 1930s meant primarily Marxists. Though in Hitler's own world-view Jews and Marxists were synonymous, his public vilification of Marxism predominated during the rise to power. Even Nazi members at this time, let alone more casual ballot-box supporters, tended to be first and foremost anti-Marxists – though, of course, this could often subsume (as it did with Hitler himself), or coexist with, violent antisemitism. Measured by their chief objects of hostility, close on two-thirds of the respondents in the sample of rank-and-file Party members mentioned earlier were above all anti-Marxists of one variety or another.[13] The most dominant ideological themes of the members in the sample reflected the vague 'positive' side of the Nazi appeal – expectations of a unified, solidaristic 'national community' (31.7 per cent of the 739 responses) and the supernationalism (22.5 per cent) associated with a strong, expansionist Germany. Anti-Semitism, pronounced or incidental, predominated in only 13.6 per cent of the responses.[14]

There was nothing specifically Nazi, let alone Hitlerian, about the general thrust of such vague imperatives. They had been a commonplace on the extreme Right before the Nazi Party came to corner the *völkisch* nationalist market. In the building of mass support, it was less an intrinsic Nazi doctrine than the style of articulation and presentation of fears, phobias, and nebulous expectations far more generally prevalent than among the traditional core support for the *völkisch* Right that was decisive. And when it came to presentation, Hitler was peerless.

In the full-scale crisis of the state which the Depression ushered in, with the economy in turmoil and political authority in complete disarray, Hitler's brand of rhetoric came into its own. He was more adept than any other Nazi leader – even Goebbels – at giving voice to grass-roots anger and popular prejudice in the most down-to-earth black and white colours. The force of his expression, the simplicity of the alternatives he posed, the strength and certainty of his convictions, and the grandiose future vision he held out – all combined to provide a compelling message for the already half-persuaded who wanted to hear it. The cold text of his speeches reveals them as a catalogue of banalities and platitudes. But the atmosphere, the staged setting, the mystical aura of messianic greatness which Nazi propaganda had by now wrapped around Hitler – all these made his words electrifying to the mass audiences whose emotions had already been prepared by a build-up and razzmatazz resembling a religious revivalist rally more than a conventional political meeting.

Some key passages in *Mein Kampf* had been about propaganda. Hitler noted that he had regarded the management of propaganda as by far the most important task in the infant Nazi Party.[15] The task of propaganda, he wrote, was 'to see that an idea wins supporters'; it 'tries to force a doctrine on the whole people'. 'Organisation', on the other hand, had its function in winning members – the active advocates of the cause who 'really make possible the victory of the movement'.[16] He attached the greater significance in leadership to agitation rather than to a theoretical programme. The great theoretician, he wrote, seldom made a great leader. Leadership qualities were more often to be found in the agitator. 'For leading means: being able to move masses.'[17]

Hitler's contempt for theoretical concern with narrow points of ideological doctrine in winning the masses was made categorically plain in a private speech in 1926 to the select audience of the Hamburger Nationalklub. 'Above all,' stated Hitler, 'one has to make short shrift of the attitude that the masses can be satisfied with ideological concepts. Comprehension is a shaky platform for the masses. The only stable

Figure 2.3   The 'Brown House' in Munich, which became the Nazi Party's headquarters in 1931.

emotion is hate.' He added that the masses felt strength more than all else, and that the individual in a mass crowd stood 'like an insignificant worm', feeling only the strength and righteousness of the movement, seeing '200,000 people all of whom fight for an ideal, which he himself cannot even understand, which he does not necessarily have to understand. He has a faith, and this faith is daily reinforced by its visible power.'[18]

As a contemporary commentator, writing in 1931, noted:

> All propaganda, according to Hitler, has to limit its intellectual level to the understanding of the most stupid among his audience. Banal 'Black against White!' rather than intricate thoughts. . . .The theme must be explosive. . . .No wisdom from the council table. Stir up anger and passion and stoke the fire until the crowd goes berserk.[19]

One early convert to Nazism, a German–Russian aristocrat, recalled that at the end of the first Hitler speech he heard, in Mecklenburg in 1926, 'There were tears in my eyes, my throat was all tight from crying. A liberating scream of the purest enthusiasm discharged the unbearable tension as the auditorium rocked with applause.'[20] This type of emotional experience was far from unusual among those ideologically open to the image and the message.

Hitler's propaganda techniques for winning the masses could achieve little success, however, without the external conditions which exposed an electoral 'market' to the Nazi political alternative. Without the Depression, the worsening crisis of government and state, and the disintegration of the bourgeois liberal–conservative parties, this mass 'market' would not have become available and Hitler would have continued to have been an insignificant minority taste on the lunatic fringes of the political system.

Even in the Depression, as we hinted earlier, the 'masses' were won to Nazism usually by more prosaic routes than being swept off their feet at a Hitler rally. For the most part, Hitler was preaching to the converted or half-converted in such rallies. Among the non-committed and merely curious who attended, the impact was often far from charismatic. 'What sort of an impression did he make? Always a crackpot, with his haircut and little moustache,' recalled a then middle-aged housewife, while a sixteen-year-old youth told his parents, after his curiosity had led him into a Munich beer-tent where Hitler was speaking in 1932, that they had no need to worry: 'Nobody will vote for him; such ranting can't convince anybody.'[21]

Support for Hitler was stronger in the predominantly Protestant north and east of Germany than in the mainly Catholic south and west, in the countryside and small towns (except in Catholic regions) than in the big cities, and within the cities in the middle-class suburbs than the proletarian slum districts. The self-employed, farmers, white-collar workers and civil servants were disproportionately inclined to back the NSDAP. But despite the propaganda that he was their 'last hope', most of the unemployed did not turn to Hitler. The Nazi Movement was more 'youthful' than any other political party except the Communist Party. But although the 'macho' image of an overwhelmingly male 'fighting movement', coupled with an emotive idealism, had distinct appeal to many young Germans, the Hitler Youth remained down to 1933 dwarfed by the size of the socialist, Catholic and bourgeois youth organisations. The Nazis were more successful than any of their rivals in drawing from all classes of society and building a socially heterogeneous following. But there were nevertheless significant deviations in the pattern of support and limitations in penetration.

Above all, of course, the socialist and communist Left and political Catholicism remained relatively immune to Hitler's appeal down to 1933 and beyond. Before 1933, something like two-thirds of the German electorate found Hitler an unattractive proposition. His full conquest of the masses came only after the Nazis had silenced oppositional opinion and had acquired total control of the media.

Nevertheless, the winning of the support of a third of the voting population between 1929 and 1932 was an extraordinary achievement of political mobilisation. As the bandwagon picked up from autumn 1929, rolled through the summer of 1930, and went into full gear after the remarkable triumph in the September election in 1930, the wave of new activist recruits enabled further extensive mobilisation, with success feeding success. Greatly swollen in numbers, the Party faithful could now unleash an extraordinary level of agitation which, through ceaseless meetings, rallies, marches, and not least through the battle for control of the streets in the towns and cities, put the 'Hitler Movement' repeatedly in the headlines, projecting an image of vitality and action.

With the Party propaganda machine centralised in the hands of Goebbels since April 1930, the image was shaped with increasing skill and direction. Campaign slogans, themes, speakers and publicity were centrally orchestrated, but with attention to local or regional emphases. New, striking techniques were deployed, as in the second presidential campaign in spring 1932 when an aeroplane was chartered to carry Hitler to his election rallies under the slogan 'the Führer over Germany'. The image was suggestive of a modern, technological world, though one in which true German values would be restored and would dominate. Above all, the image that Nazi propaganda ceaselessly portrayed was that of power, strength, dynamism and youth – an inexorable march to triumph, a future to be won by belief in the Führer.

By summer 1932 the bandwagon seemed more like an unstoppable juggernaut. By 1932 Hitler stood at the head of a massive Movement of some 800,000 Party members and approaching half a million storm-troopers, far from all of whom were Party members. And by 1932, thirteen million voters were to a greater or lesser extent prepared to place their trust in Hitler.

The mass base for the subsequent 'deification' of Hitler was laid. The acclamatory power at his disposal was to function throughout the Third Reich as the most important bonding agent in the Nazi state. But for now, it provided Hitler with a key to unlocking the door to power: no other Party leader on the Right could offer the conservative elites anything remotely comparable to Hitler's command of the masses.

However, Hitler's mass support was alone insufficient to bring him to power. By the end of July 1932, two presidential campaigns, a set of provincial elections, and then a Reichstag election had brought Hitler his peak level of electoral support, before the 'seizure of power', of 37.3 per cent of the vote. As the leader of by far the largest party in the Reichstag, with 230 seats, Hitler demanded the Chancellorship. At an audience on 13 August 1932, Reich President Hindenburg refused point blank to appoint him. The consequence, during the remaining months of 1932, was a deepening crisis of confidence within the Nazi Movement. Some Party members had had enough and quit. Voters, too, were for the first time turning away from the Party; the November election brought a drop of 2 million votes for the NSDAP, with a loss of thirty-four seats in the Reichstag. Goebbels had noted in his diary as early as the previous April: 'We must come to power in the foreseeable future. Otherwise, we'll win ourselves to death in elections.'[22] By the end of 1932, with finances at rock bottom and Strasser's departure bringing morale to an all-time low, the future for the Nazi Party did not look rosy. Hitler's gamble of staking all or nothing on the Chancellorship seemed a failure. The Party appeared to be in danger of breaking up. Hitler's mastery over his Party and control of the masses had proved insufficient to gain him power. Help had to come from outside. And at the direst point in the Party's fortunes, help was at hand.

Figure 2.4 A Nazi Party poster during the depths of the Depression in 1932: 'Our Last Hope: Hitler'.

The elites

✠

The handover of power to Hitler on 30 January 1933 was the worst possible outcome to the irrecoverable crisis of Weimar democracy. It did not have to happen. It was at no stage a foregone conclusion. Electoral success alone could not bring it about. Under the Weimar constitution, there was no compulsion upon the Reich President to appoint as head of government the leader of the party which had won most seats in a general election. As we noted, Hindenburg refused Hitler the Chancellorship in August 1932 with the Nazis on the crest of a wave. Five months later he changed his mind with the Party in crisis following the electoral setback of November 1932 and the Strasser affair. Hitler's appointment was technically constitutional. But the spirit of constitutionality was long since dead.

After Brüning had become Chancellor in March 1930, parliamentary government had increasingly and deliberately been by-passed and replaced by presidential government, with the Reich Chancellor ruling by the issue of 'emergency decrees' under the signature of the Reich President and authorised by Article 48 of the Weimar Constitution. Whereas under the first Reich President, Friedrich Ebert, Article 48 had been used to defend democracy against antidemocratic forces of Right and Left, it was now used under Hindenburg to undermine democracy. With the neutering of the Reichstag, which since the electoral gains of the Communists alongside those of the Nazis in the 1930 election had become increasingly unworkable, the position of the Reich President was pivotal. Access to Hindenburg was the key to power. Accordingly, the presidential palace became the focal point of intrigues of power-brokers who, freed from institutional constraints, conspired with guile and initiative in private wheeler-dealings to further their own power ambitions. And behind the maverick power-brokers stood the lobbying of important elite groups, anxious to attain a political solution of the crisis favourable to their interests.

Out of a labyrinth of power struggles, Hitler emerged the victor. Few of the non-Nazi power-brokers or elite groups in industry, commerce, finance, agriculture, the civil service and the army had Hitler down as their first choice. But by January 1933, with other options apparently exhausted, most – with the big landowners to the fore – were prepared to entertain a Hitler government. Had they opposed it, a Hitler Chancellorship would have been inconceivable. Hitler needed the elites to attain power. But by January 1933, they in turn needed Hitler since he alone could deliver the mass support required to impose a tenable authoritarian solution to Germany's crisis of capitalism and crisis of the state. This was the basis of the deal which brought Hitler to power on 30 January 1933.

Before Nazism acquired its huge mass base and became a force in electoral bargaining which could not be ignored, its relevance to elite interests had been tangential. Certainly, as we saw earlier, Hitler could not have become the 'drummer' of the Right in pre-putsch Bavaria without the patronage and protection of the Munich upper-crust. But, not unnaturally, in Weimar's 'good years' following the currency stabilisation, 'captains of industry', the landholding gentry, and the top brass of the military had little cause to show more than marginal interest in Hitler's party on the outer fringes of the political scene.

There can, of course, be no doubting the authoritarian tendencies and increasingly anti-democratic stance of prominent elite groups even in Weimar's short-lived heyday. And the Nazis did not cease to tout for their backing. Hitler addressed, or met privately with, industrialists on a number of occasions, seeking political and financial support. A few complied. But for the time being they remained exceptions. Quite apart from the off-putting anti-capitalist rhetoric of the NSDAP, there seemed for most leaders of the economy little point in putting their support behind a Party which had no influence and scant chances of power. Most probably shared the view put forward in a confidential report by the Reich Ministry of the Interior in 1927 which spoke of the NSDAP as 'a party that isn't going anywhere', an 'insignificant radical, revolutionary splinter group that is incapable of exerting any noticeable influence on the great mass of the population or on the course of political developments'.[23] It was no wonder, then, that most 'captains of industry' and big landholders put their backing behind the bourgeois liberal and conservative parties.

This continued to be the main pattern even during the Depression crisis. The Nazi Party benefited only on a relatively minor scale from 'big business' funding, which still poured largely into the coffers of its electoral rivals on the conservative Right. The NSDAP's funds came in the main less spectacularly from membership dues, collections at rallies and the like.[24] The bigger the Party became, therefore, the more funding from such sources was obtained. But the finances always remained in a parlous state. Though the Party did have friends and backers who provided financial and other material help (such as the usufruct of their property as

SA 'hostels', or the loan of vehicles to ferry stormtroopers around), it did not figure prominently in the power plans of the most dominant sectors of the elites as long as more congenial alternative scenarios were imaginable.

From 1929 onwards, however, the 'Hitler Movement' began to play a more notable role in their political calculations, even if most retained their reservations. The campaign to reject the Young Plan revision of reparations payments in 1929 provided a first opportunity for the Party to link forces with the other nationalist organisations, and to benefit above all from the publicity which they now received in the publications of media magnate Alfred Hugenberg, the leader of the DNVP. The path was now smoothed, too, in furthering contacts with prominent figures in industry and business. A number of local elections held in the autumn showed the NSDAP already substantially increasing their vote, especially in rural areas suffering from mounting difficulties in agriculture. Following the Wall Street Crash in October 1929, the rapid deepening of economic crisis in 1930, and the Nazi electoral triumph of September 1930 – the scale of which took even the Nazi leadership by surprise – the writing was on the wall for the Weimar Republic. By the time of the bank crash of July 1931, democracy was dead and buried. By 1932, reparations were effectively written off and a major shackle of Versailles was removed.

All this time, the deeply anti-democratic German elites had been looking for an authoritarian replacement of the Weimar Republic. Under Brüning there was talk of a restoration of the monarchy and a Bismarck-style system of government. When landowning interests persuaded Hindenburg to dismiss Brüning, von Papen, their own favourite, who would also have suited many other sectors in the business world, contemplated even risking civil war by deploying the police and military to suppress political parties and impose a new authoritarian constitution. Clear note of his intentions was given in the deposition of the elected Prussian government in July 1932 – a move of the utmost significance since Prussia, by far the largest of the German states and forming almost two-thirds of the Reich, was still controlled by a coalition of Social Democrats and the Centre Party. After intrigues had also brought down von Papen, his successor General von Schleicher tried to find a mass base of support by incorporating the trades unions and the Nazi Movement under Gregor Strasser as his Vice-Chancellor. When this move fell through with Strasser's defeat by Hitler and resignation, von Schleicher's days, too, were numbered.

Figure 2.5 A Nazi Party poster for the last election of 5 March 1933, emphasising the unity of the old Germany (represented by Hindenburg) and the new (embodied in Hitler), and carrying the slogan: 'Never will the Reich be destroyed if you are united and loyal'.

Hitler's contacts with leaders of business, industry and agriculture had meanwhile deepened without most of them being persuaded that the solution needed was a Nazi dictatorship. In 1931 the links with Hugenberg had been renewed in the 'Harzburg Front', named after a meeting of nationalist organisations at Bad Harzburg in Lower Saxony. Hjalmar Schacht had been one of those from the business world present, though he was by no means a mainstream figure and his enthusiasm for Hitler was unrepresentative of business circles in general. In January 1932 Hitler addressed the influential Düsseldorfer Industrieklub, winning some support but leaving many still unconvinced that he was their man. Through Schacht and Wilhelm Keppler (who had been in the chemicals business and now functioned as Hitler's link man with businessmen) much lobbying was done. Even more important, close ties developed between the Nazi leadership and east German landowners who had the ear of the Reich President, both through von Papen and as a result of Hindenburg's own vested interests as an estate owner. Military contacts, too, had been extended. The attractiveness of a commitment to massive rearmament coupled with the ending of political polarisation by the crushing of the Left without army involvement in a possible civil war was not lost on some of the Reichswehr officer corps. However, as this scenario made evident, the demolition of the Left and the provision of a mass base on the Right was the prerequisite of any form of lasting authoritarian regime. By January 1933, the prospects of von Schleicher providing the mass base which Brüning and von Papen had lacked had disappeared. Only Hitler had the masses on the political Right at his disposal.

In November 1932 Schacht had been the first signatory of a petition of a group of businessmen to President Hindenburg, requesting him to appoint Hitler to the Chancellorship.[25] Hindenburg still refused to do so. Since the elections had brought an increased communist vote alongside the fall in support for the Nazis, the prospect of interminable domestic strife seemed a real one in such circles. In the weeks that followed, von Schleicher's favouring of state-run work creation schemes and his attempt to involve the trades unions in his brand of authoritarianism deeply worried many leaders of big business, especially in heavy industry, while his plans to resettle farm labourers on the bankrupted estates of eastern Germany fatally alienated the agrarian lobby of the landowners. It was in this context, in January 1933, that the ambitious and self-seeking von Papen was able to act as the key intermediary and power-broker, liaising between the big business group around Schacht (still by no means representative of all the divided industrial and commercial interests), the Nazi leadership, and the camarilla around the Reich President, with its close links with the military and the Prussian landowning caste. Von Papen was now ready to accept a Hitler Chancellorship, though the price he demanded was a heavily nationalist–conservative, non-Nazi cabinet, with himself as Vice-Chancellor, and with only two Nazis apart from Hitler (Frick as Reich Minister of the Interior and Göring as Reich Minister without Portfolio and acting Prussian Minister of the Interior). On this agreed basis, von Papen, still Hindenburg's favourite, was now finally able to persuade the Reich President that Hitler should be made Chancellor.

The fatal miscalculation of the conservative Right was to imagine that Hitler would be 'tamed' by participation in government so that the Nazi bubble would burst. When worries about Hitler's intentions were voiced, they were assuaged by Hugenberg's claim that nothing could happen because 'we're boxing Hitler in', and by von Papen's laconic comment that 'we've hired him'.[26] In such a fashion, after the conservative elites had worked successfully to undermine Weimar democracy, but when they had proved incapable of providing the authoritarian system with a basis of mass support, they were prepared to lever into the top governmental office in the land a rank outsider to conventional power circles. The assumption was that Hitler would serve their interests for a while. The thought that he might be able to do more than a job for them was one they had not considered.

Notes and references

1. Tyrell, 'Trommler', p. 33.

2. Hitler was the seventh member of the Party's working committee but not, as he claimed (MK, p. 244), of the Party itself. His membership number was 555 (since membership numbers, for 'image' reasons, began with no. 501). See Maser, Hitler, pp. 173, 553, n. 225.

3. Cit. Dirk Stegmann, 'Zwischen Repression und Manipulation. Konservative Machteliten und Arbeiter- und Angestelltenbewegung 1910–1918', Archiv für Sozialgeschichte, 12 (1972), p. 413.

4. Hellmuth Auerbach, 'Hitlers politische Lehrjahre und die Münchener Gesellschaft 1919–1923', Vierteljahreshefte für Zeitgeschichte, 25 (1977), p. 18. This section makes much use of this excellent survey of Hitler's early years in Munich.

5. Kurt Lüdecke, I Knew Hitler, London, 1938, pp. 13–14.

6. Heiber, Tagebuch, p. 60.

7. Cit. Dietrich Orlow, *A History of the Nazi Party, 1918–1933*, Pittsburgh, 1969, p. 70.

8. Heiber, *Tagebuch*, pp. 71–2.

9. Tyrell, *Führer befiehl*, p. 163; trans. Jeremy Noakes and Geoffrey Pridham, *Documents on Nazism*, London, 1974, p. 84.

10. Tyrell, *Führer befiehl*, pp. 187–8.

11. N&P, i, 114.

12. Peter Merkl, *Political Violence under the Swastika*, Princeton, 1975, p. 453.

13. Merkl, p. 522.

14. Merkl, p. 453.

15. MK, p. 649.

16. MK, pp. 651–2; trans. MK Watt, p. 529.

17. MK, p. 650; trans. MK Watt, p. 528.

18. Cit. Martin Broszat, *German National Socialism, 1919–1945*, Santa Barbara, 1966, pp. 58–9.

19. Cit. Broszat, *German National Socialism*, pp. 63–4.

20. Cit. Merkl, pp. 105–6.

21. Walter Kempowski, *Haben Sie Hitler gesehen? Deutsche Antworten*, Hamburg, 1979, pp. 17–18.

22. Joseph Goebbels, *Vom Kaiserhof zur Reichskanzlei*, 21st edn, Munich, 1937, p. 87.

23. Cit. Thomas Childers (ed.), *The Formation of the Nazi Constituency, 1919–1933*, London/Sydney, 1986, p. 232.

24. See Henry A. Turner, *German Big Business and the Rise of Hitler*, Oxford, 1985, pp. 111–24.

25. The petition is printed in Eberhard Czichon, *Wer verhalf Hitler zur Macht?*, 4th edn, Cologne, 1976, pp. 69–72.

26. Theodor Duesterberg, *Der Stahlhelm und Hitler*, Wolfenbüttel/Hannover, 1949, pp. 38–9; Lutz Graf Schwerin von Krosigk, *Es geschah in Deutschland*, Tübingen/Stuttgart, 1951, p. 147.

Chapter 3

Repression and power

Portrayals of Hitler's rule in the years following the demise of the Nazi regime focused heavily upon extreme terror and repression as its chief characteristics. From within Germany, the claim was frequently heard that any opposition was futile in such a repressive totalitarian state. And from those who had grievously suffered under Nazism and those who had barely escaped the clutches of the regime through emigration there were depictions in graphic and moving terms of the exposure of the individual to brutal terror. A further strand of the same emphasis was added by scholarly analyses of totalitarianism produced under the impact of the Cold War and of revelations about the brutalities of Stalinism as well as of the Nazi regime. Hitler's power, from contrasting perspectives, apparently needed no further explanation than that of the coercive force of the totalitarian police state.

Post-war generations which mercifully have not had to suffer such barbarities as occurred under Hitler need a due sense of humility in attempting to qualify such an emphasis. Indeed, any explanation of the character and extent of Hitler's power which did not lay stress upon Nazi coercion and repression would be seriously flawed. Nevertheless, some points of qualification are necessary at the outset, which will at the same time help to define the contours of our enquiry.

To suggest that Hitler's power rested on 'totalitarian terror' – leaving aside difficulties with the concept of 'totalitarianism' – is to state only a partial truth. If we confine our attention to Germany itself and bracket out of consideration here the untrammelled terror unleashed in the wartime occupied territories (especially in Poland and the Soviet Union), terror and repression were highly selective in their application. Workers associated with left-wing parties were thrown into concentration camps in their thousands, especially during the initial onslaught of the new regime in 1933. Industrialists, landowners (apart from those suspected of implication in the 1944 bomb plot) and bankers were left untouched. Jews, an unloved tiny minority, were terrorised. Gypsies, homosexuals, beggars and other 'anti-social elements' also fell under the lash of Nazi oppression. But no German Catholic bishop, despite the 'church struggle', found himself incarcerated in a concentration camp. Police harassment was far more prevalent in working-class than middle-class areas of big cities. There was no assault on the farming and small property-holding population of the countryside. There was no army purge other than the actions connected with the removal of Blomberg and Fritsch in 1938 and the vengeful acts against those involved in the 1944 bomb plot. Most of the 'intelligentsia', apart from the minority of intellectuals forced into emigration, needed no terror to make them fall in line with Nazi 'Gleichschaltung' (or 'coordination'). Indeed, 'self-coordination' applied to many sections of society which willingly cooperated in the early Nazification of their professional and representative bodies.

Generally, then, repression was aimed at the powerless and unpopular sections of society. Little or nothing was done against the 'big battalions', especially in the early years of the regime. Nor was repression a constant over time. After the early 'settling of scores' as tens of thousands of the political enemies of the Nazis were subjected to the frenzied retaliation of the Nazi hordes, there was a decline for some years in the levels of repression, reflected in the drop in the number of cases brought before the newly instituted 'special courts' (set up to deal speedily with relatively minor political 'offences') and in the falling numbers of inmates in concentration camps. The numbers started to rise again in the two years leading up to the outbreak of the war. The beginning of the war was accompanied by an extended range of offences and draconian punishment against anyone seeming to undermine or threaten the war effort. But the worst of the repression within Germany was now borne above all by racial 'undesirables' – especially Jews (before their deportation) and the swelling numbers of 'foreign workers' sustaining the war economy. When the war turned sour, repression soared to new heights as the regime struck out wildly at all forms of real or presumed oppositional

Figure 3.1 The Reichstag Fire, 27 February 1933, which triggered mass arrests of Communists.

behaviour. Outside Germany, Nazi terror had by this time blown into a whirlwind of annihilation.

As these remarks have already intimated, the coercive force which lay behind Hitler's power is inseparable from the consensus in broad swathes of German society with much of what was happening in Hitler's name. Coercion and consent were two sides of the same coin – twin props of Hitler's power.

Still, it is important even so not to lose sight of the fact that Hitler's power after 1933 rested first and foremost upon his control of the instruments of domination and coercive apparatus of the state. In modern, stable capitalist democracies the power of the state might be said to reside in the capacity of the state to penetrate intermediary organisations of civil society and thereby implement political decisions through this mediated cooperation and consent. Where this capacity is so weakened that pluralist structures break down and democracy collapses, the resort is to what might be called 'despotic power' – actions of the state leadership carried out less by negotiation with intermediary groups in civil society than by force directed from above.[1]

This stage had certainly been reached in Germany by 1933. The collapse of Weimar democracy since 1930 – the fragmentation then polarisation of civil society leading to circumstances approaching those which bring about civil war, and the ensuing vacuum of central state power – provided the framework within which the power of the German state was reconstituted on 'despotic' lines. The extreme levels of conflict in civil society prompted extreme levels of coercion under the new Nazi regime – coupled, of course, with unprecedented attempts by propaganda to 'manufacture' the consensus which had been so patently missing before 1933.

The organisational structures of the instruments of domination have been thoroughly analysed and require no further examination here. The emphasis in what follows is rather upon the ways in which the atomisation of opposition and the erosion of legality through police executive action contributed to Hitler's accumulation of power. This process had less to do with Hitler's own actions than with the forces in the state, in the Nazi Movement and in German society which were, from whatever motives, objectively 'working towards the Führer'.

The atomisation of opposition

It took Mussolini around three years to establish fully-fledged dictatorial rule in Italy. In some ways the process of fascist monopolisation of power in Italy was never fully completed. In Germany, organisational forms of political opposition were destroyed within six months. Within another six months, lingering remnants of regional autonomy – already effectively smashed within weeks of Hitler becoming Chancellor – had gone. And in the third period of six months the potential threat looming from within Hitler's own Movement was brutally eliminated.

Meanwhile, the only major societal institutions other than the army which had not been 'coordinated' (or Nazified) – the Christian churches – had been pushed on to the defensive, adopting reactive and inward-looking stances in which political compromise went hand in hand with a tenacious struggle to fend off Nazi inroads where church practices and institutions were concerned.

Already by mid 1934 a perceptive report from the exiled social democratic organisation was pointing out that 'the weakness of the opposition is the strength of the regime'. Nazi opponents were ideologically and organisationally weak, the analysis continued – 'ideologically weak because the great mass are only discontented, merely grumblers', and 'organisationally weak because it is of the essence of a fascist system that it does not allow its opponents to organise collectively'.[2]

The complete demolition of political opposition within such a short time scarcely seemed likely in January 1933. Its attainment owed more to the dynamic forces unleashed by the total discrediting of parliamentary democratic forms of rule since 1930, to the inherent weakness of opposition on all sides of the political spectrum, and to Hitler's readiness to exploit to the full and with utter ruthlessness any opportunity which arose, than it did to any Nazi blueprints for stages of take-over and consolidation of power.

Though only two Nazis (Göring and Frick) sat alongside Hitler in a cabinet dominated by conservatives, the key position besides that of Hitler was unquestionably Göring's, who as Commissary Prussian Minister of the Interior was placed in control of the police in Germany's biggest and most important state. Moreover, Hitler held the aces from the outset in his relations with his conservative partners. They were united in the aim of destroying Marxism once and for all; but only Hitler presided over the mass political army which could ensure control of the streets.

With the huge, if potentially unstable, Nazi Movement at his bidding, and with the important added personal bonus of never having sullied his hands with participation in the Weimar system, Hitler's position on assuming power was, if seemingly precarious, actually, therefore, one of considerable strength in the Nazi–Nationalist coalition.

The coalition partners were agreed on 30 January 1933 on two essentials: the need to put an end to parliamentarianism in Germany, and the need to wipe out Marxism for good. On how to attain these ends opinion was divided. Hugenberg, the new Minister of Economics, wanted an immediate ban on the Communist Party. Hitler demurred. This could spur a Communist rising and bring the Reichswehr into a civil war – something which the army leadership were most anxious to avoid, and which the new War Minister von Blomberg had already regarded as best prevented by giving the Nazis a free hand politically in return for benefits to the army through massive rearmament. Papen suggested going for an enabling act. But an immediate move for an enabling act would have made the coalition dependent upon the support of the Catholic Centre Party. Hitler preferred first to push for new elections.[3] This amounted to practically his only opening gambit.

All that was at stake in such elections from the point of view of the governing parties was plebiscitary backing, since Hitler gave the assurance that these would be the last elections for a very long time, and that the composition of the cabinet would be unchanged whatever the outcome. This was sufficient to persuade the conservative members of the cabinet to concur in an immediate dissolution of the Reichstag and setting of new elections.

In the campaign which followed, the conservative anxiety to smash the Left again played wholly into Hitler's hands by supporting the legal framework within which violent repression could take place. In the weeks preceding and then following the election of 5 March 1933, this inordinately strengthened the position of the Nazi Movement at the expense of the remaining non-Nazi parties. The smashing of the Left at the behest not simply of the Nazi leadership but also of conservative elites was the first stage of a two-fold process of the atomisation of opposition in 1933, culminating in the dissolution of the bourgeois parties and the establishment of one-party rule by 14 July 1933.

The existing machinery of the presidential decree sufficed to provide, on 4 February 1933, for a ban on newspapers and public meetings attacking the new state. Such provisions had in fact been drafted by civil servants before Hitler took power. Full use was made of these powers,

73

Figure 3.2 Police arresting Communists.

particularly against the Communists, in the 1933 election campaign. In mid February Göring ordered the Prussian police to support the Nazi paramilitary forces and invited, with his full backing, the ready use of firearms to crush 'subversive organisations'.[4] The licence for an orgy of violence from stormtroopers against Communists and Socialists was given further sanction when 50,000 men from the 'national associations' of SA, SS and Stahlhelm were officially deployed as auxiliary police in Prussia. In response to appeals from the Centre Party to Hindenburg, to put an end to 'the unbelievable conditions', Hitler and Göring called for discipline.[5]

Hitler was careful in these weeks to do nothing to disturb the cooperation with his conservative partners. But the burning down of the Reichstag on the night of 27 February 1933 now gave him the opportunity to weaken their position still further and significantly tighten his own hold on power. Believing the Reichstag Fire – started by a young former Dutch Communist Marinus van der Lubbe as his own form of protest against the capitalist system and the government of 'national concentration' – to be the signal for the expected Communist uprising, Hitler and Göring reacted with near hysterical fury. Hitler apparently demanded the hanging of every Communist deputy that very night.[6] Though matters did not quite go that far, Göring issued a string of breathless orders for mass arrests of Communists.

By the time the cabinet met the following day, Hitler had calmed down. He explained that the 'psychologically correct moment for the showdown [with the KPD] had arrived', a struggle which must not be constrained by juridical considerations.[7] The last item on the agenda was an emergency decree rapidly drafted by Frick, using Article 48 of the Weimar Constitution, to suspend indefinitely all personal rights and freedoms, including freedom of speech, of association and of the press. Under its provisions, political prisoners could now be held for unlimited periods without having to be brought before a court.[8] By April there were around 25,000 of them in 'protective custody' in Prussia alone.[9] The Reichstag Fire Decree inaugurated, therefore, a 'state of emergency', which in practice lasted as long as the Hitler regime itself. It was a crucial prop in the consolidation of Hitler's power.

The next weeks were decisive in the elimination of organised left-wing opposition and the submission of remaining non-Nazi political organisations. Following the election of 5 March 1933 (in which the NSDAP gained 43.9 per cent of the vote and its Nationalist partners a further 8 per cent), the Nazi seizure of power in the Länder brought a drastic escalation of violence in the states which had not previously been under Nazi control. Tortures, beatings and murders of countless political opponents took place in hastily devised prisons and camps run by the SA. Though, to appease conservative sentiment at home and abroad, Hitler publicly appealed to the SA to end the molesting of individuals and disturbance of business life, he still openly encouraged the 'extermination of Marxism', and behind the scenes reacted to weak conservative protests at the violence with scorn and anger.[10]

On 20 March the Munich Police President Himmler announced the establishment of the first concentration camp near Dachau. Similar camps sprang up in numerous parts of Germany for the detention of political prisoners – for the most part Communists and Socialists. By the time of the Reichstag assembly on 23 March at which, with the support of the Catholic Centre Party and with only the SPD offering courageous opposition, Hitler was duly given his Enabling Act (allowing the government to pass legislation without consulting the Reichstag and without the necessity of obtaining decrees from the Reich President), Communist deputies were all interned or had fled, and the KPD had been forced into underground opposition. No law formally banning the Communist Party was ever passed; it would have been irrelevant.

The KPD had grossly underestimated Hitler and the Nazis from the beginning. Notions of open defiance of the new regime through a general strike rapidly proved futile. And, despite preparations for underground resistance, the party was caught completely off guard by the speed and ferocity of Nazi repression following the Reichstag Fire. Though the courage and commitment of those involved in resistance work saw to it that, despite brutal repression, underground opposition was never totally eradicated, as a political force and genuine threat to Nazi power the Communist Party was effectively destroyed in February and March 1933.

Meanwhile, despite its brave last flourish of resistance to the passing of the Enabling Act, the once-mighty SPD was also finished. The SPD, the massive *Reichsbanner* (its paramilitary arm) and the trades unions had acted with extreme caution during the first weeks of Hitler's Chancellorship in order to offer no provocation. But it was all to no avail. The *Reichsbanner* was forced into dissolution during March and April. The trades unions, despite announcing in March their willingness to break the bonds with the SPD and to work loyally with the new government, were dissolved on 2 May. The SPD itself lasted officially until a ban imposed on 22 June 1933. But for many members the game was already up in March and April. Party branches closed down, leaders of the Party went into exile, many activists were arrested, countless others sought to keep a low profile. Fear, confusion, dismay and deep disillusionment with social democracy dominated.

As with the Communists, underground work never ceased, though the main concern was less to challenge the might of the regime through continued agitation than to retain and bolster solidarity among socialist comrades. Visions of illegality had largely been preshaped by the experience of the ban under Bismarck's anti-socialist legislation. But as one former SPD functionary pointed out in 1935, compared with Hitler's, Bismarck's Reich had been a 'heaven of freedom'.[11]

With the destruction of the Left, a common aim uniting the Nazis with the conservative Right had been achieved. But in the process, far from 'boxing in' Hitler, the conservatives had found themselves increasingly outflanked, their political organisations exposed to a triumphant Nazi Movement swelling daily through the influx of new members, predominantly from the middle classes, determined to jump on the bandwagon. Towards the 'bourgeois' parties, relatively little Nazi coercion was needed. Certainly, the seizure of power in the Länder had seen scores settled with political opponents not just from left-wing parties. But the main effect of the terror of the early months had been to point up the futility of organised resistance – unthinkable in any case from the small 'bourgeois' parties which far from disapproved of all of the political objectives of the Nazis.

The former liberal parties (DDP/*Staatspartei* and DVP) dissolved themselves in late June. The Nationalist coalition partners, increasingly under pressure since the March election, gave up their independent organisation around the same time. The Catholic Centre Party and its Bavarian wing, the BVP, held out until early July. By the end of June they had lost their links with the clergy since the Vatican, in its Concordat negotiations, had agreed that Catholic clergy must take part in no political activities. Short-term arrests of Party functionaries in late June provided the final touch. The Catholic parties, the last autonomous political entities, dissolved themselves. Little more than a week later, on 14 July 1933, the NSDAP was officially declared to be the only legal political party in Germany.

Hitler's authority was by now unchallengeable by any organised opposition external to the regime itself. Interest groups, professional bodies, guilds, clubs, associations of the most harmless kind had in the meantime Nazified their forms and leadership personnel. The civil service had been purged of all adherents of the former left-wing parties, as well as of Jews (except those with a war record). In local government, mayors and other representative figures not sympathetic to the regime had been displaced. Outside Prussia, which had already come under Reich control at the time of the Papen coup of 20 July 1932, the problem of potential opposition to Reich directives had been effectively solved by the Nazi takeover of state governments in March and by the imposition of Reich Governors (in most cases Gauleiter of the Nazi Party) to ensure adherence to the Berlin line. Legal sovereignty of the states was finally abolished in January 1934, leaving Länder administrations in place, though deprived of any independent power. A further act the same month confirmed the subordination of workers to bosses and established the legal framework for the reordered industrial relations, dominated now, in the absence of trades unions and workers' political parties, by triumphantly aggressive management backed by state coercion.

By mid 1933, the 'organisational space' which any effective political opposition needs had been removed. Despite Nazi myths of a 'legal revolution', this had been done with a level of force, repression and brutality which had far exceeded the measures undertaken in consolidating Mussolini's rule in fascist Italy. The violence had destroyed the Left, and had impressed the ruthlessness of the new regime on the rest of society. It had been carried out with Hitler's sanction, but without any need for close direction of the cascades of vengeful terror actions unleashed by the Nazi hordes. As long as these were aimed at the Left and helpless minorities such as Jews, there was little opposition – and that only feeble.

The Christian churches retained some independent 'organisational space'. Attempts to 'coordinate' the fragmented Protestant Church – an amalgam of state churches with varying doctrinal emphases and organisational structures, some intensely jealous of their traditional autonomy – were eventually abandoned. Not even an attempt was made to destroy the organisational framework of the Catholic Church, however much the Nazis tried to break down and interfere with the institutional hold over the Catholic population through youth groups, schools, festivals and symbols. Both Churches were reluctantly brought into conflict with the Nazi state. But both Churches confined their opposition as institutions largely to fending off attacks on Christian beliefs and their organisational forms.

The most powerful institution which remained intact was the army. No purge, no assault, no interference was attempted here in 1933. This was an institution of which Hitler had to be wary, particularly as long as Reich President Hindenburg posed a possible alternative source of army loyalty.

Some form of army take-over and establishment of a military dictatorship, or even of a restoration of the monarchy, could not be ruled out.
Hitler needed the army's backing more than that of any other body in the
state. It is not surprising, therefore, that, when the military leadership
began to be worried about the possible subordination of the army to a
future dominant militia formed by the SA (by early 1934 some 2,500,000
men strong), Hitler showed himself prepared in June 1934 to act with
utter ruthlessness against a part of his own Movement.

A showdown with the SA leadership had been brewing for some
considerable time before the 'Night of the Long Knives' on 30 June 1934.
Some type of clash was practically inevitable. At times, the SA had been
difficult to hold in check even before 1933. But the nearing target of
attaining power just about kept the stormtroopers in line. They had most
strongly represented the 'putschist' approach within the Nazi Movement
before 1933, and in the 'seizure of power' phase their style of open
terroristic violence had been decisive in establishing Nazi rule so quickly.
But the crudity of their 'politics' became counter-productive as soon as the
target shifted from the 'enemies of the state' to the very pillars of state
power – the civil service bureaucracy, the police executive and the army.

The SA leaders had no clear alternative vision of the future to offer. But
as soon as the dust began to settle on the Nazi revolution, they found that
it had been only half a revolution, and that the 'old guard' still controlled
the real avenues of power, while few 'jobs for the boys' (or, perhaps better,
'jobs for the yobs') had opened up. The wild utterances of Ernst Röhm
about a 'second revolution' and the arbitrary interference of SA bosses in
local government stirred up fear as well as enormous antagonism among
conservatives – and among outright Nazis – who wanted an ordered
authoritarian state, not the disruptive 'political hooliganism'[12] of the SA.

By June 1934 the seriousness of the disquiet now being openly voiced
in conservative circles and the tension between the army and the SA was
such that Hitler's own position could easily have become endangered,
particularly after the death – to be expected within the near future – of the
ailing Reich President Hindenburg. Once, from within the top Nazi leadership and for power-political reasons of their own, Göring and Himmler
had shown themselves prepared to act together to remove Röhm, deploying the SS for the purpose, the fate of the SA leaders was sealed. Hitler
was now persuaded to sanction the move against the SA. In a swift and
dramatic strike on 30 June, numerous SA leaders – on the pretext that
they were involved in the preparation of a coup against the government –
were arrested by the Gestapo and SS and immediately shot. Hitler himself

Figure 3.3   The first major assault on the Jews: the nationwide boycott of 1 April 1933. Nazi stormtroopers stand outside a Jewish shop carrying placards with the slogan: 'Germans. Defend Yourselves. Don't buy from Jews'.

flew to Bavaria and personally supervised the arrest of Ernst Röhm, who was subsequently shot in prison in Munich. The opportunity was also taken to settle scores with some old enemies, among them Gregor Strasser and General von Schleicher. The 'Night of the Long Knives' claimed at least 85 victims, according to some estimates many more.

The bloody repression of part of his own Movement was a critical moment in the consolidation of Hitler's power. In the first instance, it removed the one force within the regime potentially capable of offering serious opposition from within or, more likely, of prompting opposition from other sources (especially the army) which could have toppled Hitler. After 30 June 1934, the SA amounted to no more than a useful but wholly loyal activist agency which, as in the 1938 pogrom, expended its violent energies in attacks on helpless minorities rather than tackling the wielders of state power. From the SA's loss of power, the main profit went to the SS – Hitler's pretorian guard, and unlike his mass army, an utterly loyal force. The power-shift within the regime had, in other words, notably enhanced Hitler's own position.

This was further consolidated in that the elimination of the detested and troublesome SA leadership bound the conservative power-groups more tightly to Hitler, and to the concept of the 'Führer state'. The mutual dependence of the traditional elites and the Nazi leader was reinforced. The conservative Justice Minister, Gürtner, gave retrospective legal sanctions to the murderous actions as extraordinary measures necessary to protect the interests of state. And despite anger within the officer corps at the news that two former generals (von Bredow and von Schleicher) were among the SS's victims, Blomberg ensured that the army publicly thanked Hitler for his action.[13] A few weeks later, following Hindenburg's death, all soldiers swore a solemn oath of loyalty to Hitler personally. Given the code of ethics in the German armed forces, the significance of this oath can scarcely be overestimated. A similar oath of loyalty to the person of the Führer (and not to Hitler in his capacity as head of state) was sworn by all civil servants.[14]

The acclamation and massive popular esteem gained through his destruction of the generally hated SA was a further boost to Hitler's power. Hindenburg's own vote of thanks to Hitler for having 'saved the German nation' provided legitimation from the head of state.[15] The Chancellor's popular standing had never been higher.

Last, but not least, the episode showed once more to all would-be opponents that the regime would be absolutely ruthless in its use of force whenever its interests were threatened.

The unrestrained brutality with which Hitler disposed of a part of his own Movement at the end of June 1934 provides a further pointer to the truth in Mao's dictum that 'political power grows out of the barrel of a gun'. Faced with such unscrupulous deployment of the might of the state, it was scarcely surprising if most individuals, deprived by now of any alternative forms of political organisation, felt a sense of helplessness. From 1934 onwards, the effective possibilities of removing Hitler from within were confined to those with direct access to the arsenals and coercive capacities of the Nazi state: the army and the SS.

Both had already benefited greatly from the establishment of the Nazi regime before they joined forces to crush the SA. Both continued to be favoured disproportionately by the advances of the regime throughout the 1930s. Though some army leaders, worried at the dangers of the accelerating course of German aggression, were by 1938 engaging in the embryonic thoughts of resistance which would culminate in the attempted putsch of 1944, the great majority of the generals were more than ready to offer their full collaboration to the Nazi regime. A coup from such quarters was unlikely as long as the going was good. This was even truer of the SS, pillar of the regime, an organisation imbued with Nazi doctrine, and the executive agency of Hitler's ideology.

Outside these key coercive forces, hopes of overthrowing Hitler from within were futile. Resistance from groups hostile to the regime never ceased. Thousands of ordinary citizens from all walks of life suffered persecution, incarceration, and not infrequently death, for defying the regime. The Communist Party membership in particular suffered grievously, with an estimated 150,000 persons – roughly half of its membership on the eve of Nazi rule – subjected to imprisonment or worse during the Third Reich. Some 12,000 Germans were convicted of high treason between 1933 and 1939. And during the war, when the number of offences punishable by death rose from three to forty-six, German civilian courts handed out about 15,000 death sentences.[16]

Resistance was inevitably, however, fragmented, atomised and isolated from any possibility of growing mass support. This was ensured by the scale and intensity of repression after 1933, though the ground had been prepared by divisions, distrust and lack of common purpose before the Nazi take-over of power. An analysis in 1939 by the exiled Social Democrat leadership, based on regular reports from the underground resistance in Germany, aptly summarised the impact of Nazi repression: 'Those who used to think, still think today, and those who did not then think, think now even less. Only that the thinkers are today no longer able to lead the non-thinkers.'[17] This is another way of indicating that the massive extension of Hitler's power was possible in the first instance because opposition – real and potential – was crushed, broken, cowed and neutralised through the unprecedented and unmitigated level of repression by the Nazi state.

A high degree of repression of former political opponents is a normal feature of authoritarian regimes in the 'take-over' phase of power. But frequently such repression settles down after the initial blood-letting into an unattractive but largely negative control upon those groups regarded as capable of posing a serious challenge to the regime. Even in fascist or quasi-fascist regimes such as those of Mussolini or Franco this was the pattern. Though the early violence was far more draconian in the upheaval in Germany in 1933–34, here too there was some apparent 'settling down'. While almost 27,000 persons had been taken into 'protective custody' by 31 July 1933, the number in concentration camps by the winter of 1936–37 had fallen to around 7,500 inmates – the lowest total throughout the Third Reich.[18] But already there were plans for an extension of the camps, and for new categories of prisoner.

As this suggests, in Nazi Germany repression was not static, but dynamic. A key to this process of dynamic radicalisation is to be found in the inexorable erosion of legality under the pressure of a police state, in which the conventional repressive character of political policing was blended with the ideological drive of the Party's elite organisation, the SS. Since, in turn, this organisation was the one which was closest in ethos to Hitler's own ideological imperatives and saw itself as providing the executive implementation of the Führer's 'idea', the growth of the power of the SS, merging the state repressive apparatus and Party ideological dynamism in an agency committed more than any other to 'working towards the Führer', provides a central part of the explanation of the character and expansion of Hitler's power. We need at this stage briefly to consider the unfolding of this process.

The subjugation of legality in the Führer state

Though Germany in 1933 had only a short, chequered history of democracy behind it, the tradition of constitutional rule based upon positivist legal principles was a far stronger one. It was a tradition which, in stages but inexorably, was broken in the Nazi state. It was not that

Figure 3.4 Hitler in 1934, carrying a heavy dog-whip made from hippopotamus hide.

Hitler's regime replaced one code of law by a new, Nazified code. A new penal code, it is true, was in an advanced stage of preparation by 1935, based upon the principle of punishment for the intention to commit a crime. But even this was felt to place restrictions upon the demands of the regime, and the proposal was aborted.

The Party Programme of 1920 had spoken of the need to base society on the foundations of Germanic law. But any such hopes cherished by legal pundits within the Movement such as the Party's leading lawyer, Hans Frank, were soon to be proved illusory. The regime's approach to the law was, in fact, wholly characteristic. Few changes were made to civil law. The key area was criminal law. And here the regime was ruthlessly exploitative, opportunistic and unprincipled. Where legal norms suited the purposes of the leadership, they were deployed. Where they provided obstacles, they were by-passed, ignored or simply dumped.

As has long been recognised, Nazi Germany provided the terrain for a conflict between legal norms and arbitrary executive police action. It was from the start an uneven contest. And as the climate in which a semblance of legality could be retained sharply deteriorated during the war, the erosion of legal norms turned into a complete capitulation by the exponents of the judicial system to the demands of police executive power.

Most German judges and lawyers had been hostile to the Weimar Republic, which they had seen as threatening their judicial independence and damaging their material interests and social standing. They tended to be national–conservative rather than outrightly Nazi in their political pre-ference, but generally welcomed the new regime in 1933 for its promise of a restoration of an authoritarian state, bringing with it an enhanced authority of those responsible for upholding 'law and order'.

A prime example of such views could be found in the Reich Justice Minister himself, Franz Gürtner, a conservative not a Nazi, but anxious to establish stable authoritarian rule supported by a legal system which rejected the fundamental liberal tenet of law – protection of the indi-vidual against the state. Gürtner was prepared to sanction the blatant illegalities perpetrated in the 'take-over' phase in 1933–34 as necessary in extraordinary (and thus 'extra-legal') circumstances. He accepted the retrospective imposition of the death penalty on van der Lubbe for setting fire to the Reichstag, even though the death penalty for arson had not existed at the time of the offence. And following the massacre of the SA leadership in June 1934, he gave legal sanction to the action on the grounds 'that measures of self-defence taken before the imminent occurrence of a treasonable action should be considered not only legal but the duty of a statesman'.[19] Gürtner was concerned to uphold the legal system and to keep separate the roles of judiciary and police. But his philosophy and his actions demonstrated how open his position was to exploitation by those forces in the regime – starting with Hitler – which were wholly unscrupulous in their approach to principles of legal rectitude.

The hopelessness of the legalists' position resided ultimately in their willing acceptance of the unique nature and unlimited power of the Führer – a principle which in essence contradicted entirely the premiss of rule on the basis of legal norms.

According to the head of the Nazi Lawyers' Association, Hans Frank, constitutional law in the Third Reich represented no more than 'the legal formulation of the historic will of the Führer'.[20] Such sentiments amounted, using Max Weber's terminology, to the subjugation of legal–rational authority to charismatic authority. 'Will', based on 'outstanding achievements', had replaced abstract and impersonal legal precepts as the fundamental premiss of the law.

Such a view was formulated not only by a high Nazi like Hans Frank, but also by the most prominent authorities on legal theory in Germany, who tortuously attempted to square the circle by rationalising Hitler's authority in legal terms. The leading constitutional expert, Ernst Rudolf Huber, for example, spoke of the law as 'nothing other than the expression of the communal order in which the people live and which derives from the Führer'. It was consequently 'impossible to measure the laws of the Führer against a higher concept of law because every Führer law is a direct expression of this *völkisch* concept of the law'.[21]

Explaining that the office of Führer was in origin not a state office, but one which had grown out of the Movement, Huber deduced that it was correct to speak not of 'state power' but of 'Führer power', which was personalised political power 'given to the Führer as the executor of the nation's common will'. In his understanding, 'Führer power' was 'comprehensive and total', unrestricted by any controls, 'free and independent, exclusive and unlimited'.[22]

Such interpretations by highly regarded legal theorists were of inestimable value in legitimating a form of domination which, whatever the mystical theorising, effectively undermined the rule of law in favour of arbitrary exercise of political will.

The willingness of lawyers and judges to accommodate themselves to the most draconian demands of the regime in the vain attempt to preserve their own authority and monopoly of dispensation of 'justice' was not matched by any recognition on the part of the Nazi leadership of their service to the Nazi state. On the contrary, the more ardently the judges tried to serve their Nazi masters, the greater, it seemed, was the contempt and abuse which they encountered.

Hitler's own contempt was unbridled. His view was that 'every jurist was defective by nature, or would become so in time'.[23] It was not merely a matter of personal vituperation. He hated the 'artificial notion of law'[24] whose function it was merely to use whatever means were necessary to maintain public order, but which was not an end in itself.[25] Law could by definition never provide the 'will' which was a Nazi prerequisite for action. It was reactive, not active. It categorised, provided regulations, and was thereby an unacceptable constraint. However harsh, it could never fully reflect the 'healthy sentiments of the people'. Above all, the prospect of any limitation in theory or in practice on the exercise of Führer power was unthinkable.

The law was consequently something which could never be more than partially satisfactory from a Nazi viewpoint, something to be used and exploited, but ignored if it hindered the greater needs of the state, the Movement, the 'idea', and the Führer. The clash between 'legal' authority and 'charismatic' Führer power was, therefore, intrinsic to the very essence of Nazism.

Both through an increasing number of personal, arbitrary interventions in the legal process and through his support for police executive autonomy at the expense of judicial control, Hitler himself shaped the framework for the complete erosion of legality in the Third Reich. However hard the lawyers 'worked towards the Führer', the instrument for the implementation of the Führer's will could not be confined by legal norms, but had to enjoy full autonomy from the law. The corollary to the decline in the conventional force of law was, therefore, the massive expansion in the power of the merged police and SS – the main executive agent of Führer power.

During the winter of 1933–34, the head of the SS, Heinrich Himmler, together with his sidekick Reinhard Heydrich, who ran the Party's intelligence service (the SD), had secured control over the political police in all the states outside the biggest one, that of Prussia. Though Göring, in his capacity as Minister President of Prussia, attempted to retain his hold on the Prussian Gestapo, he was unable to head off the growing challenge of Himmler. In April 1934 Himmler was made 'Inspector of the Gestapo', nominally under Göring as Minister President, with Heydrich as Chief of the Prussian Secret Police Office in Berlin. Himmler's pressure became irresistible after the decisive role which his SS played in the massacre of the SA leadership in June 1934, and by the autumn Göring, unable to retain any practical control in Gestapo affairs, conceded all effective powers to the SS leader.

One area in which Himmler had been able to build an expanding arena of power outside the normal judicial controls and with unrestricted autonomy was in the domain of the concentration camps. By spring 1934, most of the 'wild' concentration camps which had marked the 'seizure of power' phase had been disbanded. And following the crushing of the SA, undisputed control over all the camps passed to the SS, with the organisation of the first camp, Dachau, as the model. The legal basis for the extension of power through the concentration camp build-up had been provided by the Reichstag Fire decree of 28 February 1933, which allowed for police 'protective custody' without any judicial sentence. The camps were thus technically the province of the state police, though given the successful take-over of the police by Himmler and Heydrich, they were run by a Party affiliation, the SS.

Despite the attempts by the justice authorities and by Reich Minister of the Interior Frick to curtail or even end the 'protective custody' system which functioned outside their control, the autonomy of the SS–Gestapo in the sphere of the camps and 'protective custody' was reaffirmed rather than diminished, and this was achieved with Hitler's express support.

Though in April 1934 Frick had produced guidelines on the limited scope of 'protective custody', which Hitler had publicly endorsed after the 'Röhm affair', Himmler's police could in practice reckon with Hitler's backing in the frequent cases where serious infringements of Frick's regulations took place. Thus, when the Reich Minister of Justice made representations to Himmler in 1935 about the number of deaths occurring in the concentration camps and requested the presence of lawyers when persons were taken into 'protective custody', Himmler took the issues to Hitler and came back with the support he had wanted: 'In view of the conscientious direction of the camps, special measures are not considered necessary'; and 'The Führer has prohibited the consultation of lawyers.'[26]

The Reich Ministry of the Interior, still vainly hoping to gain control over policing, protested at the abuses of 'protective custody' and the ensuing 'lack of legal security' in a lengthy memorandum written in 1935.[27] But Frick's hopes of success against the expanding Gestapo–SS machine under Himmler, and backed in all essential matters by Hitler, were faint. Nominal concessions were made by Himmler in a new Prussian Gestapo Law of 10 February 1936, though ambiguity in the wording could not conceal the fact that the autonomy of the Gestapo was left intact. In the Gestapo's own interpretation, the law sealed the distinction between the Gestapo, which operated 'according to special principles', and the administration, with its 'general and regularly legalised rules'.[28]

With Hitler's decree of 17 June 1936, creating a new state office of Chief of the German Police but amalgamating this with the Party post of Reichsführer of the SS, Himmler's victory over Frick was complete. Though still, as Chief of Police, nominally subordinate to Frick, as head of the SS Himmler was personally subordinate only to Hitler. Little more than a week later, the merging of the political and criminal police in a new entity, the 'security police' under Heydrich's command, rounded off the process of creation of a massive sphere of autonomy, influence and policy formulation. With this step, conventional 'criminal' actions too were brought under the aegis of the political police, now an immensely powerful apparatus functioning outside orthodox governmental control as the direct executive organ of the 'Führer's will'. A further notable step was the amalgamation of the Security Police with the Party's Security Service (the SD) in 1939, to form the Reich Security Head Office (RSHA). Compared with the magnitude of the changes of 1936, however, this was an organisational reshuffle rather than a shift of substance.

The changes in the relationship of the law and the police which took place between 1933 and 1936 – further shifts during the remainder of the Third Reich were in essence a consequence of this early transformation – were of fundamental importance to the character and extent of Hitler's power. Hitler had supported on all significant occasions the extra-legal power of the police. By 1936 the police was institutionally amalgamated with the most ideologically dynamic Party affiliation, the SS. The judicial authorities were in every respect on the defensive. They accepted Hitler's supreme power in and over the law, and that this power had origins lying outside those of conventional state office. They compromised on illegalities. They could not penetrate the police domain of 'protective custody' and the concentration camps. In a grotesque parody of legality, defence lawyers sometimes felt compelled, by the later 1930s, to demand unduly stiff sentences for their clients in the hope that they would at least be confined in state prisons and not in concentration camps. This did not prevent prisoners on release being taken into police custody, nor the removal into 'protective custody' of persons whose sentences were

Figure 3.5 Leader of the SS Heinrich Himmler (left) and Reinhard Heydrich, head of the Security Service, who extended their control to the entire German police by 1936.

regarded by the police as too lenient or even those found not guilty by the courts.

When, a week after the outbreak of the war, the Reich Justice Minister Gürtner enquired with astonishment at the authority behind Himmler's press announcement that he had ordered the execution of a number of persons for offences for which they had not stood trial, he was informed that Hitler had personally authorised the shootings.[29] Hitler's personal arbitrary interventions in judicial proceedings increased in number during the war. And once the arch-Nazi Thierack was appointed as Gürtner's successor in 1942, the total capitulation of the judiciary to police executive power was rapidly completed. By then, the last ever assembly of the Reichstag, meeting on 26 April 1942, had formally acknowledged Hitler's position as supreme head of justice bound by no formal law.[30]

It is not necessary here to detail the vast expansion of the SS–police domain which occurred during the war. It needs only to be noted that with that expansion came the pinnacle of Hitler's personal power and the implementation of the ideological goals which in general rather than specific terms he had held to since the early 1920s. With the erosion of law and the build-up of a political police imbued with the ethos of Nazi ideology, the climate was provided and the instrument forged for the full enhancement of Hitler's power and with that the realisation of the central facets of his *Weltanschauung*.

On the day of his appointment as Chief of German Police, Himmler had announced his aim as being to 'build up the police, welded into the SS order, as a force for the internal defence of the people' in 'one of the great struggles of human history' against 'the universally destructive force of Bolshevism'.[31]

In the same year, 1936, Heydrich's deputy in the Secret State Police Office, Dr Werner Best, described the task of the political police as supervising the 'political health' of the nation and rooting out all symptoms of disease and germs of destruction. For this task, the police needed 'an authority which is derived solely from the new conception of the State and one which requires no special legal legitimation'. Hence, a new concept of the political police had developed, that of a 'unique body for the protection of the State whose members . . . regarded themselves as belonging to a fighting formation'.[32]

Infused with this doctrine, and given the autonomy with which to develop it, the political police were able to expand their activities in precisely those areas which 'worked towards the Führer' by persecuting those almost unlimited 'enemies of State and people' – Jews, Communists (and other Marxists), Freemasons, 'politically active' church representatives, Jehovah's Witnesses, homosexuals, gypsies, 'anti-socials', 'habitual criminals' – who formed target groups in Hitler's personal ideology. The screw of discrimination was thus kept turning.

The creation of a repressive organisation with a dynamic ideological aim closely tied to the 'charismatic' mission of the Führer is of decisive importance for the exercise of Hitler's power. We began this chapter, however, by pointing out how mistaken it would be to dissociate repression from consensus, and to presuppose a population subjugated against its will to the might and tyranny of the Gestapo. Although in the final stages of the war, with consensus undermined, the escalating level of repression was crucial in preventing an internal collapse as had taken place in 1917–18, for much of the Third Reich not only Hitler personally but also the police apparatus which provided such a crucial prop to his power had widespread support.

In fact, without such support within the population, the repressive capacity of the political police, which in its early stages after 1933 was far from massive in numbers or comprehensive in its surveillance possibilities, would have been greatly diminished. As late as 1937, there were only 126 Gestapo officers in Düsseldorf for a population of around half a million, 43 in Essen for a population of 650,000, and 22 in Würzburg to cover the whole population of Lower Franconia of 840,000 persons.[33] The greatest single proportion of cases dealt with by the Gestapo followed denunciations by ordinary members of the population.

The 'Malicious Practices Act' of 21 March 1933, banning offensive or subversive remarks about the state and its leadership, opened the door to a massive wave of denunciations which often combined political with personal motives. Social 'outsiders' were particular targets for denunciation, often in the workplace, the tenement block or the pub. The result was usually that the denounced person was taken into 'protective custody' or came before the 'Special Courts' which had been set up in 1933 for speedy judgement in political cases.

The surviving files of the Munich 'Special Court' number about 10,000 cases between 1933 and 1945 and there is nothing to suggest that Munich was unusual among German judicial districts, each of which was provided with a 'Special Court'. The extant files of the Gestapo itself, for its office in Würzburg, total some 19,000 individual cases, most involving, 'protective custody' and heavily reliant for their information on denunciations from the public.[34] The personal files which survive from the Gestapo office in Düsseldorf (reckoned to be about 70 per cent of the original total) come to a staggering 72,000 cases.[35] Without the 'snoopers' and denouncers, prepared to do their usually self-serving part in 'working towards the Führer' by handing over fellow citizens from whatever motives to the tender mercies of the Gestapo, such a system based upon an all-pervasive fear and anxiety could not remotely have functioned with such efficiency.

Notes and references

1. Michael Mann, 'The autonomous power of the state: its origins, mechanisms, and results', *Archives européennes de Sociologie*, 25 (1984), pp. 188–90.
2. DBS, 26 June 1934, pp. B22–3; trans. N&P, ii, 579–80.
3. *Akten der Reichskanzlei. Die Regierung Hitler, Teil I: 1933/34*, Boppard, 1983, pp. 1–10.
4. N&P, i, 136.
5. Martin Broszat, *Der Staat Hitlers*, Munich, 1969, p. 95.
6. Rudolf Diels, *Lucifer ante Portas*, Stuttgart, 1950, p. 194; and see Hans Mommsen, 'Der Reichstagsbrand und seine politischen Folgen', *Vierteljahreshefte für Zeitgeschichte*, 12 (1964), p. 385 and n. 143.
7. *Akten der Reichskanzlei. Regierung Hitler*, p. 128.
8. *Reichsgesetzblatt*, 1933, Pt I, p. 83; trans. N&P, i, 142.
9. Hans Buchheim *et al., Anatomie des SS-Staates*, 2 vols, Olten/Freiburg im Breisgau, 1965, ii, 20.
10. Walther Hofer, *Der Nationalsozialismus. Dokumente 1933–1945*, Frankfurt am Main, 1957 (1982 edn), pp. 56–7 (trans. N&P, i, 150); Broszat, *Staat*, pp. 110–11.
11. Archiv der Sozialen Demokratie, Bonn, Bestand Emigration Sopade, M32, report of the Border Secretary of Northern Bavaria, Hans Dill, of 18 Nov. 1935.
12. For the term 'politics of hooliganism', see Richard Bessel, *Political Violence and the Rise of Nazism*, New Haven/London, 1984, p. 152.
13. For the actions of Gürtner and Blomberg, see N&P, i, 182.
14. For army and civil service oaths, see N&P, i, 185–6.
15. N&P, i, 182.
16. For the above figures, see Richard Löwenthal and Patrick von Zur Mühlen, *Widerstand und Verweigerung in Deutschland 1933 bis 1945*, Bonn, 1984, p. 83; and Hedley Bull (ed.), *The Challenge of the Third Reich*, Oxford, 1986, p. 93.
17. DBS, 12 July 1939, pp. A83–4.
18. *Anatomie des SS-Staates*, ii, 25–6, 75.
19. N&P, i, 182.
20. Frank, pp. 466–7; trans. N&P, ii, 200.
21. N&P, ii, 476.

22. Ernst Rudolf Huber, *Verfassungsrecht des Großdeutschen Reiches*, Hamburg, 1939, p. 230; trans. N&P, ii, 199.

23. Picker, *Tischgespräche*, 2nd edn, p. 225.

24. Werner Jochmann (ed.), *Adolf Hitler. Monologe im Führerhauptquartier,* Hamburg, 1980, p. 59; trans. *Hitler's Table Talk* (introd. H. R. Trevor-Roper), London, 1953, p. 30.

25. *Monologe*, p. 350.

26. *Anatomie des SS-Staates*, ii, 46; trans. *Anatomy of the SS State*, London, 1968, p. 424.

27. *Anatomie des SS-Staates*, ii, 39; trans. *Anatomy of the SS State*, p. 419.

28. *Anatomie des SS-Staates*, i, 54; trans. *Anatomy of the SS State*, p. 156.

29. Lothar Gruchmann, 'Rechtssystem und nationalsozialistische Justizpolitik', in Martin Broszat and Horst Moeller (eds), *Das Dritte Reich*, Munich, 1983, p. 84.

30. Max Domarus, *Hitler. Reden und Proklamationen, 1932–1945*, Wiesbaden, 1973, pp. 1865–77. And see Dieter Rebentisch, *Führerstaat und Verwaltung im Zweiten Weltkrieg*, Stuttgart, 1989, pp. 418–22.

31. *Anatomie des SS-Staates*, i, 118; trans. *Anatomy of the SS State*, pp. 203–4.

32. *Anatomie des SS-Staates*, ii, 51; trans. *Anatomy of the SS State*, p. 427.

33. Robert Gellately, 'The Gestapo and German Society: Political Denunciation in the Gestapo Case Files', *Journal of Modern History*, 60 (1988), p. 665.

34. Gellately, p. 656.

35. Reinhard Mann, *Protest und Kontrolle im Dritten Reich*, Frankfurt am Main/New York, 1987, p. 66.

✠

Chapter 4

Plebiscitary power

Nazism in power revealed a dynamism which distinguished it markedly from other right-wing authoritarian regimes in existence at the time, whether fascist or partially fascist. The restless energy, the acceleration of momentum, the 'cumulative radicalisation'[1] of the Hitler regime were not remotely matched even by Mussolini's Italy, let alone in Franco's authoritarian state with fascist trappings in Spain. At no stage did the Hitler state lose its driving force and 'settle down' to 'mere' repressive conservative–reactionary authoritarianism.

This took many contemporaries by surprise. Whether on the Left or on the Right, inside or outside Germany, the most frequent assumption on Hitler's accession to the Chancellorship was that the initial revolutionary impulses would subside and that the traditional ruling elites would then regather the reins of power. The gross underestimation of Hitler's ability to consolidate and extend power was compounded by continuing notions – epitomised in the sphere of foreign relations in British and French appeasement policy – that below the surface, below the level of propaganda and mobilisation, conventional power structures and traditional political aims would prevail in Germany. This overlooked the extent to which, by the later 1930s, the traditional elites had been displaced in vital areas of decision-making by those forces allied to the increasingly absolutist power of Hitler.

The expansion of his power and – part cause and part effect of this – the progressive radicalisation and ceaseless dynamic of the regime cannot, however, be attributed simply to Hitler's personality and ideological intentions. This chapter suggests they are inextricably bound up with the motivation of Nazism's mass following. The wide variety of social expectations invested in the regime, resting upon an extensive underlying consensus, had a common denominator in the image of the Führer. This in turn engendered a level of acclamation and plebiscitary support which could repeatedly be tapped, thus reinforcing Hitler's increasingly deified position as leader, and contributing thereby to the growth of 'Führer absolutism' and the relatively high level of autonomy from the traditional ruling elites which Hitler was able to attain by the later 1930s. The drive of the regime, once power had been attained, was to this extent rooted in the pressures for radical change which found expression during the crisis of late Weimar in the utopian hopes and expectations lodged in the prospect of national regeneration.

Hitler embodied these hopes of a 'new deal' for the thirteen million who voted for him in 1932, and for the additional millions who were prepared to place their trust in him after 1933. The mass following, as we have already commented, was not for the most part drawn to Hitler because they shared his specific ideological obsessions or his particular way of viewing the world, but because he came to voice more plainly than anyone else their hopes of national rebirth and the destruction of the nation's enemies. This partial identity of motivation between Hitler and his mass support sufficed, however, to provide a plebiscitary basis of legitimation for the power of the Führer. Indeed, in a certain sense, the need, which Hitler plainly felt, to sustain this plebiscitary backing, to uphold his popularity, and to retain his prestige, formed a significant condition of his exercise of power.

The underlying consensus

✠

As a 'catchall party of protest',[2] the NSDAP had succeeded, already prior to 1933, in superficially uniting widely disparate sections of society by its mélange of hate propaganda and evocation of German renewal through creation of a 'people's' or 'national community' (*Volksgemeinschaft*). After a fashion, the Nazi Movement acted as a type of 'super interest group', linking quite different, sometimes even incompatible, social demands to a unifying vision of national regeneration. The spread of its organisational framework from 1929–30 onwards made the NSDAP far more capable than any other contemporary political party of appealing to a wide range of the population, above all but not merely in the fragmented middle classes, by incorporating their material anxieties and expectations into the psychological, idealistic belief that the problems could be resolved by the national rebirth which Nazism alone, under Hitler, was able to bring about.

As long as a pluralist system remained in operation the Nazi Party remained only one of a number of competing political organisations. Adherents of the working-class and Catholic parties in particular remained hostile and singularly unimpressed by Nazi agitation. Even in the last pluralist election of March 1933, with Hitler already Chancellor and communist and socialist opponents exposed to intimidation, violence and persecution, the Nazis could not win the support of even half of the electorate.

Even so, not all of those who continued to support other political parties in March 1933 rejected everything which the Nazis claimed to stand for. In the next few years, many of them would find something, often even a great deal, to admire in the Third Reich. The 'majority of the majority'[3] who did not vote for Hitler in 1933 became at least in some respects converts by 1939. This was, of course, in part because those who would have continued to oppose Nazism openly were after 1933 no longer able to do so, having been repressed into silence or incarcerated. Naturally, too, after 1933, with monopoly control of the mass media at the disposal of the Nazis, propaganda had altogether new opportunities to distort reality and manipulate opinion.

However, even Goebbels' full bag of tricks could not turn black into white. The successes of propaganda depended heavily upon the ability to build upon, exploit and 'interpret' existing social and political values.

The strains of political culture which Nazi propaganda could play upon had been forged by the expectations and disappointments of the recently unified German empire, and even more intensely by the traumas of war, defeat and revolution and profound antipathy to the experience of a crisis-torn democracy. Weimar Germany was riven by upheaval and crisis. Class, region and religion provided powerful sub-loyalties challenging allegiance to the nation-state which itself, far from acting as an integrating or unifying focus of political identity, was utterly divisive. But outside the counter-ideologies of socialism and communism, a number of prevailing attitudes and values lent themselves to ready exploitation by Nazi propaganda.

Figure 4.1 Reich Propaganda Minister Joseph Goebbels in his office, beneath a picture of Frederick the Great.

All the currents of opinion which Goebbels was able to tap, articulate and reinforce flowed together in the feeling that there must be a new start for Germany, a national rebirth. The very depths of division nurtured the longing for unity which found resonance in Nazi slogans of a 'national community'. The politicians' bickerings in a weak and fragmented democracy heightened belief in the virtues of strong, authoritarian, 'law and order' government. The visceral fears of Marxism widely prevalent among the German middle and upper classes, and given concrete shape after 1917 in the perceived horrors of the Soviet Bolshevik state, offered the prospect of instant approval for any government which could remove such fears once and for all. The national humiliation and fury – which extended into sections of the Left – at the post-war treatment of Germany by the victorious Allies, and anxiety about the nation's future, surrounded as it seemed to be by a ring of hostile countries, fostered the readiness to acclaim a bold foreign policy asserting Germany's rights from a position of military strength. Not least, any government which could rescue Germany from the depths of economic collapse and offer the hope of new and lasting prosperity could reckon with support which transcended party-political boundaries.

In addition, widely held prejudices and resentments fuelled by the social strains of war, hyper-inflation, then depression, offered the basis of a consensus extending beyond the immediate Nazi following. Hostility to trade unionism and the new status and bargaining power won by organised labour during the Weimar Republic – sentiments particularly prevalent in the middle classes and among the farming community – frequently went hand in hand with a populist anti-capitalism which denounced the exploitation of the 'little man' by big business but which, unlike the anti-capitalism of the Left, was concerned to sanctify rather than undermine private property – as long as it was 'useful' to the 'national community'.

Such 'gut reactions' formed part of a social outlook which turned away from any prospect of attempting a mere restoration of the class-bound hierarchies of imperial Germany, In sweeping away the egalitarianism of the Left, they also favoured uprooting the elitism deriving from birthright and money. Instead, a new elite of 'achievers' – the best, strongest, most able who had been given equality of opportunity and struggled to the top by dint of their own qualities – should enjoy their rightful place. A state showing ruthless determination not only to destroy the Marxist threat to property, but also to 'weed out' and eliminate social weaknesses – 'parasites', 'wasters', 'harmful' and 'undesirable elements' – could reckon, therefore, with much support. Social envy and resentment at the position of Jews – regarded as somehow 'different' despite (or because of) all their efforts to assimilate – easily fitted into such 'gut feelings'. The notion that Jews were not only different but a negative influence deepened sharply under the impact of Nazi propaganda. But here, too, rabid Jew-haters could operate in a climate of opinion in which latent antisemitism had been a traditional component.

The same type of outlook rejected what was seen as state interference by Weimar governments – for instance in social welfare or worker protection – while welcoming the intervention of an authoritarian state which, it was imagined, aimed at enhancing the opportunities, status and wealth of the deserving by promoting the 'national interest' and by destroying those forces 'harmful to the people' and 'alien to the community'. While the democratic state had, in such a view, been dominated by sectional interests, specially those of labour and big capital, the authoritarian state of national regeneration, it was naively presumed, would be 'their' state, the state of the 'little man', whose talent and ability would at last find proper support and recognition. It amounted to a search for a return to a mythical 'normality' in which the 'rightfully deserving' would receive what was 'rightfully' theirs. That many cherishing such hopes were to be sadly disillusioned during the course of the Third Reich ought not to lead to an underestimation of the potential extent of the underlying consensus which could be exploited by the Nazi idea of the 'national community'.

Among Germany's upper crust – the social elites which had traditionally produced the country's leaders – there was little direct identification with the NSDAP or the crudity of its ideology. Contempt for social upstarts muscling their way into the corridors of power, distaste for the vulgarity of mob politics, and anxieties about the strain of populist anti-capitalism in the Nazi Party's pot pourri of an ideology mingled to prevent any wholehearted embrace of the Hitler Movement. Significant partial ideological affinities with Nazism nevertheless existed. The termination of the hated experiment in democracy, the destruction of Marxism, the restoration of authority to those who had traditionally exercised it, and – externally – the revision of the postwar territorial settlement, were attractive propositions to all sections of the traditional elites. Senior figures in state administration, landowners, industrialists, financiers and army leaders all found, for different reasons, distinct appeal in the idea of a renewed authoritarian state. Such a state, it was presumed, would once more rest on the shoulders of civil service experts, would restore the primacy of support for agriculture, would uphold the free hand of economic leaders in unshackling industry from the fetters of trade unionism, and would offer new prospects to army professionals hamstrung by the restrictions of Versailles. The identification of such groups with Nazism seldom became complete, and in some cases the waxing disenchantment led in the direction of total rejection. But, in general, the affinities were strong enough to signify that a broad, multi-layered consensus underpinned relations between the Nazi leadership, the social 'establishment' and the traditional power groups. Such a partial consensus continued in good measure to exist until the later phases of the war, when the looming defeat of Germany and the increasing irrationality of the Nazi regime could patently no longer be regarded as compatible with the self-interest and self-preservation of the traditional pillars of society.

In the transmission of social values, a key role continued to be played, even during the Third Reich, by the two major Christian denominations. The Protestant (or Evangelical) and the Catholic Churches enjoyed between them in 1933 at least the nominal allegiance of more than 90 per cent of the German people. Neither Church hid its dislike of the Weimar Republic. In both cases there were strong preferences for an authoritarian system of government – though this for the most part did not mean a preference for a Nazi take-over, and areas of friction with Nazism already present before 1933 (especially in the Catholic Church) were of course to be greatly magnified in the Third Reich itself.

The departure of the Kaiser and the end of the traditional authoritarian state broke, for most Protestant Church leaders, links between Church and state which had been embedded in Reformation theology. A decline in churchgoing was seen in connection with the rise of godless atheism and the triumph of Marxist materialism. By the end of the Weimar Republic, the more radical elements in the Church were openly supportive of *völkisch* nationalism of the Nazi variety as the vehicle to producing a unity of Christian and political revivalism among the German people. 'The swastika on our breasts, and the Cross in our hearts' ran the slogan of the 'German Christians' – the Nazified wing of the Protestant Church.[4] The more mainstream sections of Protestantism avoided such excesses of association. But they, too, even where they took some aspects of Nazism to be disagreeable or worrying, saw in the 'national uprising' which was proclaimed at the 'seizure of power' the hope of the moral renewal which national rebirth would bring about. Enthusiasm for the new regime was seldom muted at first and, though disillusionment was to set in within a short time, the ideological common ground between the Protestant

Figure 4.2 A poster of 1936: 'All Germany hears the Führer with the People's Radio'. The rapid spread of cheap radio-sets after 1933 greatly helped the effectiveness of Nazi propaganda.

Church and the Nazi regime was to remain considerable. Nationalist chauvinism, fervent anti-Marxism, emphatic authoritarianism and belief in the Führer were among the factors attaching the Protestant Church to the Hitler regime, despite serious conflicts on Church policy and the ultimately total alienation of a minority of Church leaders increasingly unable to reconcile Nazism with the theological principles of Reformation Christianity.

The Catholic Church shared with German Protestantism the antipathy towards Weimar democracy. One of its outstanding leaders, Cardinal Faulhaber, the Archbishop of Munich and Freising, had even refused to have church bells rung in his diocese at the burial in 1925 of Friedrich Ebert, the first Reich President of a Republic which Faulhaber regarded as founded on treason and rebellion. The members of the hierarchy were in the main products of the Wilhelmine era. Both their social background – many of them coming from aristocratic families – and their traditional Catholicism led them to favour a renewal of authoritarianism, though one less antagonistic towards Catholicism (which had in reality flourished under Weimar democracy) than had been the Bismarckian and Wilhelmine Reich. The brand of authoritarianism which appealed to them was, however, distinctly not of the Nazi variety.

Relations between the Catholic Church and the Nazi Party remained chequered throughout the period of the rise to power. The evident anti-Christian strain in Nazi doctrine, epitomised above all in Rosenberg's writings, evoked stringent condemnation from the Catholic hierarchy. Prohibitions, warnings and admonitions about Nazism on the part of the Catholic clergy were numerous. Hitler's own concerted efforts to deny the slur that he headed an anti-religious Movement were far from convincing to Catholic opinion-leaders. Despite its origins in Munich, the Party's bastions of support even in its early years had lain mainly in the Protestant stretches of northern Bavaria, and in Franconia, rather than in the overwhelmingly Catholic south. Even after 1929, the Catholic 'sub-culture' and support for the Catholic political parties (Centre Party and Bavarian People's Party), stayed relatively impermeable to Nazi penetration. The Nazi vote remained, therefore, low in Catholic areas, whereas the big Nazi breakthrough occurred in Protestant regions. But heavy gains were made among Catholic voters at the election of March 1933. This may have been among the factors which helped persuade the bishops, following Hitler's promises in his speech to the Reichstag on 23 March 1933 justifying the introduction of an Enabling Act, to uphold the rights of the Catholic Church, to lift all prohibitions and loyally endorse the new regime.[5]

Despite the high expectations placed in the Concordat with the Papacy, ratified in summer 1933, it soon became obvious that the fears about the anti-Church thrust of Nazi ideology and policy were well founded. The 'Church struggle', a war of attrition reaching peaks in 1936–37 and again in 1941, alienated much support for the regime in the Catholic sub-culture which the Nazis had always found relatively difficult to penetrate.

Tenacious though the Church was in defending its institutions, practices and beliefs, there were nevertheless here too significant strains of consensus – outside the domain directly concerning the Church – in central aspects of Nazi policy and ideology. The assault on 'godless' Marxism was above all an area in which the regime could count upon the approval of the Church. Bishops whose aversion to Nazism was beyond question could, therefore, view the invasion of the Soviet Union in 1941 as a 'crusade' against Bolshevism. The building of an authoritarian state (though not, of course, one which would attack the fundamentals of Christianity), an assertive foreign policy to uphold the rights of the German nation, and a willingness to detach the person of Hitler himself from the evils of the system provided further components of a partial consensus with the regime.

We have glanced here at prevailing attitudes towards Nazism among the mass of 'ordinary' people, of whom only a minority were organised in one or other affiliations of the Nazi Movement; among the upper classes, who for the most part favoured a different style of authoritarian solution to Weimar's crisis than that offered by the Nazis; and among the leaders of the institutions which possessed the greatest independent influence upon the formation of opinion in wide sectors of the population once the pluralist political system had been ended in 1933 (and which in different ways experienced great conflict with the regime). In each case, important facets of an underlying consensus behind the Hitler state existed at the outset of the Third Reich. It was a consensus which, whatever the mounting reservations on many sides, was to hold in all essentials until the middle of the war.

Excluded from the consensus were, of course, those groups terrorised into submission – remaining adherents of the beliefs associated primarily with the banned worker parties, persecuted racial minorities, social 'outsiders' and others who could not be accommodated in the 'community' of national comrades'. Nor, as we have emphasised, did the consensus usually amount to an unqualified identity with Nazism. It meant a partial congruence of interest which by no means excluded significant spheres of dissent. But the underlying consensus did provide the basis for wide support and approval for the Nazi regime after 1933, in conditions where oppositional voices were forced underground and where public opinion formation was a Nazi monopoly. Before assessing the implications for Hitler's power, we must briefly consider the mobilisation potential of this underlying consensus.

Agencies of acclamation

✠

It was plain from the beginning that the regime would attach a high priority to the steering of opinion. One of the first steps taken following the election of 5 March 1933 was the creation, eight days later, of a Ministry of People's Enlightenment and Propaganda under the control of Joseph Goebbels who, since 1929, had been in charge of Party propaganda.

In his first speech to representatives of the press, two days after taking office, Goebbels outlined the ambitious aims of his ministry, emphasising the dynamic, not passive, role of propaganda. It was not enough, he declared, to terrorise non-supporters into submission, or to be satisfied with their tacit acceptance or neutral attitude. The objective must be 'to work on people until they have capitulated to us'. The intention was, therefore, no less than to win over the entire people to the idea of Nazism. The aim of his ministry, Goebbels asserted, was none other than 'to unite the nation behind the ideal of the national revolution'.[6] It set itself the 'task of achieving a mobilisation of spirit in Germany', and Goebbels significantly drew the comparison with the First World War, when defeat – in Nazi eyes – had allegedly been the product not of a lack of mobilisation in material terms, but because Germany had not been mobilised in spirit.[7] As these comments intimated, the ultimate goal, once people had been won for Nazi ideals, was already envisaged: the psychological preparation of the German people for the inevitable war to establish supremacy – whenever it might come.

The press, the rapidly expanding radio and film media, literature, music, the visual arts were all quickly brought into line in order to leave no channel of public expression untouched in the attempt to mould opinion behind the political philosophy and policies of the leadership, and to stir enthusiastic acclamation for the achievements of the regime. With a near monopoly of media control at his disposal, it was not difficult for Goebbels to build upon the varying strands of the underlying consensus in order to expand the plebiscitary backing for the regime. Nazi

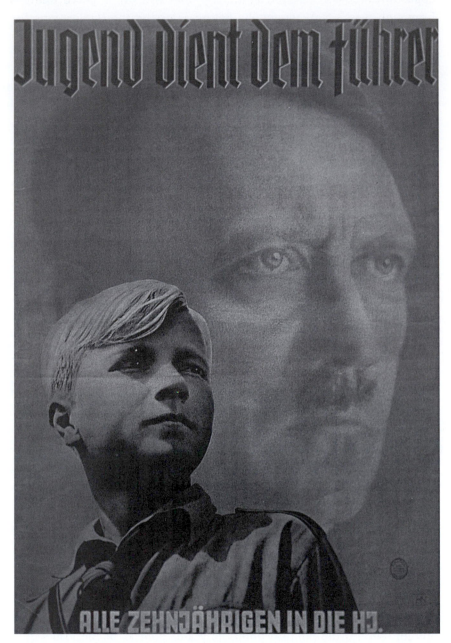

Figure 4.3 The Hitler cult is spread through membership of the Hitler Youth. A poster proclaims: 'Youth serves the Führer. All Ten-Year-Olds into the HJ (Hitler Youth)'.

'philosophising', such as Rosenberg was given to, would have been counter-productive. Under Goebbels, the message had to be couched in simple black and white terms. But the Nazi doctrine was left open-ended and vague. A 'positive' appeal to national unity and the subjugation of all sub-loyalties to class, region, religion or political party to the supreme good of the united 'national community', with its claim to total, unquestioning loyalty and self-sacrifice, had its counterpoint in the exhortations to suppression of any humanitarian feelings towards internal 'enemies of the people' and stimulation of chauvinist nationalism and sense of German superiority in dealings with other peoples.

The grandiose ambitions of Goebbels' propaganda ministry could, of course, never be fully realised in practice. Beneath the surface uniformity trumpeted by propaganda, many of the earlier antagonisms and divisions within German society remained barely concealed. Despite appeals to the idealism of the harmonious 'national community', attitudes and behaviour continued to be strongly influenced by material self-interest. Particularly among the older generation of industrial workers, schooled in the thinking of social democracy, class-based attitudes and class loyalties could not easily be swept away by Nazi chauvinism. Among hard-nosed farmers, the slogan of placing 'community good before individual good' continued to be turned on its head, as political idealism was subordinated to private benefit. Even the middle-class groups which had formed the backbone of Nazi support never ceased to find something to complain about in the policies and practice of Nazism. And when the Christian churches came under fire, the result was to alienate church-goers and, if anything, to strengthen their allegiance to their faith. But behind the daily dissent lay areas where there was little disagreement with what the regime was doing. Most of these found their representation in the image of Hitler. They offered a fruitful terrain for the one-sided barrage of channelled information provided by the Propaganda Ministry after 1933.

One such area upon which propaganda could firmly build was a widely prevalent acceptance of 'strong' authoritarian leadership which pre-dated Nazism. Extreme nationalist belief, long before Hitler, had been that Germany's salvation could be attained only through a 'great leader'. And the 'market' for such notions became greatly enlarged during Weimar's crisis. The extension of the Führer cult after 1933 as a pillar of the new state rested heavily upon this predisposition, which was far from confined to members of the Nazi Movement.

Goebbels, both genuine believer and propaganda technician, had a firm grasp of the importance of unquestioning faith in the supreme leader.

The Hitler cult became the pivot of the propaganda effort; and Goebbels was proud of his achievement in the construction of the 'Führer myth'. What was required was unthinking belief that the Führer would always do what was right for his people, and unthinking obedience which followed from that faith. The 'idea' of Nazism, it was suggested, however vaguely, was symbolised by the Führer. The achievements of Nazism were those of the Führer. The final 'goal', which was never defined, could be reached only by blindly following the Führer. In this sense, propaganda sought to convey the notion that 'working towards the Führer' was the duty of every German.

Addicts of the full excrescence of the Führer cult were doubtless a minority. For level-headed citizens, the excesses of Führer-worship were ludicrous. But there can be little doubt that Hitler's popularity was massive in the years after 1933, and extended into groups of society which otherwise found much to criticise in Nazism. The smashing of Marxism, the restoration of 'order', the removal of the scourge of mass unemployment, the economic revival, the renewed strength of German arms, and – not least – the run of spectacular foreign-policy triumphs which upturned the detested Versailles settlement and reawakened national pride: all these, in the trumpetings of Nazi propaganda (and there were no voices left within Germany publicly to contest the inter-pretation), had been made possible only by the Führer. The brutality, injustice, persecution, repression and international tension which under-lay these 'achievements' naturally found no disapproval among Hitler's uncritical supporters. But among a broader swathe of the population, too, such 'negative' aspects were at least taken on board, were frequently blamed upon others than Hitler, or were regarded as regrettable but inevitable by-products of the otherwise healthy national regeneration which was being carried out in Hitler's name. Those who found 'his' 'achievements' unconvincing or abhorrent were naturally for the most part careful to keep their feelings to themselves.

The Führer cult permeated in some fashion or other all sides of public life in the Third Reich. Civil servants were required from July 1933 onwards to make an outward sign of loyalty by use of the 'Heil Hitler' greeting, mandatory within the Nazi Movement since 1926. Physical disability offered no escape. Where the right arm was incapacitated, the left arm had to be raised.[8] Teachers began their classes with the same greeting as schools came under heavy Nazi influence after 1933. Writers, performers, artists and intellectuals – those not persecuted or forced into exile – were often quick to ingratiate themselves with the new rulers of

Germany by offering unstinted admiration for the work of the Führer. Leaders of both major Christian denominations were ready, in public at least, to exonerate Hitler from the opprobrium they attached to Party radicals for attacks on the churches. There was as good as no form of organised or institutional life which did not offer a further vehicle for public acclaim of the Führer. Above all, the Party affiliations and the Hitler Youth movement – which from 1936 became the state youth organisation – provided a vast source of fanatical backing which could be tapped whenever needed.

The numerical and organisational expansion of the Nazi Movement after 1933 meant that it was omnipresent in German society. Opportunists swarming on to the bandwagon after the 'seizure of power' brought a swift rise in the membership of the Party from 850,000 to around two and a half million by 1935, increasing to over 5 million by the outbreak of war. Further rises during the war led to a peak membership of around 8 million by 1943.[9] The membership of the SA (which overlapped with but was by no means synonymous with Party membership) also swelled rapidly in size from around 450,000 in early 1933 to almost 3 million by the time of the 'Röhm purge' in June 1934, though it fell back thereafter to only 1.2 million by 1938.[10] The Hitler Youth expanded after 1933 to embrace almost 4 million young Germans (almost half of the nation's youth) by the end of 1935. As the monopoly state youth organisation from 1936, it grew to well over 7 million by early 1939.[11] Though these were the most significant agitatory mass organisations, the extension of the Party affiliation through a panoply of sub-organisations covering practically all avenues of social or professional activity meant that it was as good as impossible to avoid some exposure to propaganda.

Before 1933 the Nazi Movement's united aim had been to attain power. Once that had been achieved, the task was a more diffuse one of social control together with propaganda and indoctrination directed at leading the people to the goals associated with the Führer's great vision. These goals were, of course, never spelled out. Even for the most devoted and fanatical Hitler believer, the goals to be worked towards had no more precision than a visionary, long-term, hazy utopia – a brave new world, with Germany on top of it. Meanwhile, on the road to that goal, the activists were motivated not only by Nazi idealism. For hundreds of thousands of Nazi followers, jobs, status and material benefits depended upon their commitment to the Party and bound them closely to the regime.

In 1934 Hitler defined the role of the Party as 'to make the people receptive for the measures intended by the Government; to help to carry

Figure 4.4   Hitler reaching out to adoring female supporters.

out the measures which have been ordered by the Government in the nation at large; and to support the Government in every way'.[12] While government policies were to be directed at the implementation of the will of the Führer, the Party's role was *par excellence* to 'work towards the Führer' in making what was interpreted as his will acceptable to the population at large. Party members were 'always and everywhere to regard themselves as carriers of the Führer's word' and to demonstrate visibly their subordination to the will of the Führer.[13] Propaganda was to be carried down to the very grass roots of society, through the personal contact of the local Nazi Block Leader with those living in his tenement block. Compulsion and control were never far removed from techniques of mobilisation. The 'Heil Hitler' greeting, a visible gesture of support for the Führer, committed even the half-hearted to an often reluctant sign of identity with the regime. To refuse it, particularly in a rally or mass meeting, demanded courage. The Party's propaganda was all-encompassing. According to one description, drawing on propaganda themes in the Munich area in 1936, 'the Party had an answer or opinion for every subject: art, peace, equality, churches, Sunday walks, farming, and, of course, Jews'.[14] And underlying all themes was the ubiquitous acclaim for the Führer, his 'achievements', and his future goals.

Führer acclamation and regime dynamism

In the years after 1933, then, the organisational framework was developed for translating the underlying consensus of the Third Reich into acclamatory backing. Such backing was never anything like total. But it provided none the less extensive and seemingly irresistible plebiscitary legitimation for Hitler's actions. The state propaganda machine determined the parameters of acceptable public opinion. The Party and its affiliations supplied a huge and fanatical activist base, the essential vehicle of agitation and mobilisation. Both were vital instruments of power. Both were totally committed to the fulfilment of the 'idea', which they interpreted as being indistinguishable from the 'will of the Führer'. The effective deification of Hitler by the state propaganda machine and by the Nazi Movement into a leader of supradimensional qualities, the embodiment of a historical 'mission', constituted a vital element in the power structure of the Third Reich.

As a consequence of the all-embracing, 'charismatic' Führer authority which stood beyond criticism or question, the 'mode of discourse' in Nazi Germany was heavily determined by the perception of Hitler's ideological precepts. It was not that Hitler laid down plain directions for action in a stream of commands from above. In practice, his normal method was, in fact, to avoid wherever possible difficult decisions which involved a choice between options proposed by two or more of his trusted followers. But this was no hindrance to the furtherance of policies which pushed in the direction of the realisation of his ideological 'vision'. The practical operation of 'charismatic rule' usually ran along more indirect paths. It was, for instance, impossible to advance an argument, let alone propose a policy, which ran diametrically counter to what was regarded as a central feature of Hitler's thinking. In fact, an important tactic in taking an initiative was to emphasise its importance to the fulfilment of the Führer's goals. And to ensure Hitler's *imprimatur* for such an initiative was usually (though there were exceptions) the key to success.

For Hitler's own actions, his central obsessions with *'Lebensraum'*, ridding Germany of Jews, and the coming showdown with 'Jewish Bolshevism' were real enough motivating factors (even if the weight of emphasis attached to them could vary over time and in accordance with tactical or strategic considerations). But for his mass following, such ideological precepts simply shaped the parameters of action in the form of distant goals to be aimed at.[15] In this way, a degree of self-selection went on, in which 'working towards the Führer' pushed towards the promotion of those elements of ideology closest to Hitler's presumed wishes, while pruning or excluding those possibilities which ran counter to or could not be accommodated to the 'idea' of the Führer.

In internal affairs, the radicalisation of different strands of racial policy provides an obvious example. The aim of creating a homogeneous 'national community' was predicated upon the exclusion of various socially or racially 'tainted' groups. In fact, only through the negative definition of excluded groups could the nebulous 'national community' acquire its practical identity. In this way, to work actively towards the vague 'positive' ideal of a 'national' community – an ideal which unquestionably had powerful suggestive force, and not only among ardent Nazis – explicitly necessitated discrimination against groups whose identity was far from vague and could be determined with some precision. Moreover, the psychological adhesive binding this 'national community' together comprised not only the 'positive' nebulous quest for German greatness but the 'negative' and concrete quest to root out apparently ever more numerous and seemingly ever more powerful forces 'alien' to the community. But since only a relentless purge, aiming finally at *total* elimination of such groups from German society, could be envisaged in order to bring about the ultimately perfectable society, the task implied an inbuilt dynamic of discrimination rather than a superficial 'reckoning' with the 'people's enemies'.

With the figure of the Jew as the symbolic antithesis to the German virtues embodied in the 'people's community', antisemitism offered the possibility of a wide range of actions in which ideological principle could easily intermarry with material forms of social motivation. 'Working towards the Führer' through discrimination against Jews could, therefore, mean ousting a business rival, removing an undesirable neighbour, acquiring a piece of property at a knock-down price, or simply letting off steam as release from a variety of life's frustrations. Given the centrality of the Jewish hate-figure to the Nazi Movement, therefore, Hitler needed to do remarkably little to channel existent pressures from below into an intensifying radicalisation of discriminatory policy. It was enough for him to give the green light or merely to offer tacit approval in order to ratify a further wave of anti-Semitic violence. The momentum of such waves – as in spring 1933, spring and early summer 1935, and summer and autumn 1938 – was more than sufficient to pressurise the civil service into legislative initiatives or to encourage the police to develop more 'rational' executive strategies. Whichever paths the anti-Jewish initiatives took, there was no reversing the spiral of discrimination.

In other spheres of racial policy, a not dissimilar process of radicalisation was at work. In a variety of ways, the barriers to permissible forms of behaviour towards disliked or 'dubious' marginal groups in society were progressively seen to fall after 1933. Not only Nazi thugs, but also modern professional experts in a range of fields could take advantage of this, justifying their inhumanity through recourse to the 'wishes', 'intentions' or 'aims' of the Führer, the interests or needs of the 'national community' and 'racial health'. Thus, for example, the removal of restrictions on the compulsory sterilisation of those with hereditary mental or physical defects, or other social or racial 'undesirables', opened the door for enthusiastic cooperation by doctors and psychiatrists to work in collaboration with police and local government authorities through the so-called Hereditary Health Courts. More than 400,000 individuals suffered at their hands.[16] The logical culmination of the emphasis upon eugenic purity, racial health and national virility was the programme to liquidate 'useless life' which was begun in 1939.[17]

Graf Baillet-Latour   Der Führer   Staatssekretär a. D. Dr. Lewald

„Ich verkünde die Spiele von Berlin zur Feier der
XI. Olympiade neuer Zeitrechnung als eröffnet"

Der Führer am 1. August 1936

Figure 4.5   Hitler opens the Berlin Olympics, 1936, which were exploited by propaganda to present the 'good side' of the Third Reich to the world.

Since, then, in striving for the completion of the task of national rebirth, the achievement of the 'positive' side of the equation – the creation of the harmonious 'people's community' – was an open-ended objective, it was scarcely just by chance that the 'negative' side – the elimination of 'unacceptable' and 'undesirable' elements – attained priority as a mobilising agent, gaining increasing ascendancy as a more realistic and tangible goal. The presumed wishes of the Führer served thereby to bind together disparate and fragmented forces within the regime, to galvanise them into action, and to justify the consequences of their activism. 'Working towards the Führer' in this way pushed policy along, without close direction from above but operating in a mutually reinforcing fashion with the interests of the policymakers and wholly eliminating the possibility of any contrary lines of policy development. The plebiscitary support for the Führer, implicit in good measure in the underlying consensus and activated by the agencies of acclamation, constituted, therefore, a crucial strand in the radicalising dynamic of the Third Reich, and in the growing autonomy of Hitler's power.

The acclaim which Hitler won through his triumphant exploitation of western diplomatic weakness between 1933 and spring 1939 also contributed notably to the strengthening of his position, particularly vis à vis the military leadership and the other traditional ruling elites.

Hitler himself was well aware of the value of the plebiscitary support which he gained through his immense personal popularity. If Hermann Rauschning can be believed, Hitler justified his first major snub of the western democracies – the withdrawal from the League of Nations in October 1933 – chiefly in terms of its domestic significance in binding the German people closer to him, claiming that he had felt compelled to take the step on the grounds that whatever foreign policy difficulties ensued would be compensated for by the trust which he would win among the German people through this action.[18] Looking back, in the middle of the war Hitler recalled that he had seen to it that plebiscites were staged after his major coups because of their impact 'both externally and internally'.[19]

Only one of the four general plebiscites to take place during the Third Reich – that on 19 August 1934 to approve Hitler's assumption of the position of head of state after the death of Reich President Hindenburg – did not follow a major foreign-policy triumph. The withdrawal from the League of Nations in 1933, the reoccupation of the Rhineland in 1936, and the Anschluß of Austria in 1938 – the occasions for the other plebiscites – were hugely popular, whatever the palpably absurd official plebiscite results (particularly in 1936 and 1938). Such triumphs in unifying 'national' questions rather than in potentially divisive issues close to the heart of the specifically Nazi creed were guaranteed to tap the maximum possible consensus, and to send the signal both to doubters in Germany and to the world outside that Hitler had the mass of the German people behind him.

The march into the Rhineland on 7 March 1936 – when German troops, in breach of the Versailles and Locarno treaties, reoccupied the former demilitarised zone – offers the clearest indication of how a foreign-policy coup could, temporarily at least, deflect attention from genuine internal difficulties and help the regime regain the momentum at home as well as abroad. Though diplomatic gains were doubtless uppermost in Hitler's mind, it was in fact thought in some high places in the government that the reasons for the timing of the coup were in fact solely domestic – the need to stir up the masses again, to renew enthusiasm in the Party, to win back confidence after the serious crisis of food provisions during the previous winter, and to overshadow the mounting conflict with the Catholic Church.[20]

Indeed, the plebiscite on 29 March did provide an excellent opportunity to revamp the flagging morale of the Party by engaging activists in a massive propaganda operation in the weeks before the 'vote'. The optimal 99 per cent 'yes' vote was this time attained. Even taking account of some 'creative vote-counting', as well as the deployment of indirect and less subtle forms of coercion, which had gone into producing the result, it was one which could not be altogether ignored, either inside Germany or outside. Externally, the western Allies had not merely missed an opportunity of halting German expansion; they had been forced to witness the enormous popularity boost which such a move had given Hitler.

And for those isolated groups within Germany working towards the downfall of the regime in endangered illegal organisations, the inaction of the west and the plebiscitary support for Hitler further took the wind out of their sails, after signs the previous winter that even Hitler's own popularity was beginning to suffer in the wake of the growing difficulties of coping with food shortages. An observer from the exiled SPD caught the relationship of the plebiscitary acclamation for Hitler's actions and the shaping of Nazi policy when he noted that Hitler could 'no longer escape from his policy'. Through the undoubted overwhelming endorsement of his action which the announced plebiscite on 29 March would bring, 'the Dictator lets himself be bound by the people to the policy he wanted!'[21]

Plate 9 Hitler flanked by Professor Leonard Gall and architect Albert Speer during construction of the 'House of German Art' in Munich, 1934.

Plate 10   Adolf Hitler in 1934.

Plate 11   Hitler attends the International Automobile Show in Berlin, 1935.

Plate 12 Nazi Rally at Nuremberg 1936, parading airship Hindenburg overhead.

Plate 13 Adolf Hitler and Heinrich Himmler, leader of the SS, at Nuremberg in 1938.

Plate 14 Hitler and Mussolini meet at Munich in 1938.

Plate 15 The new Reich Chancellery built by Albert Speer, completed in 1939; SS men guard the door to Hitler's office.

Plate 16 Hitler meets Molotov, Soviet Commissar for Foreign Affairs, in Berlin, November 1940.

If Hitler's popular support among the masses was a source of great strength to him, the potential loss of such support could only mark a weakness. Hence, he was sharply allergic to anything which might damage his popular standing or undermine his prestige. He expressed more than once his dark fears in the event of a serious drop in his popularity.[22] And since he accepted that 'the grey daily routine' was a constant threat to political 'enthusiasm'[23], he recognised the need for repeated success to bind the masses to him and to produce the necessary recurrent psychological mobilisation. Otherwise, in his view, 'sterility' would set in, 'and in its train disorders of a social character must arise'.[24] In this way, the legitimation through plebiscitary support could be ensured only by recurrent success – a classical hallmark of 'charismatic rule' in Max Weber's conceptualisation. Refusal to let the momentum sag was in this respect, therefore, intrinsic to the very essence of Hitler's 'charismatic' power.

Notes and references

1 . For the term, see Hans Mommsen, 'Der Nationalsozialismus: Kumulative Radikalisierung und Selbstzerstörung des Regimes', in *Meyers Enzyklopädisches Lexikon*, vol. 16 (1976), pp. 785–90.

2. The phrase is that of Thomas Childers, *The Nazi Voter*, Chapel Hill/London, 1983, p. 268.

3. Sebastian Haffner, *Anmerkungen zu Hitler*, Munich, 1978, p. 43.

4. J. S. Conway, *The Nazi Persecution of the Churches 1933–45*, London, 1968, p. 45.

5. N&P, i, 156–7, 159.

6. Paul Meier-Benneckenstein, *Dokumente der deutschen Politik*, vol. 1, 2nd edn, Berlin, 1937, pp. 263–4; trans. N&P, ii, 381.

7. Helmut Heiber, *Goebbels Reden*, vol. 1, Düsseldorf, 1971, p. 90; trans. N&P, ii, 382.

8. BAK, R43II/1263, ff. 93, 164.

9. Aryeh H. Unger, *The Totalitarian Party*, Cambridge, 1974, p. 84; Michael H. Kater, *The Nazi Party. A Social Profile of Members and Leaders, 1919–1945*, Oxford, 1983, p. 263.

10. Mathilde Jamin, *Zwischen den Klassen. Zur Sozialstruktur der SA-Führerschaft*, Wuppertal, 1984, pp. 2–7; Conan Fisher, *Stormtroopers*, London, 1983, p. 32.

11. N&P, ii, 421.

12. Hans-Adolf Jacobsen and Werner Jochmann (eds.), *Ausgewählte Dokumente zur Geschichte des Nationalsozialismus 1933–1945*, vol. 1/C (no pagination); trans. N&P, ii, 234.

13. Cit. Unger, pp. 87, 89.

14. Dietrich Orlow, *The History of the Nazi Party, 1933–1945*, Pittsburgh, 1973, p. 173.

15. See on this point the important article by Martin Broszat, 'Soziale Motivation und Führer-Bindung des Nationalsozialismus', *Vierteljahreshefte für Zeitgeschichte*, 18 (1970), pp. 392–409.

16. Gisela Bock, *Zwangssterilisation im Nationalsozialismus*, Opladen, 1986, pp. 8, 238.

17. See the documentation in N&P iii, pp. 997 ff.

18. Hermann Rauschning, *Gespräche mit Hitler*, Zürich, 1940, pp. 102–3; serious doubt on the authenticity of Rauschning's evidence has been raised by Wolfgang Hänel, *Hermann Rauschnings 'Gespräche mit Hitler' – Eine Geschichtsfälschung*, Ingolstadt, 1984.

19. Picker, *Tischgespräche*, 2nd edn, p. 169.

20. See Manfred Funke, '7 März 1936. Fallstudie zum außenpolitischen Führungsstil Hitlers', in Wolfgang Michalka (ed.), *Nationalsozialistische Außenpolitik*, Darmstadt, 1978, pp. 278–9.

21. Archiv der sozialen Demokratie, Bonn, Emigration Sopade M33, Hans Dill to Otto Wels, 7 March 1936.

22. See Albert Speer, *Erinnerungen*, Frankfurt am Main/Berlin, 1969, pp. 173, 229.

23. Helmut Heiber (ed.), *Hitlers Lagebesprechungen. Die Protokollfragmente seiner militärischen Konferenzen 1942–1945*, Stuttgart, 1962, p. 718.

24. N&P, iii, 681.

Chapter 5

✠

Expansion of power

There was no sweeping away of the existing forms of government and replacement by the Nazi Party during the 'seizure of power'. Only a minority of the important offices of state in the Reich government down to the end of 1937 were held by Nazis. The Ministries of Foreign Affairs, War, Economics, Finance, Labour, Justice and Transport remained to that date (some of them beyond) occupied by national–conservatives.[1] Within the Party there were frequent signs of disappointment and frustration in these years at the limits of influence and control over state policy and administration.

The period between the 'Röhm crisis' of 1934 and the 'Blomberg–Fritsch crisis' of 1938 appeared to offer some indications that the turbulence following the 'seizure of power' might now be subsiding into a relatively stable authoritarianism. In reality, the radicalism of the Nazi Movement was never halted, let alone reversed, by the conservative forces – which, despite their aversion to some of its manifestations, had their uses for Nazi 'actionism'. Nevertheless, the emasculation of the SA, the decline in the scale of political arrests, and the replacement of the anti-Jewish agitation of Party fanatics after the frenetic summer of 1935 by 'legal' (and therefore seemingly 'regulated' discrimination) appeared to offer hints that a stabilisation and 'systematisation' of Nazi rule might be possible. The calm imposed by the need to impress foreign visitors to Germany during the Olympic year of 1936 helped to sustain the illusion.

In external affairs, too, there was little in these years to suggest that the regime's foreign policy, under the conservative Baron von Neurath, would go beyond 'revisionism' and the liquidation of the Versailles and Locarno settlements.

The mid 1930s were years in which the dramatic radicalisation of Nazi policies which set in on a whole number of fronts from 1938 onwards could scarcely be accurately foreseen even by the most perceptive observer. They were years when Hitler had to tread somewhat carefully in his relations with the traditional elites, when the more extreme demands and dynamic drive of the Nazi Movement were kept under relative restraint.

The regime in this period comprised in effect a set of differing power entities – the Nazi Movement, the state administration, the army, big business, the police – with separate but interlocking interests which found a common unifying factor in the authority of the Führer. The different entities in this 'power cartel' did not remain static, however, but fluctuated in their relationship to each other, and to the authority of the Führer. Hitler's power, in turn, derived from his position as the fulcrum, linchpin and mediating element of the differing interests. But the very centrality of his unique position in the overall power constellation allowed his own authority to expand and develop an increasing autonomy relative to the other spheres of power. And as it did so, the 'power cartel' itself shifted in its base, with those spheres closest to Hitler expanding in importance at the expense of those with a more distant relationship to the Führer. Beneath the signs of seeming 'normalisation' of Nazi rule in the years 1934–37, therefore, the process of expansion of Hitler's power was taking place. And accompanying it, part as cause, part as result, the underlying radical dynamic of Nazism, far from subsiding towards stagnant authoritarianism, was gathering pace.

How and why did the autonomy of Hitler's power position expand so significantly during this period? A part of the answer has already been provided by our consideration of the growth of the police–SS organisation and of the plebiscitary acclaim for Hitler's actions. But we need now to extend our examination to the changing structure of government in the Third Reich and to the ways in which Hitler could gain through the weakness and compliance of the traditional ruling classes within Germany and through the acquiescence and feebleness of the leaders of the western democracies.

The erosion of collective government

Government in the Third Reich was increasingly an attempt to reconcile the irreconcilable: to accommodate bureaucratic structures of governmental administration to the will of a leader whose authority derived from his 'charismatic' claims and not from a formal position. The consequence was a progressive overlayering of the bureaucratic structures of the state by arbitrary Führer power, resulting in a gradual undermining and corrosion of formal patterns of government and administration – a process reaching its apogee only during the war years.

Initially, Hitler's 'charismatic' claims counted for little in the practice of government. His authority resided in the fact that he had been appointed head of government like the Chancellors who had preceded him. And like them, he had to work within the framework of a complex and sophisticated governmental system and bureaucracy. Unlike his predecessors, he had no governmental experience and – something which was to become a distinctive feature of his style of government – had a pronounced distaste for bureaucratic procedures and conventional administrative work routines. On the other hand, he could depend upon the backing of a huge mass movement. And his entry into government had been celebrated – not solely by Nazi fanatics – less as a change of administration than as the dawning of a new epoch for Germany. The seal was symbolically set upon a rebirth supposedly building on the most glorious and 'true' German tradition (in which Weimar democracy was seen as a treacherous interlude) at the 'Day of Potsdam' on 21 March 1933, when President Hindenburg and Chancellor Hitler – the 'old' and the 'new' images of Germany – joined hands before the tomb of Frederick the Great at the ceremonial opening of the recently elected Reichstag.

Despite his inexperience in office, Hitler's mass following and the atmosphere of 'national uprising' which embraced the beginning of his Chancellorship offered him from the outset an advantage denied to other Chancellors. Moreover, Hitler rapidly demonstrated how fatally flawed was the condescension with which established politicians and many in the upper classes and intelligentsia viewed this 'vulgar upstart'. Far from revealing a naiveté and an incapacity which would have made him putty in the hands of the traditional power groups and would rapidly have rendered him dispensable, he showed a quick and sharp appreciation of the realities of governmental power.

Figure 5.1 Hitler's greatest foreign-policy triumph to date: the reoccupation of the Rhineland, 7 March 1936. Crowds of onlookers give the Nazi salute to German troops at Mainz.

Though Hitler was initially careful not to provoke conflict within a coalition cabinet in which the Nazi members were in a minority, both the status of the Chancellor's position and the role of the cabinet and its members in the promulgation of legislation rapidly changed sharply and decisively. From the very beginning there was no voting of any kind in the Hitler cabinet. And following the passing of the Enabling Act on 24 March 1933, the Reich Chancellor himself was empowered to promulgate and execute laws which had been agreed upon by the cabinet. The Reich President's signature was no longer necessary. In any case, Hindenburg saw no need to involve himself in the procedure. The important difference between laws (which had passed through parliament) and executive decrees was thereby effectively removed at a single stroke.[2] And with it, the actual power of Hitler in the Reich cabinet increased significantly. By April, Goebbels could note with satisfaction that the authority of the Führer was now fully established in the cabinet.[3]

Though in the first months the cabinet continued to meet frequently, once his regime had become established in power Hitler neither liked nor had use for cabinet meetings. The number of meetings declined sharply: whereas the cabinet met on seventy-two occasions in 1933, by 1935 ministers came together only twelve times, in 1937 six times, and in 1938 on one final occasion.[4] Nor were all meetings held under Hitler's chairmanship. The end of collective government (though there were faint-hearted attempts to revive it at the start of the war) could hardly be more plainly illustrated.

Already in the summer of 1933 a novel procedure for the promulgation of legislation was introduced, whereby it was no longer necessary for there to be verbal discussion among ministers. Such a procedure gradually took over. Ministers prepared legislative drafts on their own initiative, sent these round to other ministers with relevant interests, and redrafted until there was general agreement. Only at this stage was Hitler interested in seeing the draft legislation before, providing he agreed with it, appending his signature and turning it into formal law. Hitler thereby retained the power to reject or confirm the legislation; but its preparation scarcely concerned him.

Central government thus fragmented into a number of separate offices of state, each preparing legislation in quasi-autonomous fashion, without any coordinating hand, and in any contentious issues striving to uphold its policy and strengthen its departmental standing against opposition from other departments of state. It was scarcely a recipe for rational decision-making.

As the only link between individual ministers, and between any minister and the Führer himself, stood the newly appointed head of the Reich Chancellory, Hans-Heinrich Lammers (who from November 1937 also enjoyed the status of a Reich Minister). Any minister wishing to address Hitler had to go through Lammers. Memoranda sent in to the Reich Chancellor landed on Lammers' desk. Communication between Hitler and a minister (unless, like Goebbels, he happened to be a favoured minister with close and frequent personal access to the Führer) was again via Lammers.

Lammers' own role as the intermediary between the Führer and the ministers became vitally important. He could influence Hitler's opinion on a matter decisively by the way he chose to present it. He could, of course, decide that the Führer was too preoccupied with weighty affairs of state to have to consider a particular piece of draft legislation or an 'urgent' memorandum from a minister. The upshot was then that such legislation was shelved – sometimes more or less indefinitely.

Hitler was thus paradoxically the indispensable linchpin of the governmental apparatus, but at the same time largely detached from and scarcely involved in its deliberations. The distance he preserved from the daily business of government was both a strategic necessity – to avoid being sucked into factional in-fighting and thereby to enhance his aura of untouchability – and a reflection of his own character make-up: his impatience with bureaucratic routine, his reluctance to deal with petty detail, his instinctive 'Darwinism' of letting opponents slug it out before a winner emerged, his reliance on the 'loyalty' of chosen favourites – his tried and tested 'old comrades' – rather than government ministers and their state secretaries.

While Reich President Hindenburg was still alive, Hitler complied with more or less regular office hours and a largely conventional style of government. Once he had been confirmed as head of state, with the sworn support of army and civil service as well as the popular acclaim provided by the plebiscite of August 1934, Hitler's working style as head of government changed. Increasingly, now, he reverted to the irregular, non-bureaucratic style which had characterised his Party leadership prior to 1933. His temperament and personal indolence inclined him more towards the 'genial' idea on the spur of the moment and a premium upon public display and maintaining appearances than to poring over lengthy memoranda and complex government papers. According to a former adjutant, 'he took the view that many things sorted themselves out on their own if one did not interfere'.[5] Access to Hitler was increasingly difficult for all but the most favoured ministers, impossible for some. Pinning him down to a clear, reasoned decision in disputes, especially on sensitive issues, was far from easy. Important matters could be shelved for months before a decision could be extracted from him. When they came, his 'decisions' were often arbitrary, even casual utterances in an informal setting.

They were, however, regarded by those who took them away to use in defence of some policy initiative as anything other than loose recommendations. Where, on occasion, such an initiative, apparently backed by Hitler, met with such hostility that it proved unworkable, it was not revoked – which would have been incompatible with the Führer's prestige – but simply left as a dead letter, or remained 'pending' indefinitely.

Hitler's non-bureaucratic style was a recipe for general structural governmental disorder. That it was the product of a well-conceived Machiavellian strategy to 'divide and rule' is scarcely likely, even though Hitler had extremely sharp antennae towards any move to impair his authority. Rather, it was the practical application of the principle of letting the stronger in a dispute arise through a process of struggle. Even more so, it was the inevitable consequence of a heavy dependence upon the need to uphold prestige and preserve image.

Given the vague and open-ended nature of the mandate to restructure and 're-educate' German society in line with Nazi philosophy, there were bound to be clashes and conflicts in formulating policy. Unclear lines of authority intensified personal rivalries and enmities immeasurably. Struggles to establish supremacy in policy-making were time-consuming and energy-sapping. Hitler's authority as the last instance of appeal in any contentious issue was unquestioned. But he was notoriously unwilling to come down unequivocally on one side or the other, where the issue had not in effect already resolved itself.

This was particularly the case in internal affairs and in the broad arena of 'social policy', where decision-making often stumbled its way along without coherent or consistent indications of the 'will of the Führer'. But Hitler's limited interventionism in policy-making enhanced rather than restricted his power as Führer at the same time as it distanced it from the conventional agencies of government. Despite clashes in the shaping of specific policies, there was little or nothing that was irreconcilable with the broad imperative to prepare society materially and psychologically for the coming great war or with the utopian dream of the German paradise once that war had ended in victory.

Figure 5.2 Joachim von Ribbentrop, Reich Foreign Minister from 4 February 1938.

In foreign affairs, to which we will return, Hitler did intervene more frequently and directly in the formation of policy. There seems no doubt that he took the crucial decisions which set the 'diplomatic revolution'[6] in train, sometimes acting against the thrust of policy from his own Foreign Ministry.

In race policy, on the other hand, Hitler's general stance during the 1930s – for tactical and prestige reasons – was to remain aloof as far as possible. The initiatives tended to come from others, certain of course in the knowledge that they were 'working towards the Führer'. But where a matter seemed of importance to him, Hitler could intervene decisively. As early as 1933, for example, he overrode opposition from his own Vice-Chancellor, von Papen, in cabinet to ensure the passage of the sterilisation law.[7] In anti-Jewish policy, Hitler's primary role at this date was to endorse the conditions within which at times conflicting policy initiatives unfolded, rather than to provide clear and consistent direction. He intervened more frequently than used to be imagined, at times taking an interest in even relatively minor details.[8] Usually, however, at least before the war, his interventions followed requests to resolve some contentious issue. His decisions, when they came, even in this policy area were not always consistent. And sometimes here, too, he avoided making any decision at all.

Hitler's style of rule ensured that free rein was given to every form of competitive urge, leading less to directed government than to pre-datory opportunism and arbitrary, uncoordinated initiatives. But the key factor was that such initiatives could be taken only within the parameters of what were perceived to be Hitler's ideological intentions. The 'rising stars' in the Nazi constellation were those who accurately 'second-guessed' such intentions and the opportune moment to 'work towards' them, and those whose drive, energy and ruthlessness in political in-fighting were most visible in areas proximate to Hitler's own interest.

The erosion of collective government under Hitler meant, then, that instead of a central body deliberating and formulating a relatively coherent and consistent set of policies, there was – below the position of the Führer himself – a fragmentation and proliferation of rival and often conflicting agents of power, each agent finding justification only by recourse to the implementation of the 'will of the Führer'. Power relations in the Third Reich, it has been suggestively argued, were those of a latter-day feudal system, built upon personal loyalties rewarded by private fiefdoms.[9] If the full enormity of this collapse of regulated government was reserved for the war years, its process of development can none the less be located in the earliest phase of the Third Reich.

Outside the ministries of state, the Party itself claimed an input into policy formulation on every front. This was articulated at the centre by Rudolf Hess, head of the Party administration, with a seat in the cabinet and a veto right on legislation. In practice, however, 'Party policy' itself was seldom defined in clear terms. At the provincial level, relations between Party and state were, if anything, even less clearly defined than they were at the centre. The Party's provincial chieftains, the Gauleiter, frequently enjoyed a high degree of independence from control both by the central Party office and by central and regional agencies of the state administration. Attempts by Reich Minister of the Interior Frick to create a unified and systematic structure of authoritarian rule were vitiated by Hitler himself – unable to contemplate any institutionalised restrictions on his own freedom of action, and welcoming therefore the unclarity of overlapping and competing agencies of Party and state. Rather than providing a systematic involvement in government, the Party tended to act more as a populist stimulant forcing legislative action (as in the case of the anti-Semitic legislation of spring 1933 and September 1935), thereby preventing radical dynamism from subsiding into stagnant authoritarianism.

More important than the unresolved Party-state dualism was the creation of new institutions, usually straddling Party and state though belonging as such to neither, and owing their very existence and their power to their position as direct executive agencies of the 'Führer will'. They were an expression of the fact that from the very outset the 'Führer will' formed a separable – theoretically all-encompassing and in practice increasingly dominant – category of power to that of the apparatus of state government and administration itself. 'The State', which in German political thought since Hegel had enjoyed such an elevated status, was, as a structured apparatus of 'rational' government and administration, for Hitler no more than a means to an end – to be exploited where possible, but to be discarded where the end could be better achieved without it. Hence, in policy areas which Hitler regarded as of especial importance, new instruments of executive implementation were established. The Todt Organisation for administering public building and works programmes, the Hitler Youth organisation under von Schirach, the huge Four Year Plan apparatus run by Göring, and, above all, the combined SS–police empire under Himmler and Heydrich constituted immense loci of power derived specifically from their position, subordinate to neither Party nor state but only to the will of the Führer.

Through the erosion of central government, the accompanying proliferation of agencies of policy-making and administration, and the creation of new hybrid executive organisations, the autonomy of the 'Führer will' could expand dramatically, freed of any constitutional or institutional restraints. Even Hitler's official title suggested the change which was taking place: in 1933 he was officially 'Reich Chancellor'; after Hindenburg's death this was altered to 'Führer and Reich Chancellor'; and after 1939, in accordance with Hitler's own wish, this was reduced to simply 'Führer'.[10]

The detachment of Hitler from the conventional apparatus of government and administration was by no means complete by the beginning of 1938. But the development which during the war led to the complete fragmentation of government into a set of competing power fiefdoms was already well advanced by that date. With the gradual undermining of the 'state' itself and the legitimation of all action by the 'Führer's will', the potential scope for more cool and 'rational' considerations to put the brakes on 'dangerous' initiatives and to contain the more radical forces in the regime diminished. Correspondingly, the uncoordinated but dynamic impulses in the regime working in different ways 'towards the Führer' and the implementation of his vaguely formulated ideological aims gradually gathered impetus. And with them, without the need for careful central direction, Hitler's own ideological 'vision' increasingly came into focus as a realisable objective.

The seizure of opportunity

As this last remark intimates, the immense – in theory wholly unconstrained – power of the Führer as it had developed by the later 1930s was by no means a product of a pre-conceived and consistently executed plan on Hitler's part. The expansion of Hitler's power was in good measure the mirror reflection of the weakness of both the domestic and the international order in the 1930s. The crisis of Weimar had gone so deep that Hitler only had to touch the remaining structures for them to fall apart. And the post-war international order remained so fragile that it fractured irredeemably in the face of a new, determined German revisionism. Hitler's advantage in this context lay in no small measure in his gambler's instinct – a supreme opportunist's knack of seizing the precise moment to exploit the weakness of others. This opportunism, though one which was

Figure 5.3   The Anschluss. German troops parade through Vienna, 13 March 1938.

anchored in the absolute certainty that the future would bring the fulfilment of his own world philosophy, was Hitler's own vital contribution to the inflation of his power. This can most clearly be witnessed in the course of foreign policy.

Hitler had no ready-made programme for proceeding, no blueprint for action. The general thrust of policy was to appear conciliatory, tread warily, but rearm with all speed in order to be ready to seize the main chance when it presented itself. Germany's military weakness and diplomatic isolation offered in any case little alternative to such a strategy. There was as good as nothing in Hitler's early foreign policy which was specifically Nazi in intonation. It was broadly consonant with the wishes of the armed forces' leadership, the Foreign Ministry, and other dominant revisionist forces. A similar line in foreign policy would presumably have been adopted by any nationalist German government at the time.

Hitler's hallmark in the early years was less the nature of the foreign policy itself than his capacity to perceive the weakest point of opposition and to push diplomatic relations into completely new terrain through a bold forward move. This can already be seen in the conditions accompanying the withdrawal of Germany from the League of Nations in October 1933, and in the conclusion of the non-aggression pact with Poland in January 1934.

Germany's position seemed less than promising in early 1933. The public shows of brutality which had accompanied the 'seizure of power' had done little to enhance the new regime's international acceptability. But the divisions between the major western powers – France worried about the militarist tone already rampant in its eastern neighbour, Britain unhappy about refusing Germany the parity accepted in principle by the disarmament conference of the League of Nations which had been meeting in Geneva since 1932 – offered Hitler the opportunity for his first foreign-policy coup and for a major fillip to his prestige at home.

Hitler's first major foreign-policy speech, on 17 May 1933, had been a passionate avowal of his desire for peace and at the same time a protest at the Allies' unfair treatment of Germany in the disarmament question.[11] The speech was favourably received in London and Washington, though the French continued to block any recognition of Germany's claims to equality. When French pressure eventually persuaded the British to go along with a continued limitation in German armaments (though not in their own), Hitler, in a dramatic step on 14 October 1933, took Germany both out of the Disarmament Conference and out of the League of Nations itself.

   Little other than the timing and the propaganda exploitation were the specific contribution of Hitler. Much of the running, and the adoption of a hard line, had been the work of Foreign Minister von Neurath and the military leadership. But Hitler knew how to make the most of such an opportunity. He immediately dissolved the Reichstag, called a new 'election', and combined it with a plebiscitary vote of confidence in his action. Nazi propaganda brilliantly exploited the mood of the people. The three-week-long campaign culminating in the 'election' of a new Reichstag and a plebiscitary vote of confidence in Hitler provided the first orgasm of national euphoria. The 95 per cent vote in favour of Hitler, even given the pressure to conform, was without doubt a statement of massive popular acclaim for the Reich Chancellor. The British Ambassador noted: 'One thing is, however, certain. Herr Hitler's position is unassailable, even in circles which do not approve altogether of National Socialism.'[12]

   A second significant foreign-policy coup followed only a few months later, with the signing of a ten-year non-aggression pact with Poland. Here, too, Hitler showed himself a master of seized opportunities.

   The initiative came not from Hitler himself, but from the Polish head of state Pilsudski, reflecting anxiety in Poland about Germany's intentions following the departure from the League of Nations. Hitler responded with an offer of a non-aggression treaty which, in its apparent generosity, both took the Poles by surprise and had to overcome the hostility of a traditionally anti-Polish German Foreign Ministry. It indicated a shrewd ability to appreciate the fragility of Poland's alliance with France and at the same time to exploit his 'statesmanship' and apparently peaceful intentions to probe for better relations with Britain and drive a further wedge between the western democracies.

   After the gathering internal crisis of 1934 had been terminated by the destruction of the SA and the take-over of headship of state – events cumulatively amounting to a second 'seizure of power' – Hitler's domination moved on to a new plane in the course of the following two years. Above all, the series of remarkable triumphs in foreign policy in 1935–36 formed the basis for the further significant strengthening of his position vis à vis the old power elites. They also led to Hitler being swallowed by the all-embracing cult of Führer worship which increasingly enveloped him.

   Hitler's aloofness, his presumption of his own Olympian greatness and sense of his own infallibility became notably magnified in the years 1935–36. He was apparently increasingly allergic to the slightest sign of criticism, surrounding himself more and more with a court of flattering cronies. The growing feeling of confidence, that he himself could single-handedly determine events, the mounting contempt for critics and opponents within and without Germany, amounted to a deepening hubris of power, the early stages of what was to develop into catastrophic *folie de grandeur* and detachment from reality.

At the beginning of 1935 the foreign political situation did not appear rosy for Germany. The assassination of Austrian Chancellor Dollfuss by Nazis in July 1934, though a 'local initiative' and not carried out on orders from Berlin, had again brought the opprobrium of the world on the German government. The initiative was restored to Hitler by chance circumstances. According to the Versailles Treaty, which had separated the Saar territory from Germany as from January 1920, a plebiscite was to be held after fifteen years to determine whether the inhabitants wished to return to Germany, to retain the status quo, or to become part of France. The plebiscite fell on 13 January 1935. Though Nazi propaganda was intensive, the vote itself was a free one, and in a largely Catholic and heavily industrialised area where the Nazis before 1933 had received only minuscule support. The result was an overwhelming vote of 90.9 per cent for a return to Germany. In terms of prestige at home and abroad, it meant a massive and much-needed boost for Hitler.

This was followed up in March by the announcement of the reintroduction of military service to the new German Wehrmacht – another clear breach of Versailles. Again, Hitler accurately gambled on the weakness of the western Allies – especially the uncertainty of Britain – and proved without equal in the propaganda game. He used the British announcement of rearmament plans (made in response to the increase in German armament, which it was now impossible to hide) and the French announcement shortly afterwards of the extension of military service as a provocation warranting the declaration of a German airforce, a peacetime army size of 550,000 men, or thirty-six divisions (which had been requested by the army leadership), and general conscription. All of this flouted the Versailles Treaty. But Hitler's gamble came off: the British response, other than a token protest, was restricted to a request that the visit of the British Foreign Secretary, which Hitler had a few days earlier called off at short notice, be reinstated. The accommodating attitude of the British delegation during the discussions which followed indicated once more, not only to Hitler himself but also to the military and to the Foreign Ministry in Germany, that a gambler's *'fait accompli* policy' paid greater dividends than careful negotiation. This was noted by Hitler's

Figure 5.4 Terror in Vienna. Onlookers enjoy the spectacle of Jews being forced to scrub the streets.

interpreter Schmidt, who commented on the receptivity of the British to Hitler's claim for full military parity, whereas two years earlier 'the heavens would have fallen in if German representatives had posed such demands'.[13]

The popular mood in Germany was one of exhilaration. And for the non-Nazi national-conservative elites, especially the army leadership, Hitler had again demonstrated his ability to deliver.

Hitler drew great advantage in diplomacy from his wholly amoral position. He regarded treaties as simply temporary devices, means to an end. The end was the destruction of Versailles and the preparation as rapidly as possible for the coming great war which he saw as inevitable. The immediate future meant all-out German rearmament. But for the time being he could afford to show generosity in weakness to allow time to build strength, after which – one of his core beliefs – force alone would determine. The Polish treaty had been one example. The naval agreement with Britain was another. Britain's benevolence was central to Germany's future strategy as he saw it. Hitler was prepared to do more or less anything to secure it.

Hitler's determination to reach a naval agreement with Britain over-rode the objections of the navy that he was conceding too much in offering a ratio of 35: 100 (compared with the navy's preference for a 50 per cent weighting). First feelers for a naval treaty had been made in November 1934. A date was set for negotiations when the British foreign delegation went to Berlin shortly after the breach of the Versailles Treaty in March. Now, in June 1935, Britain itself was party to another major nail in Versailles' coffin, not to mention the effective destruction of the Stresa Front (the united declaration in April 1935 of France, Italy and Britain, in response to the German announcement of remilitarisation, of their readiness to protect the integrity of Austria). Hitler described the signing of the naval treaty on 18 June 1935 as 'the happiest day of his life'.[14] The keystone alliance with Britain now seemed within reach.

When, in mid August, the Abyssinian crisis arose, Hitler, delighted at the new turmoil in Europe, spoke to Goebbels and others in his inner circle of his expectations of the foreign-policy development. He regarded the alliance with Britain as 'eternal', indicated expansion to the east as the goal, and foresaw opportunities arising through Britain's entanglement in the Abyssinian conflict, and Russia becoming embroiled within a few years in a struggle with Japan. 'Then our great historical hour will arrive. We must then be ready.' A 'grandiose vision. We are all deeply moved,' commented Goebbels.[15]

During 1936 external events continued to play into Hitler's hand. Against the backcloth of the continuing diplomatic disarray of the western democracies caused by the Abyssinian conflict, and using the pretext of the ratification in Paris on 4 March 1936 of the 1935 mutual assistance pact between France and the Soviet Union, Hitler pulled off his greatest coup to date: the reoccupation of the Rhineland, thus tearing up the Locarno settlement of 1925.

Hitler's decision to reoccupy the Rhineland on 7 March 1936 followed weeks of anxious deliberation. The Foreign Ministry was advising caution. The army, too, was nervous about the consequences. Hitler himself considered pulling back at the very last minute. Again, however, he was ultimately prepared to gamble. And on the gambler's principle of 'nothing ventured, nothing gained',[16] Hitler was ready to back his instinct on the divisions and weaknesses of Britain and France and take the risk. Goebbels noted Hitler's unbounded jubilation once it rapidly became clear that the gamble had paid off: 'The Führer beaming. England remains passive. France takes no action on its own, Italy is disappointed, and America uninterested. We have sovereignty over our own country again.'[17]

The remilitarisation of the Rhineland was important in the context of rearmament; it matched the revisionist expectations of the traditional conservative–nationalist elites; and it was hugely popular among the masses of the population – even in circles otherwise distinctly cool about the Nazi regime. As the re-establishment of German sovereignty over territory which no one disputed was Germany, it would have been on the agenda of any nationalist German government. And given the well-known divisions between Britain and France in their stance towards Germany, it was an issue which more than most stood a likely chance of success. But precisely the manner in which Hitler achieved his notable triumph was guaranteed to give a massive boost to his leadership position. He had been proved right again, in the teeth of Foreign Office hesitancy and military anxiety. And his popularity among the masses, who were mobilised anew by the dissolution of the Reichstag and 'election' campaign in March 1936, had never been higher.

In foreign affairs, opportunities for great steps forward presented themselves readily in the early years of the Third Reich. Versailles would have been a tottering system even without Hitler. But as the western democracies dithered and the post-war settlement crumbled, Hitler was able – with some tactical adroitness as well as the gambler's bluff – to exploit the opportunities beyond anyone's expectations to undermine further the international order, to weaken his opponents abroad and at home, and thereby to enhance immeasurably his power base.

Foreign policy, already Hitler's main preoccupation (other than his passion for architecture), was ideally suited for the technique of the bold leap forward – the surprise effect of the coup and the *fait accompli* – which characterised his approach. Internal developments, especially in economic and social affairs, lent themselves less easily to bold coups. Here, Hitler showed a distinctly less sure touch. In fact, with no patent solutions to offer to Germany's underlying economic problems, he refrained as far as possible from direct involvement, remaining for months aloof in 1935–36 as Germany's economy plunged into a new raw materials and foreign currency crisis which threatened to overturn all rearmament plans.

Mounting problems in 1934 had been temporarily overcome through the appointment of Hjalmar Schacht as Minister of Economics with quasi-dictatorial powers over the economy, and through the 'New Plan' which Schacht introduced that summer. But economic difficulties gripped Germany even more tightly towards the end of 1935. At their root was the impossibility, given Germany's limited reserves of foreign exchange and deteriorating terms of trade, of financing the necessary scale of imports both of foodstuffs and of raw materials necessary for rearmament. Inefficiency in the Reich Food Estate compounded the difficulties in food supplies, so that by winter 1935–36 a first-rate 'provisions crisis' was raging, bringing in its wake significant signs of serious social unrest.

Conservatives – prominent among them Reich Price Commissar Goerdeler and Economics Minister Schacht, who had supported rearmament so far – now advocated reining back on armaments spending in order to build up the consumer economy, a prospect which was, of course, ideologically anathema to Hitler. Even so, an indication of how worrying the situation had become was that spending on rearmament did indeed temporarily have to take a back seat to the provision of foodstuffs.

Raw materials dwindled by spring 1936 to a level where there were only two months' supplies left. By now the choices, with Hitler as good as wholly inactive, had reduced themselves effectively to two: gradual reversal of the trend towards autarky in favour of reintegration in international trade (the policy favoured by Goerdeler); or the bold leap forward to a policy of maximum autarky within the shortest time.

Only the second alternative was, of course, acceptable. But with it would come, inevitably, economic strains sustainable only over a relatively short period of time. In these circumstances, reached in the spring

Figure 5.5 The Munich Agreement, which conceded the Sudetenland to Germany. Hitler with Neville Chamberlain, the British Prime Minister (left), Edouard Daladier, French premier (second from left), and Benito Mussolini, Italian dictator (right), at Munich, 30 September 1938.

and summer of 1936, Hitler was faced with a decision in which he essentially had no choice. His own power in effect stood or fell by a course of action which could be upheld only by an all-out autarky policy. The forward move had to be taken.

The opposition of the Economics Ministry together with the export-geared industries forced Hitler in August 1936 to take what was for him the highly unusual step of composing a written memorandum, justifying the Four Year Plan. It began with the unalterable premiss that a show-down with Bolshevism was unavoidable and concluded that Germany's armed forces and economy had to be ready to wage war within four years.[18] An indication of Hitler's authority was that oppositional voices could no longer be heard on the matter. Goerdeler's memorandum putting forward a different line was dispatched by Göring at the subsequent cabinet meeting as 'absolutely useless'.[19]

Hitler's authority was in this instance, however, in effect confirming an economic shift in course not only made inescapable by the irreconcilability of the economic problems with rearmament priorities but also favoured by the grouping which had by spring 1936 come to establish a dominance in economic planning: the powerful combined lobby of the giant chemicals combine IG-Farben, and the Luftwaffe (headed by Göring). In the face of this mighty faction – whose own interests in autarkic policy and synthetic fuel production closely matched, therefore, the thrust of Nazi ideological aims – the economic conservatives fronted by Schacht and Goerdeler, supported by the export-orientated sections of industry, had little hope of success. It was no more than a logical consequence when Göring, who in April had been put in charge of the allocation of raw materials, was appointed by Hitler as plenipotentiary for the new Four Year Plan announced at the Party Rally in September 1936.

The year 1936 was in a number of ways a highly significant one for the unfolding of Hitler's power. At the beginning of the year, the regime faced a crisis over economic policy, prognostications about a further likely rise in unemployment, a worrying decline in popularity on account of the difficulties in food supplies, an increase in the activity of the communist underground opposition, a slump in Party morale, and – on the foreign political front – Germany's relative isolation with no firm allies or friends.

The 'break-out' was achieved through the Rhineland spectacular and the decisive lurch into all-out autarky with the Four Year Plan. Internally, as we have seen, the same period witnessed the renewed crushing of internal opposition and the triumph in internal security affairs of

Himmler and Heydrich and their combined and centralised Gestapo–SS apparatus.

By the end of the year, with the German–Italian axis secured (reversing the cool relations which had prevailed between 1934 and 1936), the creation of the anti-Comintern pact with Japan, the Spanish Civil War providing renewed evidence of the passivity and uncertainty of the western democracies, and the German economy committed full tilt to preparation for war, the contours of growing international tension and an escalating arms race in the latter 1930s were set. And out of the various interwoven crises of 1936, Hitler's own power position had emerged buttressed and reinforced.

After 1936 the options for changing course diminished sharply. The economic pressures from the accelerated rearmament programme began to mount visibly and could not be contained indefinitely. Militarily, too, time was not in Germany's favour. Other nations would begin to catch up, and Germany would within a few years be at a disadvantage.

As regards international support, Britain's coolness was leading to a reappraisal of the old alliance notion. Far greater weight was now attached, under Ribbentrop's influence, to the axis with Italy and the anti-Comintern pact. With the Spanish Civil War, Hitler began, too, to concern himself more and more with the coming final struggle with Bolshevism. In other words, economic, strategic and ideological considerations were coming increasingly to be intermingled and to reinforce each other. The dynamic which had been set in train, partly by Hitler's own actions but in good measure also by events outside his control, was, therefore, pushing heavily in the direction of continued, even accelerated, high-risk policy. In these circumstances, with such oppositional voices as existed within the regime scarcely able to make themselves heard, the Hitlerian argument for the forward push in the face of an unthinkable alternative of stagnation and ultimate decline could carry the day.

The argument was put most forcefully in Hitler's address to the leaders of the armed forces on 5 November 1937, noted and summarised by his military adjutant Colonel Hossbach.[20] The meeting had been called in response to Admiral Raeder's request for the Führer to act on the acute shortage of raw materials for the navy.

Hitler took the opportunity to outline at length his strategic thinking to the military top brass and his Foreign Minister. He began by asserting that the subject of the meeting was too important for a cabinet meeting. Germany's problem of 'living space', he stated, could be solved only by the use of force. Germany would be properly prepared for war only in the mid

1940s but under no circumstances could wait any longer than that. However, a chance might present itself for expansion before that date, and could not be missed. The first objective would be the overthrowing of Austria and Czechoslovakia – a goal which Hitler referred to on a number of occasions around this time. In contrast to his high hopes after the signing of the naval pact in 1935, Hitler now regarded Britain as hostile, though too preoccupied with the problems of its weakened empire to oppose German expansion.

The seriousness of Hitler's intentions was not lost on his listeners. And action followed: within weeks of the meeting, the army had worked out a strategic plan for an offensive against Czechoslovakia.[21]

While a sense of urgency was increasingly preoccupying Hitler (whose ill-health around this time prompted him to believe that he might not have long to live), it was precisely the pace of events which was beginning to cause anxiety in sections of the military leadership and Foreign Office. At the meeting on 5 November, Hitler's lengthy monologue had prompted heated rejoinders from War Minister von Blomberg and Werner Fritsch, the head of the army. Fritsch voiced his anxiety about the implications of precipitate German military action again a few days later, as, in January 1938, did Foreign Minister von Neurath.[22] On the other hand, Hitler was receiving more accommodating advice from Ribbentrop – who had long served as an alternative source of advice in foreign affairs. When a chance opportunity arose, then, in February 1938 to change the personnel at the very top of the military and Foreign Office establishment, Hitler was not slow to take it.

Nothing suggests that the 'Blomberg–Fritsch crisis' of January–February 1938 was a premeditated move on Hitler's part. War Minister Blomberg had, with the Führer's permission, married on 12 January 1938. Hitler and Göring had been the chief witnesses. Within ten days it transpired that the past of Blomberg's bride had been a colourful one. The German War Minister had, in fact, married a former prostitute; and the Führer had been 'best man'. Hitler had known nothing of this until told by Göring on return from a stay at his house in the Bavarian Alps. He was visibly shaken at the news, but agreed that Blomberg would have to go. The ex-War Minister and his bride departed for a lengthy sojourn abroad – sweetened by a 'golden handshake' of 50,000 marks.[23]

Meanwhile, an old scandal concerning Werner Fritsch, the supreme commander of the army, had been resurrected by the Gestapo. The story of his homosexual activities had first come to the fore some two years earlier, but Hitler had then refused to act upon it. This time, too, he was, it

Figure 5.6 'Danzig is German'. A Nazi postcard of 1938 prepares the ground for Hitler's claim the following year that the city, still under League of Nations protection, should become part of the Reich.

seems, initially inclined to take the side of Fritsch, whose name had been mentioned as a possible successor to Blomberg. But Göring, who had pretensions to Blomberg's position (for which Hitler thought him wholly unsuited), and Himmler, keen as ever to embarrass the Wehrmacht given his own hopes for an armed SS, now exploited Hitler's discomfiture over Blomberg to bring down Fritsch as well. Hitler soon became persuaded by the case put forward by Fritsch's accusers, and the head of the army also had to go. A court later established that Fritsch had been the victim of mistaken identity.

The intrigue over Fritsch was, however, a secondary stage in the affair. Hitler had not been planning major changes in government and military. His own reactions were initially shock and dismay.[24] For ten days he was unsure how to proceed. Goebbels called the crisis the worst since the Röhm affair.[25] But faced with lack of alternatives, Hitler responded then characteristically by seizing the opportunity and, with a typically daring forward move, turning the initial embarrassment into a bloodless purge of the old-guard national-conservative power elite.

Blomberg's office of War Minister was abolished. Instead, at Blomberg's own suggestion, Hitler himself took over as commander in chief of the armed forces, appointing the pliant General Wilhelm Keitel as head of the newly established supreme command of the Wehrmacht. The new head of the army, recommended by Keitel, was General Walther von Brauchitsch, who declared himself prepared to work for an improved attitude of the army towards Nazism. Göring was given a field marshal's baton as a consolation prize. Around sixty generals were replaced or pensioned off. Major changes took place, too, in the Foreign Ministry. Ribbentrop was put in charge of foreign affairs and von Neurath 'kicked upstairs' to an advisory role. New ambassadors were appointed to the key cities of Rome, Tokyo and Vienna. The Economics Ministry, where Schacht had resigned the previous November, was handed to the malleable Walther Funk, with a number of other personnel changes ensuring that the days when the ministry could cause difficulties were over.

Hitler's relationship with the traditional elites was decisively altered through the outcome of the Blomberg–Fritsch affair. Time and again since 1933 he had proved his indispensability to them. But his own power, relative to theirs, had grown, not diminished. And precisely at the moment when, in foreign as in domestic policy, the radical dynamic of the regime began rapidly to gather momentum, and the conservatives hesitantly began to distance themselves from Nazi adventurism, Hitler was once more able to grasp the initiative and, through the events of

February 1938, to establish outright supremacy over them. Above all, the army was largely emasculated as an independent force. The former power elite of the German officer corps was now reduced to a mere 'functional elite'[26] serving the Führer and the Nazi state. Hitler's own contempt for the old-style officer corps was greater than ever.

Following the Reichstag Fire and the Röhm crisis, the Blomberg–Fritsch affair was the third great milestone on the way to Führer absolutist power. As has been rightly said, it amounted practically to a coup d'état against the remnants of the old order.[27] From early 1938 onwards, Hitler was increasingly surrounded by his own sort: adventurers, hard-liners, all-or-nothing gamblers, ideologues. And with the establishment of Führer absolutism, embodying a course whose unstoppable momentum was carrying Hitler, too, along with it, the grandiose 'vision' – whatever the risks – inevitably came increasingly to replace any lingering semblance of policy-making aimed at limited, 'rational' objectives.

Notes and references

1. Broszat, *Staat*, p. 327.
2. See Broszat, *Staat*, p. 351.
3. Elke Fröhlich (ed.), *Die Tagebücher von Joseph Goebbels*, 4 vols, Munich, 1987, ii, 410.
4. Lothar Gruchmann, 'Die "Reichsregierung" im Führerstaat', in Günther Doeker and Winfried Steffani (eds.), *Klassenjustiz und Pluralismus*, Hamburg, 1973, p. 192.
5. Fritz Wiedemann, *Der Mann, der Feldherr werden wollte*, Velbert/Kettwig, 1964, p. 69; trans. N&P, ii, 208.
6. The phrase of Gerhard Weinberg, 'The foreign policy of Hitler's Germany', *Diplomatic Revolution in Europe 1933–36*, Chicago/London, 1970.
7. *Akten der Reichskanzlei. Regierung Hitler*, pp. 664–5.
8. See David Bankier, 'Hitler and the Policy-Making in the Jewish Question', *Holocaust and Genocide Studies*, 3 (1988), pp. 1–20.
9. Robert Koehl, 'Feudal aspects of National Socialism', *American Political Science Review*, 54 (1960), pp. 921–33.
10. Broszat, *Staat*, p. 353.
11. Domarus, pp. 273 ff.
12. *Documents on British Foreign Policy*, vol. 6, London, 1957, p. 85.
13. Paul Schmidt, *Statist auf diplomatischer Bühne 1923–1945*, Bonn, 1953, p. 307.
14. Joachim von Ribbentrop, *Zwischen London und Moskau. Erinnerungen und letzte Aufzeichnungen*, Leoni, 1953, p. 64.
15. *Die Tagebücher von Joseph Goebbels*, ii, 504.
16. *Die Tagebücher von Joseph Goebbels*, ii, 577.

17. *Die Tagebücher von Joseph Goebbels*, ii, 582.

18. Trans. of text in N&P, ii, 281–7.

19. N&P, ii, 288

20. Trans. of text in N&P, iii, 680–7.

21. N&P, iii, 691–2.

22. See N&P, iii, 688.

23. *Die Tagebücher von Joseph Goebbels*, iii, 419.

24. See *Die Tagebücher von Joseph Goebbels,* iii, 414–25; Hildegard von Kotze (ed.), *Heeresadjutant bei Hitler, 1938–1943. Aufzeichnungen des Majors Engel*, Stuttgart, 1974, p. 20.

25. *Die Tagebücher von Joseph Goebbels*, iii, 416.

26. Klaus-Jürgen Müller, *Armee, Politik und Gesellschaft in Deutschland 1933–1945*, Paderborn, 1979, p. 44.

27. Harold C. Deutsch, *Das Komplott oder die Entmachtung der Generale*, Eichstätt, 1974, p. 231.

✠

Chapter 6

Absolute power

The years between 1938 and 1943 were the most fateful in Germany's traumatic recent history. They were the years when Hitler's power was absolute.

With the coup of February 1938, Hitler's supremacy over the one institution of state which could still topple him – the armed forces – was firmly established. There were no institutional constraints on his exercise of power; no decision of any significance could be taken without his approval; no organisation presented an oppositional threat.

Opposition was, of course, not eliminated. But it could take no organisational form which was a danger to Hitler. The possibilities of an internal strike against Hitler were confined to the activities of small conspiratorial groups within the army (with links to individuals from among the other sections of the traditional elites, increasingly anxious at the direction Nazi policy was taking, but scarcely capable of action as long as Hitler's 'triumphs' continued); or to the isolated actions of persons unattached to any grouping or organisation (such as the remarkable solo attempt on Hitler's life in the Munich Bürgerbräukeller in 1939 by the Swabian joiner Georg Elser).

This chapter explores the exercise of Hitler's absolute power in those fateful five years when the deformation of the power structure had left him in a position to shape events in a measure unusual even for dictators, let alone for democratic heads of government. It attempts to explain how the 'idea' of Nazism, located in the person of the Führer, came to be implemented as practical policy.

It finds part of the answer to this question in the character of Hitler's leadership and decision-making in these years. The war for him was no conventional military conflict. It represented the decisive step towards the fulfilment of his 'idea', the accomplishment of his 'mission'. In the war, it has been rightly said, Nazism returned to its essence.[1] The activist dynamism built into the Nazi Movement, bottled up only partially and with difficulty before the war, was fully uncorked in the climate of a war which, in Nazi eyes, amounted to a 'crusade'. Hitler's diplomatic manoeuvrings and strategic shifts of the 1930s, based on rational political calculation, gave way increasingly to the readiness to 'go for broke', and to decisions founded upon the ideological 'truths' of his irrational 'world philosophy' of the once-and-for-all great quest for German supremacy, racial domination and 'living space'.

But another, equally crucial, part of the answer is found in the impact upon government of the now untrammelled Führer power. In conditions of feverish preparation for war, then war itself, the process of the collapse of rational structures of government and administration into a fragmented and competing set of executive agencies of Führer power accelerated sharply. 'Government' and 'administration' were replaced by pure domination – 'rule' in the most despotic, unconstrained, arbitrary fashion imaginable, defined only by reference to a number of uncontradictable but generalised ideological precepts. Government disintegrated, therefore, into a 'Behemoth'[2] of rival fiefdoms whose overlords, to boost and retain their own power, strived to outdo each other in 'working towards the Führer', in putting Hitler's 'idea' into practice. This was both a reflection of Hitler's concept of power, and provided the framework within which the underlying ideological driving force behind the war could find implementation in specific policies of barbarism and genocide. The first part of what follows examines the corrosion of systematic government through the impact of the power of the Führer.

The disintegration of the state

✠

When government ministers gathered on the evening of 5 February 1938 to hear a lengthy statement by Hitler about the Blomberg–Fritsch crisis and outcome, there was no indication that there were to be no more

Figure 6.1 Hitler at the height of his power after his triumph over France, on his brief visit to Paris on 28 June 1940.

cabinet meetings. In fact, with incompleted business piling up, the head of the Reich Chancellory, Lammers, who from 1937 himself enjoyed cabinet-minister status, pressed Hitler into accepting dates for further meetings to follow on a number of occasions in 1938 and in early 1939. In each case, Hitler cancelled the meetings at short notice.[3] As the cabinet size had grown, its significance had dwindled. It was, in fact, by now utterly supernumerary to the legislative process in the Führer state.

But Hitler's dislike of cabinet meetings, present from the beginning, was more deeply rooted than consideration of mere matters of procedure. The very notion of a collectivity of ministers, deriving their authority from their constitutional office, and thereby presenting the possibility of a check on his expression of power, was anathema to Hitler. Bureaucratic regulations, drawing their binding force from abstract legal and constitutional concepts, were incompatible with the principles of personalised rule, which underlay Hitler's 'charismatic' Führer authority. Lammers' attempts to resurrect cabinet meetings in 1942 predictably, therefore, came to nothing. With sharp antennae alert to anything which might limit his freedom of action, Hitler refused to countenance even informal gatherings of ministers around a beer table.[4]

Alternative forms of partially collective central government came to nothing. The so-called 'Secret Reich Cabinet' (*Geheimes Reichskabinett*), announced by Hitler's decree on 4 February 1938, which supposedly brought a group of relevant ministers together, under von Neurath's chairmanship, to advise on foreign policy issues, never met a single time. It was simply a device to camouflage to the public the true significance of the shift in personnel at the Foreign Ministry.

At the outbreak of war, the establishment of a 'Ministerial Council for the Defence of the Reich' – under Göring's chairmanship and comprising Frick (as Plenipotentiary for Administration), Funk (Plenipotentiary for the Economy), Lammers (Head of the Reich Chancellory), Keitel (Head of the Supreme Command of the Wehrmacht), and Hess (Head of the Party) – appeared to signify a resurrection of some kind of inner cabinet, particularly since, to release Hitler from the legislative burden, it was allowed to promulgate laws under Göring's signature (unless Hitler reserved the legislation to himself). But it met only six times – promulgating a number of decrees on administrative and economic matters – and never reassembled after 15 November 1939.

Göring, whose administrative style was practically as arbitrary as Hitler's own, somewhat surprisingly ignored the opportunity to build the Ministerial Council into a vehicle of his own power. Hitler himself was more than ready to see the potentially significant institution wilt before it had flowered. Though the Council continued to promulgate decrees, these were carried out by circulation of drafts, not by collective gatherings.

Nor did the so-called '*Dreierkollegium*' or 'Three-Man Directive' (Frick, Funk and Keitel, whose plenipotentiary powers of decree in the spheres of administration, economy and civil defence derived from a Reich defence law of September 1938) come together to work collectively. Draft legislation was merely cleared with the other two offices.

The central governmental apparatus of the Reich, therefore, which as a collective entity had already been strongly in decline in the first years of Hitler's rule, under conditions of war now splintered into its constituent parts. The Reich Chancellory no longer played a practical coordinating role in the bulk of legislation.[5] And Reich Chancellory chief Hans-Heinrich Lammers often now found it difficult himself to gain access to the Führer. By the later 1930s weeks would sometimes go by without his being able to attain an audience to discuss pressing government business.[6]

During the first years of the war, Lammers' access was again more frequent than this: he had the opportunity for brief discussions with Hitler about once a week on average. But after the invasion of the Soviet Union there was a sharp decline in the number of such meetings, to thirty-nine in 1942 and to only eighteen the following year.[7] By this time, he was having to present a written summary of the points he wished to raise with the Führer to the person who now controlled access to Hitler: Martin Bormann.

The road to the top for Bormann was taken behind the scenes. His talent lay not in demagoguery and agitation but in organisation, where he combined ideological fanaticism with bureaucratic skill, Machiavellian deviousness, indefatigable energy and a remarkable capacity for hard work. He was little known in the Party rank and file, and to begin with universally underestimated by Nazi leaders. But during the 1930s he laid the twin foundations of his power position in the later years of the Third Reich. The first foundation was his control of the central Party apparatus, which he built up after 1933 as the head of the staff of Hess's office as Deputy Führer. The second foundation was his personal contact to Hitler, which expanded notably after 1934 when he managed the funds at Hitler's personal disposal and also the acquisition of property for the mountain retreat at the Berghof near Berchtesgaden. Once war broke out, Bormann remained constantly at Hitler's side in his field headquarters.

After the débâcle of Hess's flight to Scotland, the running of the Party was handed over to Bormann as head of the newly titled Party Chancellory, along with the rights which Hess had exercised in vetting government legislation and appointments and holding the authority of a Reich Minister. With the radicalisation, once war had started, of policy relating to central aspects of Nazi ideology, the influence of the Party itself became far more pervasive than it had been in the early years of the Third Reich. Bormann's role, from this point of view alone, was a crucial one. He intervened more and more in the business of the Reich government. At times, he simply by-passed the government in empowering legislation in the annexed territories. And he was more responsible than anyone for the revitalisation of the 'church struggle' in 1941. It was, however, the combination of the control of the Party (with its ever more intrusive impact on government and administration), together with his initially unofficial position as Hitler's private secretary – he was given the official title of 'Secretary of the Führer' on 12 April 1943 – which provided him with his unique power base.

At first, Bormann continued to share with Lammers – according to their relative spheres of competence – the control over access to Hitler of those wishing to see the Führer. But the waning influence of the head of the Reich government was inevitable. By 1944 Lammers effectively had access to Hitler only when the 'Secretary of the Führer' was prepared to permit it. In October that year he had to give up his place in the field headquarters and saw Hitler only once more on official business – for a quarter of an hour on 27 March 1945 in order to attain his signature on some draft legislation.[8]

In the exercise of Hitler's power during the wartime years, therefore, Bormann had the vital, pivotal position. He controlled in good measure not only which persons were admitted to Hitler's presence, but also what information reached the Führer. With pad and pencil at the ready to note down any utterances of Hitler which seemed of significance, Bormann increasingly channelled, in addition, the emission of the 'Führer will' into directives for action, sometimes interpreting casual remarks over dinner as binding directives for legislation.

Powerful though he was, even Bormann could not deny access to Hitler of a number of other Nazi leaders. But as the war progressed and Hitler's isolation increased, the number of those who could see the Führer when they wished dwindled to a mere handful: apart from Bormann himself, Göring, Goebbels, Himmler, Ribbentrop, Ley, Sauckel, Speer and Keitel, together with most of the regional Party bosses, the Gauleiter. Even when they themselves were not present, Göring, Himmler and Ribbentrop ensured that their interests were watched over by their own attachés in the Führer headquarters. Others, notably Goebbels and, after 1942, the Reich Justice Minister Thierack, sent in frequent reports – so-called 'Führer Information' – to which Hitler sporadically reacted.[9] The internal routes of information to Hitler, therefore, even where they did not go directly through Bormann, were largely and increasingly self-selecting – deriving from a leadership clique which was fanatically committed to Hitler personally and to the implementation (through differing apparatuses of power) of the 'idea' of the Führer.

Away from the central locus of power, in the provinces and in the occupied territories, the strong bonds of personal loyalty which existed on a mutual basis between Hitler and the regional chieftains, the Gauleiter, meant that the scope and licence they were given to work for the implementation of the loosely defined 'will of the Führer' ensured a continued radicalising of policy initiatives.

Already in the peace-time years of the Third Reich, the Gauleiter had been decisive in the exercise of Nazi rule in the provinces – especially where a Gauleiter also acted as Reich Governor. Despite having no obvious function once the autonomy of the Länder had been abolished in 1934, the position of Reich Governor had typically been retained by Hitler. Its retention avoided offending his trusty Gauleiter by depriving them of a component of their power, at the same time reinforcing their direct ties with Hitler himself and thereby continuing to function as a vehicle of his power in the regions. Though there were exceptions, most Gauleiter had the chance to come into contact with Hitler either individually or through periodic meetings of Gauleiter which continued even when collective state government had long since faded. During the war, Gauleiter would sometimes take away from such meetings directives – or broad guidelines from Hitler – for action which they themselves would then deploy to pressurise the central state bureaucracy.

In the war, too, numerous new tasks of 'leadership' were passed on to the Gauleiter in their capacity as 'Reich Defence Commissars' with wide-ranging powers in the mobilisation of population and resources for the war effort. Once more, this brought an extension of the role of the Party fanatics and activists at the base of society, and with it a further strengthening of the hold of those whose own power was a direct derivative of that of Hitler.

In their own provinces, the Gauleiter amounted almost to independent viceroys of Hitler. The influence of the central state administration on the

Gauleiter was extremely limited. Even towards the central Party office their stance was not subservient. The personal bonds with the Führer formed the decisive underpinning of their position. This was the case even in the 'old Reich' of the 1937 borders. With the annexation of Austria and Czechoslovakia, and then especially with the conquest of Poland and large tracts of the Soviet Union, even more extensive powers were delegated to the Gauleiter who took over the new Nazi provinces and needed no second bidding to make what they could of the annexed territories put under their charge. The broad mandate for action from the centre was thus reciprocated by initiatives 'on the ground' to comply with the presumed 'will of the Führer' – 'initiatives' which then in turn could usually reckon with approval from Berlin.

If the state bureaucracy was helpless against the territorial fiefdoms of the Gauleiter – who represented a personalised power in the provinces which could bypass, block, override or usurp state prerogatives – and had to come to terms with the fact that there were huge tracts of the extended German Reich in which its writ simply did not run,[10] it was also completely undermined as a central agent in the power structure by the proliferation and extension of the 'special authorities' (*Sonderbehörden*) which, as we noted, had already been a feature of Hitlerian government before the war.

By 1942 it was scarcely possible, even for the Reich Chancellory, to acquire an overview of the cancerous growth of the multi-layered, and often overlapping and competing, organs of policy-making. Göring's own empire of the Four Year Plan had now expanded to take in no fewer than twenty-two spheres of 'special authority' including price control, chemical production, mining output, roads, waterways, shipping and exploitation of plundered Polish property.[11] The Minister for Armaments and Munitions (Fritz Todt, then after his death Albert Speer), Reich Commissar for Housing (Robert Ley) and the Plenipotentiary for Labour Deployment (Fritz Sauckel) ran other major power complexes which had direct channels to Hitler and stood outside the normal agencies of government administration. As the vehicles of ideological implementation, the most crucial 'special authorities' of all were the police–SS domain, the overlapping empire of Himmler in his capacity, from October 1939, as Reich Commissar for the Consolidation of Ethnic Germandom (RKFDV), and the Chancellory of the Führer under Philipp Bouhler.

Despite its grand-sounding title, the Führer Chancellory was in essence a fairly insignificant office. It had been set up by Hitler at the beginning of the Third Reich to handle petitions and appeals which were sent to him

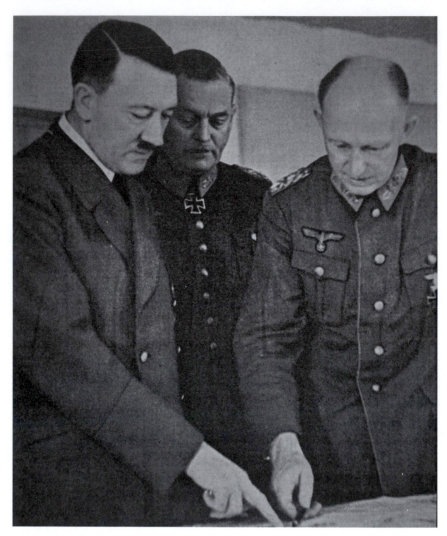

Figure 6.2 Hitler, studying a map in 1940 with Field Marshal Wilhelm Keitel, head of the High Command of the Wehrmacht (centre), and General Alfred Jodl, head of the Wehrmacht Operations Staff (right). By the end of July 1940, Hitler had already indicated that he wanted to invade the Soviet Union the following spring.

as head of the Party. But by the end of the 1930s its power-hungry leaders Bouhler and his deputy Brack were able to use their proximity to Hitler to assert the position of the Führer Chancellory in the competitive jungle and acquire a significance for it out of all proportion to the modest role which the office had originally been meant to play. For it was from this office that the initiatives were taken which culminated in its orchestration of the murderous 'euthanasia action'.[12]

A chance petition to the Führer Chancellory from the father of a badly deformed child, seeking permission to have it 'put to sleep', prompted Hitler's authorisation to his personal doctor, Karl Brandt, to carry out the request, and subsequent empowering of Brandt and Führer Chancellory boss Bouhler to act in the same way in similar instances. Hitler's ideological intention to settle the 'euthanasia question' had been indicated much earlier, but he had intimated that the issue could be tackled only in the context of a war. Following the authorisation to carry out 'euthanasia' in the cases of children, feelers were put out about possible Church objections and, partly in the light of the response, an 'action' regarding adults, too, was decided upon. Bouhler was prodded by his deputy Brack into seeking responsibility to organise the 'programme'. Since Hitler was keen on an 'unbureaucratic' solution and on utmost secrecy, he was anxious to keep it out of the hands of the health authorities in the cumbersome Ministry of the Interior.

By October 1939 the machinery and organisation had been set up within the Führer Chancellory and, based on the ready cooperation of doctors who supplied lists of patients who were 'candidates', the 'action' was set in motion. The death of more than 70,000 mentally ill and deformed patients in German asylums was the result. Later, the Führer Chancellory acted as a quasi-employment agency in finding the personnel for 'Aktion Reinhard' – the extermination of Polish Jewry in the death camps of Belzec, Sobibor and Treblinka.

The 'euthanasia action' is a classic example of how a murderous 'initiative' could take shape in the Third Reich. In the unfolding of the 'action', a number of key components meshed together: the power-lust and eye for an opportunity on the part of Bouhler and Brack; the ready compliance of doctors in the asylums, more than prepared to do their bit to 'work towards the Führer' in an issue which played upon themes of eugenics and 'racial health' long pre-dating the Third Reich; Hitler's distaste for bureaucracy and his proclivity to ignore the state administration completely in sensitive matters or where 'unfussy' executive action was required; and, not least, an ideological objective close to the centre of Hitler's 'world philosophy'.

As the example of the 'euthanasia action' also shows, not only was his authorisation essential, but, in conditions of war, Hitler did not shy away from decisions, in full accordance with his own ideological 'mission', which passed the death sentence on tens of thousands of civilians. The mode of his decisions was, however, increasingly deformalised – once more reflecting the collapse of anything resembling an organised state system (however authoritarian) in the face of the all-embracing, but corrosive, personalised power of the Führer.

In the case of the 'euthanasia action', the initial empowering of Bouhler and Brandt – evidently a purely verbal one – prompted difficulties when their authorisation was questioned. Since no state minister other than Lammers had been informed, such questioning was in itself hardly surprising, given the gravity of the issue. As a result, Hitler was pressed, around the end of October 1939, into giving written authorisation. This was provided not in the shape of a decree or law (which he refused to issue) but in a blanket mandate of a few lines on his personal writing paper – significantly backdated to the first day of the war.[13] Such was the incontestability of the incorporation of law in the person of the Führer that even this loose and informal authorisation was regarded as having binding legal power.

Hitler, for whom the precise form of legislation was in any case a matter of indifference, tended increasingly during the war to deploy the device of personal decree instead of formal ordinances or laws. Many of these decrees, including some of the most important and far-reaching in their consequences, were not even publicly promulgated. Just such an unpublished mandate appointed Himmler on 7 October 1939 to the new position of Reich Commissar for the Consolidation of Ethnic Germandom, an office which gave him blanket powers to bring about the ruthless 'germanisation' and 'racial purification' of the conquered eastern territories.[14] On the basis of this decree, Himmler was able to erect a huge apparatus, under his personal charge, to organise massive deportations of the ethnic population.

The character of Hitler's decisions was guaranteed to lead to continuing uncertainty and conflict. Sometimes difficulties were caused where a Führer decree proved impracticable – reinforcing Hitler's demands to be aware of all the arguments, pro and con, before agreeing to legislate. The open-ended nature of some decrees, bestowing extensive powers which conflicted with those of other authorities, could create serious problems of implementation. The Reich Chancellory, for instance, had difficulty (not, of course, on moral grounds but on those of its legal formalities) with a decree which Rosenberg persuaded Hitler to draw up in March 1942, effectively empowering him with the widest brief imaginable to undertake the cultural plunder of Nazi-occupied Europe. The decree nevertheless stood in the end, little amended.[15]

At every level, then, government based upon any systematic principles or abstract legal and constitutional norms was fundamentally eroded by executive agencies bound to Hitler and to the fulfilment of his ideological vision. The predatory structures which emerged can hardly be conceived of as an actual state *system*. 'Law', which forms the basis of systems of rule recognisable as 'states' (even of an authoritarian kind), had collapsed and been replaced by arbitrary force, justified by recourse to the mystical power of the Führer. The replacement of law by force – a process well developed by 1942 in Germany itself – was complete in the occupied territories. The privatisation of public coercive force through the elevation of Hitler's personal bodyguard to a position where it swallowed the state police[16] is the most obvious example of the ultimate lawlessness of the Hitler regime. The 'mafia' mob had taken over the state. It was, as has been said, 'a form of society in which the ruling groups control the rest of the population directly, without the mediation of that rational though coercive apparatus hitherto known as the state'.[17]

The 'Idea' becomes reality

Even in the later 1930s, Hitler's 'world-view', for those non-converts who cared to read his outpourings in *Mein Kampf*, appeared ludicrous. By 1941 the vision of an ultimate showdown with Bolshevism as a twin 'crusade' to win 'living space' and to eradicate the Jews was grim reality. How did this realisation of Hitler's 'idea' come about, and what was Hitler's own contribution to the fulfilment of his ideological objectives?

In the collapsing house of cards of European diplomacy, Hitler provided the push. German expansion in 1938–9 represented an amalgam of differing, interlocking causes – economic pressure, military logistics, ideological thrust, and the weakness of the western democracies – each mutually reinforcing the rapidly accelerating momentum which took Europe over the brink of the abyss and into war. Each of these preconditions of expansion existed independently of Hitler. German expansion would have been likely even had Hitler been deposed or assassinated in 1938. But the course, character and tempo of expansion bear Hitler's hallmarks. Under a German government run by Beck and Goerdeler, for instance, the 'go for broke' risks which Hitler took would scarcely have been thinkable. Even Göring was visibly backing away from Hitler's dangerous gambling act as war loomed. This points to the way in which the governmental structure had disintegrated to a position where one man – spurred on by a small band of political and military desperadoes – could wield such enormous, unconstrained power.

The two Nazi leaders who exerted most influence upon Hitler in foreign policy matters, especially following the important changes of February 1938, were Ribbentrop and Göring. In neither case were their views totally identical with those of Hitler, but nor did they pose categorical and irreconcilable policy alternatives.

Ribbentrop's approach was less fixated upon the destruction of 'Jewish Bolshevism' than was Hitler's, and more traditionally power-political in orientation.[18] For Ribbentrop, the main target was not Russia, but Britain. His hand is visible in the revamped colonial policy from 1937, clearly directed at Britain. With the icing over of relations with Britain in the later 1930s, Ribbentrop's influence on Hitler expanded, its prime moment of glory arriving in the signing of the non-aggression pact with the Soviet Union on 23 August 1939. But nothing suggests that this pact, the apparent upturning of everything which Nazi policy had stood for, was for Hitler other than what it indeed turned out to be: a strategically necessary but no more than temporary arrangement. And as the opportunity to reverse the arrangement presented itself, so Ribbentrop's influence began again to wane. Ribbentrop's 'alternative' foreign policy conception had proved no more than a passing vehicle which Hitler could use opportunistically and then discard again. At no time did it pose a fundamental alternative to Hitler's racial–imperialist 'vision', and ended by working towards that goal and being subordinated to and supplanted by it.

Göring, too, had a somewhat different conception of foreign-policy goals to that of Hitler.[19] But the more Hitler freed himself from constraints restricting his 'high-risk' proclivities, the less chance of success had Göring's more pragmatic aims.

Between 1934 and 1938, Göring's role in foreign policy had been an important one. This was particularly so in shaping relations with the countries of south-eastern Europe and with Italy, in the decision to intervene in the Spanish Civil War, in policy towards Austria, and above all else in the Anschluß crisis itself, where Göring and not Hitler had made the running. Hitler's racial–imperialist obsessions were of little direct importance to Göring, who was more concerned to establish

Germany's economic dominance of central and south-eastern Europe as the base of continental political hegemony consolidated through alliance with Britain. Whereas Ribbentrop's anti-British stance pandered to Hitler's readiness to risk war with a Britain he regarded as fundamentally weakened, Göring, partly echoing fears expressed by his many contacts in business, military and landholding circles, sought to work against the high-risk policy and, especially, to avoid the prospect of a war with Britain.

Göring's triumph – it was to be his last one – came with the signing of the Munich Agreement in September 1938. But it signified only that his star was on the wane. Hitler held it against Göring that he had been instrumental in bringing him to the conference table and deflecting him from the conflict he had all along wanted. Göring, suffering from signs of nervous depression, was seldom to be found in Hitler's company during the next few months, and was scarcely consulted about the decisions to occupy the rest of Czechoslovakia and to attack Poland at the first opportunity. Hitler's impatience – coming fully to the fore after Munich – to speed up rather than slacken the pace of German expansion, to gamble for high stakes, now clashed with Göring's more cautious approach. Göring was, therefore, found dispensable, and was displaced as the most important 'confidante' on foreign policy by the outrightly hawkish Ribbentrop.

On the very eve of war, Göring rather half-heartedly tried to intercede with Britain to prevent hostilities. He also belatedly attempted to dissuade Hitler from undertaking the risky venture which could engage the western powers and end in disaster for Germany. On 29 August 1939, Göring implored Hitler not to 'go for broke'. Hitler's reply, characteristically, was that throughout his life he had always 'gone for broke'.[20]

Ultimately, as with his arch-rival Ribbentrop, Göring's 'alternative' aims in foreign policy proved too closely aligned to Hitler's to be able to exert more than passing influence. In addition, Göring's personal subservience to and dependence upon Hitler was a major hindrance to the construction of a genuinely viable 'alternative' policy from the 'second man in the Reich'.

If different notions of foreign policy concepts existed among those in Hitler's immediate entourage, it goes without saying that variant views prevailed within the wider leadership of government, bureaucracy, military and business, and among those 'amateur' groups within the Party organisation involved in German foreign relations. Traditional pan-German colonialism, aimed at Britain, existed side by side with interests

Figure 6.3   Rudolf Hess, Deputy Leader of the Nazi Party between 1933 and 1941.

in agrarian acquisitions in eastern Europe and in commercial dominance in the Balkans. Within the Wehrmacht itself, the navy – alongside the Luftwaffe more fervent in its support of the Nazi regime than the former Prussian officer corps of the army – saw its own interests better reflected in preparation for a conflict with Britain than in the commitment of scarce resources to building up a land force for war in the Soviet Union.

Whatever the differences of emphasis, however, the basic consensus in an expansionist foreign policy and the attainment of German hegemony in central Europe remained extensive – even reaching into the ranks of those individuals tentatively finding their way into out-and-out opposition to the Nazi regime.[21] The combination of wide-ranging consensus behind expansion and the disintegration of any institutional constraints upon Hitler offered the scope for the dictator's ever more dangerous gambles, to which German society had bound itself with ever-diminishing possibilities of escape.

As the constraints upon Hitler's actions from within the regime had dwindled, so, paradoxically, had the external constraints upon his manoeuvrability increased. The economic strains could not be sustained for much longer without expansion. The problems arising from the forced rearmament programme were already serious in 1938 – acting as a major motivating factor in the expansion into Austria and Czechoslovakia – and acute by 1939. Even more important was the fact, well realised by Hitler, that time was running against Germany in the arms race. Germany's advantages in armaments would soon be negated, as other countries rearmed. The initiative would then be lost. Nor was the international constellation, notably British and French weakness, likely to remain propitious for much longer. 'We have no other choice. We must act,' he told his generals in August 1939.[22]

Within the bounds of his unchanged long-term objective – the struggle for *Lebensraum* – and within the narrowing range of options imposed by economic and military-strategic considerations, Hitler's foreign-policy decisions in 1938–39 remained highly pragmatic and opportunistic. Common to the crises over Austria, the Sudetenland and Poland were rapid – almost impulsive – policy readjustments, a readiness to resort to brutal force when diplomatic bullying provoked signs of resistance and a corresponding threat to prestige, and a mounting sense of urgency that the moment for action had arrived, time was against Germany, and the risk had to be taken. And as the feebleness of the western powers became fully exposed at Munich in late September 1938, Hitler's self-confidence grew to the point where he was convinced that they would not go to war over Poland. 'Our enemies are small fry,' he told his generals in August 1939. 'I saw them in Munich.'[23]

In each of the crises over Austria, the Sudetenland and Poland, strategic considerations were uppermost in German expansion, economic necessity was scarcely less important (certainly in the cases of Austria and Czechoslovakia), and ideological issues played only a subordinate role. Hitler's decisions and policy adjustments were opportunistic – to invade Austria when Schuschnigg unexpectedly called a plebiscite, to merge Austria into Germany only in the light of the delirious reception he encountered in Linz, to destroy Czechoslovakia at the earliest opportunity when Czech mobilisation in the 'weekend crisis' of 20–21 May 1938 made Germany look foolish, and to attack Poland only when diplomatic overtures had been repulsed and the British guarantee had been made. But underlying them was a consistency in aim of establishing German dominance in central Europe and leaving the options open for a strike either at the east or at the west, but with the ultimate goal of destroying Bolshevism and attaining *Lebensraum*. Once Ribbentrop was able to exploit the hesitancy, yet again, of western diplomacy to mastermind the pact with the Soviet Union, the way was cleared for an attack on the west – after the demolition of Poland, secretly agreed with the Soviet Union, had been completed.

Though singly none of these momentous steps in foreign policy, culminating in war, had been in the first instance driven by the demands of Nazi ideology, and had even led finally to an alliance with the ideological arch-enemy, they nevertheless cumulatively furthered in a number of ways the process of ideological radicalisation both in the newly incorporated territories and within Germany itself.

In Austria and the Sudetenland (then in the rest of occupied Czechoslovakia) the scores to be settled against political and racial enemies brought new 'tasks' for the Party and the Gestapo. It was for both Party hotheads and police bureaucrats a time reminiscent of the 'seizure of power' era. But the Party now had from the outset a strengthened position in the administration of the new territories, and the enforcement apparatus of the Gestapo–SS was even more efficient and ruthless than the police had been in Germany itself in 1933.

The climate was, therefore, provided for renewed ferocity against the socialist and communist Left, and for a viciousness in the open brutality against Austrian Jews even more savage than what had taken place in Germany to that date. The new 'organisational opportunities' for tackling the 'Jewish Question' offered the chance to Adolf Eichmann, at that time still an insignificant figure at the SD's 'Jewish Desk' in Berlin, to mastermind the rapid and brutal Jewish emigration policy of the SS in Vienna and then, from July 1939, in Prague.

Within Germany itself, the beginnings of a new wave of radicalisation in the treatment of the Jews had already been signalled in September 1937 by Hitler's furious attack on 'Jewish Bolshevism' at the Nuremberg Party Rally. This was sufficient to usher in a new wave of anti-Semitic violence and, in the context of the mounting economic problems of the Four Year Plan, to sanction the 'aryanisation' – or forcible expropriation – of Jewish businesses. Again, this process received a major boost through the annexation of Austria and the Sudetenland.

The 'green light' flashed to the Party in Hitler's September speech gave new impetus to Party activism. This found release during the months of tension in the spring and summer of 1938 in renewed and intensified violence towards Jews and their property. The aggression was now more menacing and widespread even than it had been during the previous wave of attacks in the summer of 1935.

The dénouement of the surging anti-Semitic terror was reached in the notorious '*Reichskristallnacht*' – the terrible pogrom of 9–10 November 1938. Again Hitler needed to do no more than offer his approval for Goebbels, the main instigator, to unleash the pent-up hatred of Party and SA activists in a frenzy of violence. Around a hundred Jews were killed in the nationwide pogrom, synagogues were burnt down, Jewish property was plundered and destroyed, and some 30,000 male Jews were taken to concentration camps as hostages to force the pace of emigration. Jews were now also entirely excluded from the economy and forced further on to the shadowy fringes of society. The upshot of the affair was that centralised control of the 'Jewish Question' passed into the hands of the SS, and Eichmann, reaping the rewards of his successes in Austria, was charged with organising Jewish emigration for the whole of the Reich. An important step had taken place en route from the 'emotional antisemitism' and public violence of the pogrom – with its distasteful features for many Germans – to the 'rationalised' non-public conveyor-belt murders in the death camps.

Hitler himself had done little in a direct sense to bring about the dramatic sharpening of the persecution of the Jews. He had not needed to. All that was required was his licence for his underlings to carry out what they took to be his 'wishes'. These 'wishes' corresponded not only to the convictions of rabid antisemites within the Movement. Working towards the implementation of such 'wishes' offered possibilities of promotion, of personal advancement and enrichment, of self-aggrandisement for many who were less than paranoid Jew-haters but were more than ready to use anti-Jewish policy for their own ends. Given the centrality of antisemitism in the Nazi creed, practically any action could be justified by recourse to its role in excluding Jews from German society. The 'final goal' of a Jew-free Germany served to legitimate policy initiatives from differing agencies, ministries and organisations in the Third Reich, competing with each other to implement what they took to be the Führer's will.

Later, in one of his 'table talks', Hitler conceded that he had been forced for a long time to remain inactive towards the Jews[24] – a tactical constraint directed at refraining from unnecessarily souring international relations. Throughout the whole of the year 1938, when the vital radicalisation was taking place in the extended Reich territory, he had little or nothing to say in public on the 'Jewish Question'. Even in a confidential address to leaders of the press on the very morning after the pogrom, he never mentioned the events of 'Crystal Night'.[25]

In his speech to the Reichstag on 30 January 1939, however, Hitler returned to the 'Jewish Question' with new, frightening menace in his voice. He said he would be a prophet: 'If the international Jewish financiers in and outside Europe should succeed in plunging the nations once more into a world war, then the result will not be the Bolshevising of the earth, and thus the victory of Jewry, but the annihilation of the Jewish race in Europe!'[26]

The words were partly propaganda. They repeated in more ominous language the threat, which Hitler had implied on a number of other occasions during the 1930s, to hold the Jews as 'hostages' in the event of Germany being forced into armed confrontation. But on this occasion they were more than mere propaganda. Hitler (and some of those in his close circle) went on to invoke this precise passage on a number of occasions in his speeches (but also in comments to his immediate entourage) during 1941 and 1942, precisely at the time that the 'Final Solution' came to be implemented. And he consistently misdated it to the date of the outbreak of war, 1 September 1939. It plainly signified, in his mind, that in some way or other the coming war would be synonymous with the destruction of the Jews. How that would come about, neither he nor anyone else knew. That it *would* come about, he was certain.

Meanwhile, not only the Jews had been the targets of the escalating ideological radicalisation in the later 1930s. Traditional social prejudice, the keenness of the police to extend their empire by finding ever new 'enemies of the people' to persecute, and the health and social hygiene fetish which prompted the medical authorities and health bureaucracy to comply readily with the demands of the unfolding Nazi eugenics and sterilisation programmes, combined to radicalise the drive against gypsies, homosexuals, prostitutes, 'idlers', beggars, 'drop-outs', 'anti-socials', the 'work-shy', habitual criminals, other 'racial undesirables' and 'community aliens'. Impulses and initiatives of countless individuals and myriad organisations, from a multiplicity of motives, ensured that by the eve of war new possibilities for tackling key ideological issues – and those close to the heart of Hitler's personal 'world philosophy' – were beginning to emerge. The war itself offered the opportunity, and created the context of brutalisation, in which these could then take genocidal shape.

In the occupation of Poland, Hitler again provided licence from above for barbarity in instructing his military leaders to close their hearts to pity, to 'act brutally', and to secure what were German rights with 'the greatest harshness'.[27] The racial struggle in Poland did not allow any legal limitations, Hitler commented to Keitel after victory had been attained: 'The methods will be incompatible with the principles which we otherwise adhere to.'[28]

Objections by some officers to the merciless barbarity during and after the Polish campaign were contemptuously dismissed by Hitler as 'childish' complaints of military leaders wanting to wage war with 'salvation army methods'.[29] Most military commanders, less scrupulous or courageous, complied with the draconian severity of the savage destruction of Poland and the ruthlessness of the 'germanisation' methods deployed there.

Given *carte blanche* from the Führer to proceed how they saw fit in their domains, the new Nazi bosses improvised a mounting role of terror. The western parts of Poland (together with a stretch of territory adjacent to East Prussia), now incorporated into the Reich and specifically excluded from the normal bounds of German criminal law, were turned into experimental areas for the Nazi 'New Order'. Hitler said he asked no more of his Gauleiter in the east than that, after ten years, they should be able to announce that their territories were completely German. He would not concern himself about the methods used to bring this about.[30] They in turn could push through the barbarous policies by recourse to 'special tasks' set by the Führer personally, though these were never specified in detail let alone laid out in writing.

The remainder of Poland – the 'General Government' placed in the charge of Hans Frank – became a dumping ground for 'racial inferiors'. Heydrich's 'Security Service Task Squads' (*Einsatzgruppen*) set to work to

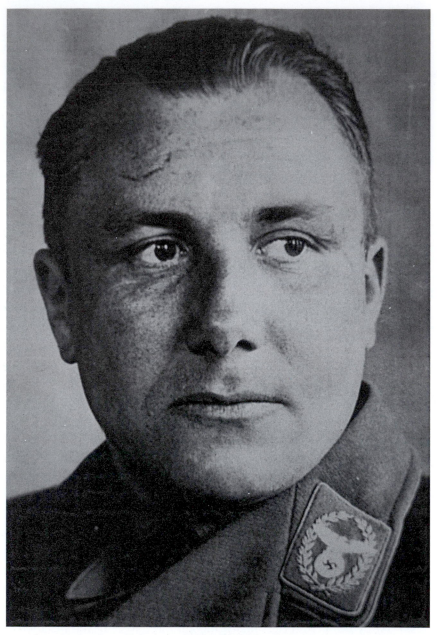

Figure 6.4 Martin Bormann, head of the Party Chancellery following Hess's flight to Scotland, on 10 May 1941, and from April 1943 officially 'Secretary to the Führer'.

wipe out the Polish intelligentsia. Himmler, in his new capacity as Reich Commissar for the Strengthening of Ethnic Germandom, orchestrated the deportations and 'resettlement' of countless thousands. On Heydrich's orders, Jews were now rounded up and placed in ghettos, where the rapidly worsening conditions and uncontrollable disease epidemics dramatically accelerated the need to find a 'final solution' to the 'Jewish problem', hugely magnified through the inclusion of around three million Polish Jews under Nazi rule. And for non-Jewish Poles, a reign of terror which left scarcely a family untouched was unleashed by the Nazi occupying administration. Whereas in the Reich itself, a semblance of law, however corrupted and perverted, remained in existence, 'law' in Poland was determined by the whim of Nazi Gauleiter and the regional SS bosses, the Higher SS and police chiefs. Hitler's mandate for action set the tone. The dirty work itself was willingly undertaken by others.

In his determination to attack Poland, Hitler had been convinced that the western democracies would not declare war over Danzig and the Corridor. By 3 September 1939, this gamble was revealed as a miscalculation – even if the western powers did nothing to prevent the dismembering of Poland (typically improvised as the destruction of the country took place). Not only the confidence won through the rapid demolition of the Polish army, but even more so the continuing spectre of time running against Germany both militarily and diplomatically – especially the doubtful durability of the pact with Russia – made Hitler impatient to turn immediately after the conclusion of the Polish campaign to open the attack on the west, on the presumption that this would lead to the final destruction of Germany's western opponents. He encountered opposition from his military commanders to the appalling risk of such a campaign in the depths of winter. Bad weather indeed brought a succession of postponements before, following upon the successes in Scandinavia, the astonishing western campaign stunned the world, left France comprehensively defeated, Britain isolated, and the triumphant Hitler at the height of his popularity and power.

A mere five weeks after the French signed the armistice, and at a time when the size of the German army was actually being reduced, Hitler ordered his military chiefs, in a meeting at Berchtesgaden on 31 July 1940, to prepare for an attack on Russia, to take place in May 1941.[31] The aim was the complete destruction of Russia within five months. The showdown with Bolshevism which had remained a constant in Hitler's thinking, even though he had no idea of the conditions in which it would occur, now began to take concrete shape.

Specifically ideological considerations played no direct role in the constellation of motives behind the initial planning of the attack. The crucial factor was the need to force Britain to come to terms, thus leaving Germany as the masters of Europe and with the desired free hand to turn the east into the required *Lebensraum*. A second key consideration was the worrying expansion of Soviet power in the Baltic and, especially, in the Balkans, where annexations of territory now posed a major threat to the Rumanian oil fields which were so crucial to the German military effort. The decision to attack the Soviet Union was hardly, therefore, a 'free choice' on ideological grounds, to put into reality the 'vision' of *Mein Kampf*. It was a strategic and economic necessity.

Once more, the dynamic of the war itself largely determined the bounds within which Hitler could act. The enormity of the gamble for hegemony in Europe imposed its own 'logic' on his decision-making. It was, then, fully in character that once more he justified the decision to strike at the Soviet Union by emphasising the impossibility of any alternative course of action – that is, the certain negative consequences of inaction.[32]

Though it meant opening up a war on two fronts – the old German nightmare – there appeared little cause for anxiety to the Nazi leadership. The gross underestimation of Soviet fighting capacity by the German military leadership meant that an optimism amounting to certainty prevailed that the destruction of Russia would be accomplished within months, leaving the way clear to attack British strength in the Middle East. The presumed victory over the Soviet Union would at one blow provide vital economic resources for Germany, leave Britain completely stranded and forced to capitulate or to face invasion, place America under further pressure from the increased opportunities in the Far East then open to Japan, and thus deter the USA from involvement in the war.

Though the Hitlerian ideological obsessions had played no major part in the actual framing of the decision to attack the Soviet Union, once that decision had been taken, and particularly once the planning of the invasion began to be worked out in detail, in the spring of 1941, the imprint of the Nazi racial philosophy became fully visible. Hitler himself spoke of his feeling of psychological freedom as soon as the termination of the pact with the Soviet Union, which he regarded as a break with his own origins and political views, was decided upon.[33] As if released from years of tactically imposed limitations on measures which could be used against enemies, Hitler now – faced with the reality of the war which he had always known he would have to fight, though in circumstances which had been impossible to foresee – came into his own. He told his generals that the war would be different to that in the west – a 'war of extermination'.[34] Political commissars of the Red Army were to be shot without further ado.[35] The army was to cooperate fully with the extermination squads of the SD, operating under the 'special tasks' accorded to Himmler.[36] The nature of these 'tasks' was revealed in Heydrich's instructions to the leaders of the *Einsatzgruppen* to liquidate Communist Party functionaries, 'Jews in the service of the Party or the State', and 'other extremist elements'.[37] The assault on the Soviet Union, whatever the strategic and economic reasons which, in Nazi thinking, necessitated it, was formulated by Hitler in the character of an ideological crusade against 'Jewish Bolshevism'. In spring 1941, the 'quantum leap'[38] into genocide was taken.

The decision to wipe out *every* Jew within German-occupied Europe was still some way off. During the first, triumphant weeks of the Russian campaign, the escalation in killing was still compatible with a 'final goal' couched in terms of a territorial settlement 'beyond the Urals'. Even this, could it have come about, would unquestionably have amounted to merely a different form of genocide to what took place. The killing process was already irreversible and rapidly developed its own momentum.

Heydrich's orders had evidently left plenty of room for interpretation to the *Einsatzgruppen* commanders. Most initially killed only male Jews; others, whole families. Probably some clarification was sought. It seems to have been provided by Himmler in August 1941.[39] At any rate, by late August and into September, with the military advance slowing and increasing numbers of Jews in German hands, the murders escalated dramatically, now being generally extended to include not just adult males but *all* Jews – including women and children. The Wehrmacht, having lost whatever vestiges of humanitarian feelings had still been present during the early atrocities in Poland, cooperated with the murder squads and committed many outrages on its own account.[40]

By the end of July, Heydrich had sought and attained the authorisation necessary from Göring (who since 1939 had nominally been in charge of coordinating the 'solution' to the 'Jewish Question') to prepare for the coming 'total solution'.[41] Until mid September this still appears to have been conceived of in terms of a territorial settlement – deportation to a Jewish reservation in the east, which would doubtless have amounted to some form of gigantic concentration camp. But at this juncture, with the prospects for a rapid victory over the Soviet Union rapidly dwindling, Hitler, who till then had vetoed deportation into the military zone,

Figure 6.5 The 'Final Solution': the notorious 'Gate of Death' at the entrance to the extermination camp of Auschwitz-Birkenau.

foreseeing the final removal of the Jews from Europe to the east as following upon a successfully concluded campaign, was persuaded to order the deportation of German Jews.[42] The crucial steps into the fully fledged 'Final Solution' – the attempted systematic murder of all the Jews of Europe – now rapidly followed, one after another.

Within a month, the first deported German Jews were arriving at the Lodz ghetto, where conditions were already indescribable and where liquidation of the inmates had been mooted months earlier as the solution.[43] Trainloads followed within a short time to Riga and Kowno, where the first German Jews were shot in late November.

In October 1941, the Police Chief of Lublin, Odilo Globocnik, was authorised by Himmler to exterminate the Jews in his district. The mandate later became extended to the Jews of the entire General-gouvernement, in what developed into 'Aktion Reinhard'. Within a short time planning began on the first of the extermination camps within Globocnik's remit, Belzec, later followed by Sobibor and Treblinka. Viktor Brack, deputy head of the Führer Chancellory, with the experience of the 'euthanasia action' behind him, supplied the experts to advise on gassing techniques and the personnel, tried and tested through the 'euthanasia action', to carry out the work. Construction now began, too, of the extermination unit at Birkenau, within the Auschwitz complex. At about the same time, a 'special command' of Himmler's men led by Herbert Lange, formerly engaged in the murder of the mentally sick in East Prussia through the device of a 'gas van', after scouring the area in favour of a suitable extermination site for liquidating the Jews of the Lodz ghetto in the Warthegau, settled upon a site near Chelmno and began operations in early December 1941. What would soon emerge as the 'Final Solution' was now under way. A systematic programme for the killing of the Jews of Europe was the subject of the Wannsee Conference on 20 January 1942, and put into operation during the following months.

During the summer of 1941, the inexorable course of events in the Russian campaign, together with the growing practical difficulties of coping with the millions of incarcerated Jews, the keenness of Nazi Gauleiter to rid themselves of remaining Jews on their territory, and the organisational ambitions of the SS, combined to produce mounting pressure from a number of sides to bring about a 'final solution' to the 'Jewish Question'. Initiatives came from many quarters. But, given the nature of the Führer state, Hitler remained the key to whatever comprehensive action was taken.

Hitler was the inspiration behind the 'Final Solution', even where the direct initiatives came from others. Goebbels called him the 'unswerving protagonist and advocate of a radical solution'.[44] The 'order' or 'wish' of the Führer was invariably invoked at every level in setting in motion and carrying out the murder of the Jews.[45] Crucial decisions required Hitler's approval. Himmler claimed Hitler's authority for the order around mid August 1941 to extend the killing in the Soviet Union to Jewish women and children.[46] At the prompting of Goebbels and Heydrich, Hitler consented in August 1941 to the introduction of the 'Yellow Star' to be worn by German Jews – something which, for tactical reasons, he had hitherto rejected.[47] There is no doubt that Hitler himself in mid September took the decision to deport the German Jews to the east, sealing their fate. No written directive from Hitler ordering the 'Final Solution' has survived. Almost certainly none was ever given. But there can be no serious doubt that Hitler gave the verbal authorisation to kill the Jews of Europe – even if such authorisation amounted to no more than a simple blanket empowering of Himmler and Heydrich.

War and the Jews had been bound up in Hitler's thinking from the beginning. He had blamed the loss of the First World War on the Jews. He had threatened them with extinction in the event of a new war. In the late summer of 1941, war and the fate of the Jews became in reality inseparable. As the progress of the German troops became slower, and doubts grew into the certainty that the vital gamble of the quick knock-out blow against the Soviet Union had failed, that Germany was faced with a prolonged war, and that the magnitude of the task to attain final victory was now enormous, the pressure grew from Nazi leaders in the east to find a 'solution to the Jewish Question'. In his own warped mentality, Hitler himself was determined that the Jews would be in no position to defeat Germany a second time. With the declaration of war on the USA on 11 December 1941, Germany was now involved in the world war that he had 'prophesied' would result in the annihilation of European Jewry. His radical reassertion in December 1941 that his 'prophecy' of 1939 would be fulfilled to the letter was, in this climate, sufficient to prompt the further drastic steps needed to transform the existing 'initiative' already in progress on a local or regional level to kill Jews in Russia and Poland into a comprehensive programme of extermination.[48]

Though the critical decisions in the extermination of the Jews were indeed taken by Hitler, the 'Final Solution' cannot be seen simply in personalised terms. The radicalisation of anti-Jewish policy during the

1930s took place with little active involvement on Hitler's part and in full view of German society. If many ordinary citizens were less than enthused by what was going on, there was as good as no opposition. The churches, too, looked to their own interests and remained, as institutions, silent in the face of gross inhumanity. Industry and commerce objected on pragmatic grounds when foreign trade appeared to be endangered, but easily reconciled themselves to a programme of ruthless economic exploitation and plunder of Jewish property. Civil servants, from the heads of major government departments down to the small fry organising the timetabling of the deportation trains, worked hard to turn ideological irrationality into bureaucratic regulations for discrimination. The army, unhappy at some of the 'excesses' in Poland, were cooperative in the fight against the 'Jewish–Bolshevik' arch-enemy. And in the SS, Hitler had the most dynamic organisation in the Third Reich, drawing its entire ethos from a doctrine of racial dominance and wedded to the centrality of the need to solve the 'Jewish Question'. German genocide, therefore, was far from one man's doing. Rather, it was the product of the readiness, on the part of widely varied sections of society, to work towards the visionary goals of a 'charismatic leader' who, by the time conditions for genocide emerged, was entirely freed of any constitutional or legal constraints.

While the death-mills of the east were going into full production, ultimate victory in the war was slipping further away from Germany. Military and economic advisers told Hitler in November 1941 that the war could not be won. He himself voiced for the first time the thought that the German people might perish in the struggle.[49] As the odds lengthened, Hitler gambled ever more recklessly. Willpower increasingly replaced strategy, irrationality more and more displaced reason. The divide with his generals deepened to a chasm in the winter crisis of 1941–42. With things going wrong, he cast around for scapegoats. Numerous generals were sacked. The head of the army, von Brauchitsch, eventually succeeded in having his tendered resignation accepted. Hitler himself now took over the army leadership, becoming thereby enmeshed in the minutiae of command details.

In the depths of the winter crisis, Japan's attack on Pearl Harbor on 7 December 1941 was the best news Germany could hope for. Germany had, in fact, been trying since the previous April to bring Japan into the war in order to keep the USA out of the European arena.[50] To this end, Hitler had already before Pearl Harbor been ready to commit Germany to war against America in the event of Japanese aggression. But a formal

Figure 6.6 Propaganda attempts, in the armed forces' magazine of 3 March 1943, a month after news of the 6th Army's surrender, to portray the catastrophe at Stalingrad as an epic of German heroism.

agreement to this effect had still to be signed. The Japanese coup gave Hitler what he had wanted for months. Germany, one might have thought, could now have refrained from action and rejoiced in the prospect of American energies being taken up in a Pacific conflict. There was no formal commitment to intervene. And all Hitler could extract from the Japanese was an agreement not to enter a separate peace with America. Nevertheless, on 11 December 1941 he announced Germany's declaration of war against the USA. It was a typical Hitler forward move, attempting to seize the initiative in a conflict with the USA which, he argued, already existed in reality and was bound before long anyway to become an open one. But it was a move from weakness, not strength. And it was more irrational than any strategic decision taken to that date. For the first time, it was an obvious loser's throw of the dice.

For a time in 1942, Germany's military successes in Russia and north Africa flattered to deceive. An internal analysis by the High Command established that the Wehrmacht was weaker in mid 1942 than it had been the previous year.[51] And the German war economy was under enormous strain. With backs to the wall, the economy, under Speer's leadership, was to show remarkable resilience between 1942 and 1944, though the hope of competing with the combined economic might of the Allies was a vain one. On the military front, the defeats at El Alamein and, above all, the calamitous sacrifice of the German Sixth Army at Stalingrad – where approaching 250,000 soldiers were lost in a terrible two-month battle which ended on 2 February 1943 with surrender and Soviet captivity for the 91,000 survivors – amounted to major turning-points in Germany's fortune.

The defeat at Stalingrad symbolised, not just in retrospect, the beginning of the end of Hitler's rule. His personal responsibility for the débâcle was widely recognised. The mounting criticism of the regime no longer stopped at the Führer. Underground resistance began to regroup. Hitler's power was shaken. But its grip was still enormously strong. Only a putsch or total military defeat could break it.

Notes and references

1. Broszat, *Staat*, pp. 380–1.
2. The title of the masterly study by Franz Neumann, *Behemoth. The Structure and Practice of National Socialism*, London, 1942.
3. Dieter Rebentisch, *Führerstaat und Verwaltung im Zweiten Weltkrieg*, Stuttgart, 1989, pp. 41–2.

4. Gruchmann, 'Die "Reichsregierung" ', p. 202.

5. See Rebentisch, p. 374 and n. 11.

6. Gruchmann, 'Die "Reichsregierung" ', pp. 196–7.

7. Rebentisch, p. 401.

8. Gruchmann, 'Die "Reichsregierung" ', pp. 211, 223, n. 115.

9. Rebentisch, pp. 399–400.

10. See Broszat, *Staat*, pp. 384–5.

11. Rebentisch, pp. 362–3.

12. Documentation on the 'euthanasia action' in N&P, iii, 997 ff.

13. N&P, iii, 1021.

14. IMG, xxvi, 255–7; trans. N&P, ii, 930.

15. Rebentisch, p. 381.

16. See Wolfgang Benz, 'Partei und Staat im Dritten Reich', in Martin Broszat and Horst Möller (eds.), *Das Dritte Reich*, Munich, 1983, p. 78.

17. Neumann, p. 384.

18. The key work on Ribbentrop is Wolfgang Michalka, *Ribbentrop und die deutsche Weltpolitik 1933–1940*, Munich, 1980.

19. The following passages rely mainly on Alfred Kube, *Pour le mérite und Hakenkreuz. Hermann Göring im Dritten Reich*, Munich, 1986, esp. pp. 299 ff.

20. Leonidas E. Hill (ed.), *Die Weizsäcker-Papiere 1933–1950*, Berlin, 1974, p. 162.

21. See K.-J. Müller, 'Nationalkonservative Eliten zwischen Kooperation und Widerstand', in Jürgen Schmädeke and Peter Steinbach (eds.), *Der Widerstand gegen den Nationalsozialismus*, Munich, 1985, pp. 28–31.

22. IMG, xxvi, 340; trans. N&P, iii, 740.

23. IMG, xxvi, 343; trans. N&P, iii, 742.

24. *Monologe*, p. 108.

25. Text of the speech in Domarus, pp. 970–3.

26. Domarus, p. 1058; trans. N&P, iii, 1049.

27. N&P, iii, 743.

28. IMG, xxvi, 379; trans. N&P, iii, 928.

29. *Heeresadjutant bei Hitler*, p. 68; trans. N&P, iii, 941.

30. Cit. Helmut Krausnick and Hans-Heinrich Wilhelm, *Die Truppe des Weltanschauungskrieges*, Stuttgart, 1981, pp. 626–7. See also Martin Broszat, *Nationalsozialistische Polenpolitik 1939–1945*, Frankfurt am Main, 1965, p. 200; trans. N&P, iii, 665.

31. Franz Halder, *Kriegstagebuch*, 3 vols, Stuttgart, 1962–4, ii, 49–50.

32. N&P, iii, 815.

33. N&P, iii, 817.

34. Halder, *Kriegstagebuch*, ii, 336–7; trans. N&P, iii, 1086–7.

35. *Anatomie des SS-Staates*, trans. *Anatomy of the SS State*, ii, 211, 225–6.

36. *Anatomie des SS-Staates*, trans. *Anatomy of the SS State*, ii, 198–205.

37. *Anatomie des SS-Staates*, ii, 364–5; trans. *Anatomy of the SS State*, pp. 62–3.

38. See Christopher Browning, *The Final Solution and the German Foreign Office*, New York, 1978, p. 8.

39. Philippe Burrin, *Hitler et les Juifs. Genèse d'un Génocide*, Paris, 1989, pp. 117–18.

40. See Omer Bartov, *The Eastern Front 1941–1945. German Troops and the Barbarisation of Warfare*, London, 1985.

41. *Anatomie des SS-Staates*, ii, 372–3; trans. *Anatomy of the SS State*, p. 68.

42. Burrin, pp. 138–9.

43. BAK, R58/954, ff. 189–91; trans. N&P, iii, 1103.

44. *Die Tagebücher von Joseph Goebbels*, ed. Elke Fröhlich, Munich, 1994, Part II, vol. 3, p. 561.

45. See Gerald Fleming, *Hitler und die Endlösung. 'Es ist des Führers Wunsch'*, Wiesbaden/Munich, 1982, for presentation of the evidence.

46. Burrin, pp. 118, 151.

47. Burrin, p. 136.

48. See Peter Longerich, *Politik der Vernichtung. Eine Gesamtdarstellung der nationalsozialistischen Judenverfolgung*, Munich, 1998, Chapter 6; and Christian Gerlach, *Krieg, Ernährung, Völkermord. Forschungen zur deutschen Vernichtungspolitik im Zweiten Weltkrieg*, Hamburg, 1998, pp. 117ff.

49. Fest, *Hitler*, p. 892.

50. For this section, see Eberhard Jäckel, *Hitler in History*, Hanover/London, 1984, ch. 4.

51. See N&P, iii, 840.

✠

Chapter 7

Hubris of power

In Greek mythology, the self-deification of Hubris in challenging the gods incites the wrath of Nemesis, the goddess of retribution, avenger of arrogant presumption, punisher of extraordinary crimes. It seems an apposite metaphor for the climacteric phase of Hitler's power.

Before 1941, the magnification of Hitler's power – and of his self-glory – had accompanied a succession of breathtaking triumphs. Astride the world, contempt for puny opposition could be boundless. But the conquests could not produce final victory. And with the failure of the Blitzkrieg in the Soviet Union and the entry into the war of the USA, the thin line between victory and inexorable defeat was crossed, the megalomaniac gamble for world power doomed. After 1941, Hitler was to experience only adversity and calamity. His volatile moods signified at the one extreme an unquenchable, increasingly irrational optimism that his will would ultimately triumph, that 'Providence' would not fail him; at the other extreme depression and resignation at the powerlessness to gain victory or to escape defeat, with a corresponding fury lashing out on all sides, stopping only at self-criticism.

Hitler's power in these last years was a paradox. Until the visible signs of dissolution set in during the final months of his rule, his power remained intact – unbroken in the sense that his orders were carried out and not disobeyed, and in the sense that he continued to function as the legitimating instance of all forms of authority in the Third Reich. On the other hand, in the face of mounting adversity Hitler had lost the power to determine the course and character of events. The initiative had been permanently relinquished. The powerlessness to turn the tide of war reflected itself in ever wilder irrationality, whose impact upon the structure and conduct of government was catastrophic. The incapacity to conclude the war either through victory or through a rational peace settlement culminated not only in a personal death-wish on Hitler's part, but in a verdict of destruction and damnation on his own people who, in his eyes, had failed him. It was the logical climax of Hitler's hubris of power.

By the second winter of the Russian campaign, the relentless pressure of the war began to take its toll of Hitler's health. From 1943 onwards he was in many ways a sick man – at times, as in autumn 1944 and again in April 1945, quite seriously ill.

The signs are that Hitler was under acute nervous strain in late 1942 and early 1943, during the months following the bitter confrontation with his generals about strategy in the Caucasus and including the Stalingrad catastrophe. In this period, Hitler usually ate alone and left his own quarters as little as possible. He slept badly. His only relaxation was a short walk with his dog. He did not even want to listen to Wagner any longer. His mood was one of deep depression, finding release in violent outbursts of uncontrollable rage, especially directed at his generals, as he cast around for scapegoats.

Hitler's detachment from reality broke new bounds in the last war years. His self-imposed isolation in his remote headquarters in East Prussia (for a short time in 1942–43 in Winniza in the Ukraine) intensely magnified his tendency to exclude unpalatable reality in favour of an illusory world in which 'will' always triumphed. He no longer visited the front, paying his last visit to any army field headquarters in September 1943; the war was conducted entirely from the map-room of the Führer bunker. His trips to Germany became ever rarer as, without successes to proclaim, he cut himself off from the German public. He did not visit a single bombed city, and was more shocked by the destruction of public buildings than by reports of human suffering. He was inaccessible to all but a favoured few Nazi leaders; and he made his only concessions to socialising in the company of his secretaries, adjutants, doctors and the ubiquitous Bormann, treating them late at night to endless monologues on future architectural plans in a post-war utopia and reminiscences on his past life and 'struggle'. For the most part, he was impersonal and distant in human relations. That he was not untouched by his growing

Figure 7.1 The V1 Flying Bomb, the first of the much-trumpeted 'wonder weapons'.

Plate 17   The politics of violence: a poster of 1932 urging the public to vote for Hindenburg.

Plate 18 Adolf Hitler in 1933.

Plate 19 Hitler in 1933 holding the legendary Blutfahne (Blood Flag) said to be stained with the blood of Nazis killed in the abortive Munich Putsch of 9 November 1923.

Plate 20 A painting of Hitler in Nazi hero style, *c*. 1935.

Plate 21 Hitler as a Teutonic Knight, painted by Hubert Lanzinger; at war's end a GI slashed Hitler's face on the painting with a bayonet.

Plate 22 Hitler postcard postmarked 10.4.1938, Innsbruck.

Plate 23 'Man Eater'. Russian cartoon *c*. 1942 depicting Hitler as a blood-dripping cannibal.

Plate 24 Adolf Hitler. Photograph by Henrich Hoffmann, published in 1940.

isolation was revealed in a remark he made to Albert Speer, that soon his only friends would be Fräulein Braun and his dog.[1] Speer's impression was of a man who was in the process of burning out.

During the last two years of the war, Hitler also increasingly became a physical wreck. His strong hypochondriac tendencies were pandered to by his quack doctor Morell, who pumped him during the war with no fewer than ninety separate patent medicines and injections.[2] Whether the twenty-eight different pills each day and regular hormone and other injections did him any good is extremely doubtful. But in any case, an unhealthy life of constant stress, sleeplessness, poor diet, lack of exercise and total absence of relaxation produced an inevitable sharp acceleration of the aging process. Göring remarked in 1943 that Hitler had aged fifteen years since the beginning of the war.[3] The shaking of his left arm, dizziness and disturbance of balance were most probably symptoms of Parkinson's Disease, though this cannot be established with certainty.

The physical deterioration accelerated following the attempt on Hitler's life in July 1944.[4] A cardiogram in September confirmed the rapidly advancing arteriosclerosis, which had first been diagnosed in spring 1943. Towards the end of the month Hitler contracted jaundice. Around this time, the shaking and trembling in his limbs reappeared more strongly than ever, after they had disappeared for a while following the shock of the explosion in the Wolf's Lair headquarters. The stomach cramps, intestinal spasms and headaches were chronic. Dizziness and sickly feeling were often present for hours at a time. Dr Morell regarded the accumulation of health problems in September 1944 as a minor collapse – a belated reaction to the attempt on Hitler's life.[5]

In the last months of the war, though he was still only in his mid fifties, Hitler's body was that of an old man. His hair was grey, his head and hands shook visibly, he was scarcely capable of shuffling more than a few steps in a bowed and unsteady gait; his eyes were bloodshot; saliva at times dripped from his mouth.[6]

In what ways and why the mentally unstable and physically decrepit man directing Germany's fortunes from a headquarters part way between monastery and concentration camp, as Jodl described it,[7] could continue to exercise power is the subject of this final chapter. Brief consideration of a number of aspects of Nazi policy indeed indicates that Hitler's authority remained paramount and incontestable. It reveals at the same time the utter absurdity and ultimate helplessness – other than the capability to destroy – built into the mounting arbitrariness of the exercise of personalised power in its full hubris.

Given the extent of fragmentation of government in the Third Reich, the major spheres of policy were linked only through Hitler. Policy deliberations involved Hitler in discussion with individuals (such as Himmler in the case of race policy and the occupied territories, or Bormann and Lammers in domestic affairs), or shifting bodies of armaments experts and military personnel (on munitions production and war strategy). But Hitler remained the only strand in the web binding all the threads together.

By the time of the defeat at Stalingrad, Hitler had in effect for long been a 'part-time Reich Chancellor'.[8] Goebbels complained on a number of occasions in early 1943 of a 'lack of leadership in domestic and foreign policy', of 'a complete lack of direction in German domestic policy', and of a 'leadership crisis'.[9] In private, Goebbels in fact spoke not only of a 'leadership crisis' but of a 'Leader crisis'.[10] He simply could not understand why Hitler had relinquished the vital field of 'politics' in favour of the wholly secondary task of military command.

Goebbels' comments arose in the context of his exclusion from a last attempt at a form of collective government, initiated by the Reich Chancellory. A 'Committee of Three' comprising Lammers, Keitel and Bormann – dubbed sarcastically by Göring 'the Three Kings'[11] – was set up, and met eleven times between January and August 1943. Göring, Goebbels, Speer and other excluded prominent leaders spent the next months scheming to undermine the committee. The idea was to break Bormann's influence on Hitler, and to revamp Göring's powers as head of the defunct Reich Defence Council. The machinations failed both because of Göring's poor standing with Hitler in the light of the failure of the Luftwaffe to combat Allied bombing, and also as a result of the personal rivalries of those involved in the intrigue.

They need have worried little, however, about the likelihood of being by-passed by a new institution of power. In practice, the 'Committee of Three' was soon stymied once again by the administrative chaos in the Third Reich. It rapidly came up against vested interests of the varied power blocks and petty fiefdoms which meant that a unified, simplified and coordinated centralised administration was vitiated from the outset. It also had to cope with arbitrary and sporadic interventions by Hitler, blocking 'for political reasons' administrative measures which the committee had worked out. These interventions ranged from preventing the conscription for labour of women over the age of forty-five, to stopping the merging of local government offices, and even to permission for horse-racing and betting-shops to continue.

The question of whether to ban horse-racing during the 'total war' highlights the chaotic nature of decision-making in domestic affairs.[12] Not least, it shows Hitler's own authority to be necessary as legitimation, but his capacity to arrive at a clear, unequivocal decision to be remarkably limited.

It began with Goebbels, particularly alert to questions of morale at the time of the Stalingrad defeat, seeking a directive from Hitler to ban horse-racing after workers in a Berlin tank factory had allegedly shown their disapproval at racing taking place nearby while they had to work on Sundays. Hitler communicated his disagreement in a telegram to the Propaganda Ministry: there was a lack of entertainment as it was, and a visit to the races was among the favourite relaxations of the tank-factory workers. Goebbels then paid a visit to the Führer Headquarters and reported to the Reich Chancellory, on his return, that Hitler had spoken out against the continuation of horse-racing – a plain contradiction of the earlier telegram.

Following hectic deliberations, in which Hitler was again consulted, horse-racing was allowed but confined to a limited number of courses, with all other courses, together with bookies' offices, being closed down. Reich Defence Commissars (who were all Party Gauleiter) were given permission to ban other races if it was felt necessary for morale reasons. But, on the contrary, a number of Gauleiter now found pressing reasons why their own localities should be excluded from the general ban. In Munich a row broke out between Gauleiter Paul Giesler and Christian Weber, a Hitler crony since the early Munich days, a former pub bouncer who had become President of the Economic Federation of German Riding-Stable Owners, about continued racing at Riem, on the outskirts of Munich. Both complained to Hitler, whose wisdom of Solomon judgement was that racing at Riem should be stopped, because of the wastage of petrol in laying on transport to the course for spectators, but that it should be allowed on the Theresienwiese in the city centre.

Soon afterwards Hitler remarked to Bormann, on seeing advertisements in a newspaper for horse-racing in Berlin, that Munich should not be less favoured than the Reich capital, and promptly gave directions for racing to be opened in Riem again. Bormann, Lammers, Goebbels and various Gauleiter continued to engage in correspondence about horse-racing in these months when the military outcome of the war was effectively being decided. Finally, Lammers and Bormann agreed, in accordance with an 'expression of the will of the Führer', that racing and bookmaking should once more be generally permitted, but that Reich Defence Commissars should be empowered to ban them if need be.

The farce had taken around five months to resolve. Hitler had been personally involved on several occasions. It was vital for all parties to obtain a 'Führer decision'. But the 'decisions' had been arbitrary, scarcely consistent, and strongly influenced by the way the case had been presented and the person presenting it. It ended in central government conceding that no ruling could be laid down, and that actual power of implementation resided with the Gauleiter.

The 'Committee of Three' had constantly sought to 'work towards the Führer', and had never contemplated any decisions which might have run counter to Hitler's expressed wishes. But the failure of the Committee was the final demonstration of the incompatibility of any systematic administration with the arbitrary and unsystematic power of the Führer.

In the last two years of the Third Reich, the progressive fragmentation and disintegration of government reached its apogee. It is true that by March 1945, Bormann was laying plans to centralise Party control (and his own power base) still further by taking over the Führer Chancellory and Ley's office as Reich Organisation Leader of the Party.[13] But this scarcely marked a rational move to a coordinated structure of government. By this time there was, in fact, a notable disproportion between the gathering stream of directives issuing from Bormann and the practicalities of their implementation as government buildings were bombed, files and records burnt, and communications networks destroyed.

Hitler remained alert to the very end to the protection of his own rights of final jurisdiction. Goebbels, for example, was empowered, as Plenipotentiary for Total War Deployment, to issue directives but not binding legal decrees, and Hitler reserved to himself the last word in instances where objections arose from Goebbels' directives.[14] Goebbels was intelligent enough to strike the right chord with Hitler's prejudices in order to gain approval for most of his actions, but on occasions where he encountered objections – often in small matters of detail which had come to Hitler's attention – he yielded without demur.[15]

Hitler's authority remained, then, unquestioned, his backing a necessary prerequisite for action. Disobedience or disloyalty was for Nazi leaders beyond contemplation.[16] But there was less coherence and rationality than ever in his exercise of power. It was impulsively and spasmodically *reactive*, rather than clear, consistent and constructive.

This was a consequence of the irrationality of the power structure itself. The disintegration of all intermediary structures of authority and the preservation of the final determining right of the Führer, which went hand in hand with the upholding of his prestige, had led to an extraordinary accretion of power, but with it to a level of personalisation in decision-taking which was incompatible with systematic government and administration. Final responsibility for the most wide-ranging and also for the most trivial policy decisions rested with Hitler. But his unwillingness to reach a decision, or search for a compromise, in complex or sensitive matters was notorious.[17] And he was increasingly reluctant to pass on such responsibility, or to delegate any authority.

As long as the run of diplomatic and military triumphs had continued, his natural indolence had been compatible with the 'genial' direction of grand strategy. But in conditions of total war, and faced with the self-imposed unrelieved burden of work and punishing routine necessitated by concentrating the direction of both civilian and military affairs in his own hands, Hitler could not cope. The demands on the intellectual resources, competence and energy needed to manage responsible decision-making on all important issues would have been beyond the capacity of any single individual. They were certainly beyond Hitler.

The lack of direction in internal affairs, of which Goebbels complained, was also a product of Hitler's unwillingness and inability to create clear systematic lines of policy control, allocate priorities, and delegate full authority. Only the manifestation of the threat from within – the recurring nightmare of another '1918' – could galvanise Hitler into belated reactive action. Hence, it took the fall of Mussolini to prompt the replacement of Frick, for years ineffectual, by Himmler at the Reich Ministry of the Interior. And only in the aftermath of the bomb plot of July 1944 could Hitler finally be persuaded to give Goebbels 'plenipotentiary powers' (which, as we have seen, were less extensive than his title suggested) for total war mobilisation. By then, with the room for manoeuvre in domestic affairs rigidly limited by external events, 'politics' had crystallised once more into propaganda and terror. Mobilisation of the masses to fight on and hold out, and repression of anything threatening that end were all that counted. They were, in fact, all that was left: a substitute for policy.

The most crucial sphere of policy in the later war years was that of armaments production. It was an area in which Hitler took the keenest and most direct interest, involving himself to the fullest. It provides a particularly telling illustration of the character of Hitler's power.

Following the untimely death in January 1942 of Fritz Todt, who had masterminded the Reich's building and construction projects from the

Figure 7.2 A V2 rocket being prepared for launch against Britain.

early years of the Third Reich, Albert Speer – the 'court' architect, and specially favoured by Hitler – found himself without prior consultation suddenly appointed to all Todt's offices, including that of Minister of Armaments. His objection that he knew nothing about armaments production was brushed aside by Hitler, who said he was sure Speer would manage it, and in any case he had no one else. Hitler provided him with the requested authorisation, and promptly blocked Göring's attempt to muscle in on the new domain which Speer had been offered.[18] The demarcation of Speer's powers and responsibilities was, however, characteristically left vague and ill-defined.

The new Armaments Minister proved an inspired choice. Ambitious, clever and dynamic, he turned around the over-bureaucratised, inefficient production of armaments which by 1941 had still not reached the level of the First World War.[19] 'Speer, I will sign everything that comes from you,' Hitler is alleged to have told him.[20] But the next years were nevertheless to show that Hitler's authorisation was never as extensive as it seemed. In the jungle of the Third Reich, Speer had to use all the considerable scheming and elbow-power he possessed to fight his way through. Not only the conflicting powers assigned to Fritz Sauckel as Plenipotentiary for Labour Mobilisation blocked his path. He had to compete with intrigues among his own right-hand men – Xavier Dorsch, head of the central office of the former Todt Organisation, and Karl Otto Saur, head of the technical office in Speer's ministry. Both were particularly trusted by Hitler. And both schemed at times against Speer, going to Hitler behind his back. By 1945 Speer was in effect indeed superseded by the thrusting Saur. Not least, Speer was to learn at first hand how Hitler's own arbitrary, impulsive and dilettante interventions could sabotage any rational formulation of armaments policy.

Self-taught in the technicalities of weaponry as in other matters, Hitler had considerable knowledge and an extraordinary memory for minute detail. He could take an informed part, therefore, in the conferences on armaments production, in which he was usually in more relaxed mood than during the strategy conferences with his generals. Despite his mastery of detail, however, his understanding of weapons systems was by no means sophisticated, wide-ranging or far-sighted. In many respects, his conception of weaponry derived from the technological developments of the First World War and the 1920s. Moreover, he was scarcely equipped to cope with the sophisticated scientific and technological principles of modern weapons systems.[21]

Hitler involved himself regularly and directly in decisions which had almost daily to be taken in the realm of armaments production. Some 2,500 'Führer decisions' are recorded between 1942 and 1945 in the protocols of the armaments briefings by Speer and his team[22] (who relied upon the leadership and technological expertise of major armaments firms for the data they presented to Hitler). The decisions were normally made either during or immediately following the verbal reports made by Speer and his technical experts, though were sometimes modified during the course of conferences which could last for several days. The recorded decisions were in any case 'doctored' by Speer and his colleagues. Phrases such as 'the Führer has decided' or 'in the opinion of the Führer' were added at every opportunity in order to lend authority to Speer's directives.[23]

Speer well knew how to couch his suggestions in order to gain Hitler's approval. Such agreement remained crucial since Hitler's decisions were indeed accepted on all sides as authoritative. Speer could then seize upon Hitler's agreement to pass on directions to government ministers and to the army. Hitler's consent, along with his requests and demands, rapidly became thus translated into a string of decrees and orders on the part of his Armaments Minister.

Speer was initially adept at exploiting his close ties with Hitler to obtain an uncritical signature on draft decrees and a nod of approval for recommendations made in the armaments conferences. Moreover, he could use the authority of Hitler to free reserves of energy in the system.[24] But the more hopeless the war situation and Hitler's desperate search for a 'miracle' became, the more Speer had to reckon with his wholly unpredictable, arbitrary and dogmatic interventions. And the more grave Germany's military position became, the more closed Hitler's mind became to counter-argument or alternative suggestions.

Hitler's tendency to over-simplification, his strategic miscalculations, his instinctive leaning towards offensive rather than defensive weaponry, his reduction of complexities to matters of will, continued readiness to be more impressed by production than performance of weaponry,[25] and his self-delusion – sometimes based upon misinformation from Speer, himself by no means always well informed[26] – imposed limitations, sometimes damaging, on policy formulation. Diffuse and suggestive insinuation by Speer's rivals to match Hitler's own known prejudices, coupled with Hitler's over-estimation of his own knowledge and ability and repeated emphasis on the experience gained as an 'ordinary front soldier' in the First World War, led to major errors in weaponry design and production.

The insistence upon a heavy, slow type of tank, ill-equipped to cope with the more mobile Soviet tanks, was one such error. Hitler demanded greater armour, not more speed, to combat the Russian T34. As a result, the German Tiger had grown from its original fifty to seventy-five tons, and the new light Panther soon expanded from thirty to forty-eight tons. Seeing advantage for his firm in allying himself with Hitler's preferences, Ferdinand Porsche – now a byword for light, fast cars – undertook to produce slow, heavy tanks. What emerged was the 'Mouse', a monster of a hundred tons, followed by even larger prototypes which proved utter non-starters.[27] Hitler's perverse directive did not lose Germany the war. Most tanks produced, in fact, remained light and by 1944 the most effective German tank was the sixteen-ton Hetzer.[28] But it did lead to a damaging multiplicity of competing projects instead of rational concentration of production.

More seriously damaging to Germany's war effort was Hitler's reluctance to commission the Me262 jet fighter.[29] This was potentially Germany's most effective defence weapon against growing allied air superiority. With a speed of up to 800 km per hour, the jet could outfly any contemporary aircraft. It was commissioned in May 1943, but production priority was removed by Hitler in September, apparently following indications of the jet's high fuel expenditure.[30] Suddenly, in January 1944, Hitler restored priority after reading reports in the press of British experiments with jet aeroplanes. But now Hitler, with his characteristic leaning towards offensive, not defensive, weaponry and misled, it would seem, by comments of designer Professor Willy Messerschmitt,[31] to the dismay of all concerned with the aeroplane insisted on its deployment as a *bomber*. And as attempts to persuade him to alter this decision mounted through the summer of 1944, Hitler refused point blank to discuss the matter any further. In late March 1945, he then astonishingly ordered the rearming of the Me262 as a fighter.[32] By that date there was no fuel; in any case, the war was as good as over.

A further serious error in armaments production was Hitler's insistence for propaganda and prestige reasons upon the production and deployment of the V1 flying-bomb and the V2 rocket in an absurdly misplaced emphasis upon offensive weapons rather than defensive ground-to-air missiles which could have offered some counter to Allied bombing. Once he had been persuaded in October 1942 by Speer of the potential of the long-range rocket-bomb, following successful trials at Peenemünde earlier that year, he had characteristically demanded on impulse their mass production on a scale which, given Germany's fuel situation, was quite incompatible with other urgent demands. A few months later, he gave the project equal priority with tank production.[33] Even had it been possible to put into operation against Britain the 5,000 rockets (or over five months' production) which Hitler wanted to assemble for simultaneous deployment, the bomb load would have been less than half that of a combined Anglo-American bombing raid.[34] As it was, a huge effort of energy and expense – deflecting from more worthwhile projects – was put into developing a weapon which, by the time not five thousand at once but twenty-five over a period of ten days came to be fired against England in September 1944, amounted to only a fringe irritant to the Allied war effort.

Serious though the mistakes were which flowed from Hitler's dilettante determination of armaments priorities, the weaknesses of Germany's armaments programmes in the last war years cannot be attributed solely or even in the main to his eccentric personal interventions. In the case of the V2, for instance, the Army Ordnance Office had striven for years to obtain recognition for its rocket programme (with a corresponding keenness of the Luftwaffe to gain funding for its own competing system, the 'doodlebug' cruise missile or V1 flying-bomb).[35] Hitler's own reservations about the V2 programme were in fact overcome by Speer only some months after the project had met with the enthusiastic backing of the Armaments Minister himself. And Speer not only approved Hitler's decision to go all out for the rocket-bomb, but regarded the V2 as his own favourite armaments project.[36] The mistakes in the case of the V2 were at least as much Speer's as Hitler's, even if the latter's intervention was decisive in the allocation of priorities. Hitler's dilettantism was, in fact, the direct expression of a supreme German leadership hopelessly positioned once the optimistic gamble of the Blitzkrieg had given way to a belated and inadequate adjustment to a defensive strategy with no way out.

Since the start of the war, and especially since the beginning of the Russian campaign, the direction of military strategy had been Hitler's dominant concern. And once he had taken over the leadership of the army as well as of the armed forces as a whole, during the winter crisis of 1941, it became his almost exclusive preoccupation.

In the western campaign of 1940, adopting General von Manstein's bold attacking ploy, Hitler had pursued an offensive strategy against much contrary advice from his generals, and achieved a remarkable military triumph. In the winter of 1941, after his personal initiative had forced the attack away from Moscow towards the flanks of Leningrad and the Kiev salient, he had insisted upon a halt to the retreat from Moscow which had saved an even worse military disaster. Such successes amplified his contempt for his generals and his own self-confidence. After the full-scale clash with the military leadership in autumn 1942, Hitler's strategic and tactical limitations, arising from his inflexibility in adversity and overestimation of will as the decisive military factor, were central to the disaster of Stalingrad.

As supreme head of army command, Hitler was centrally involved in the formulation of day-to-day tactics in a way which occupied no other head of state during the Second World War. For the German army, this was catastrophic. The command structure which he had devised placed him in charge of both the general management of military campaigns and its detailed tactics. It amounted to an absurd and counter-productive concentration of power. And it guaranteed that the clashes between Hitler and his generals continued.

The crisis of confidence in his leading generals was never overcome. In the face of adversity, and with room for manoeuvre and initiative rapidly diminishing, Hitler looked everywhere except to himself in allocating blame for setbacks. Above all, he heaped opprobrium on the incompetence or arrogance of his military leaders, towards whom his distrust was as good as paranoid even before the attack on his life on 20 July 1944. Hitler's view of his generals, in the aftermath of Stalingrad, was that they were cheating him wherever they could do so, that they understood nothing of running a war, and that they were the untrained products of a military education which had been wrongly conceived for generations.[37]

Among the ranks of the generals who met with Hitler's disfavour, even von Manstein and Guderian, who had counted as amongst Hitler's strongest supporters in the military leadership and whose military achievements had been brilliant, were dismissed towards the end of the war when, in Hitler's eyes, their will to victory and tenacity to stave off defeat had declined. A protest or hint of disobedience at such dismissals would have been unthinkable.

At the hub of the military command – and the centre-point of daily routine in the Führer Headquarters – was the two- or three-hour briefing conference each midday. The conferences were a stressful occasion for all concerned, including Hitler. The attempt to combine a strategic overview with repeated intervention in the petty detail of tactical manoeuvre was disastrous. Convinced that the experience of the First World War corporal was of greater value than the formal military training of the professionals, Hitler was often able to deploy his formidable detailed knowledge to

Figure 7.3 Albert Speer, Reich Armaments Minister from 1942, whose organisational skills greatly increased armaments production, driving an experimental tank.

embarrass his generals, but also made serious errors of judgement arising from a refusal to pay due attention to advice from his commanders in the field and his insistence on running the war in person and from the map-room of his headquarters. As the vice tightened and the impossibility of prising it open became ever more evident, Hitler's inflexibility, stubbornness, intolerance, irascibility, ready search for scapegoats for mistakes, and grasping at straws as a way out of problems intensified. It offered little prospect of sound military leadership, and every likelihood of damaging errors in the direction of the war.

However, the war was not lost for Germany as a result of Hitler's military mistakes, but because his form of politics had brought Germany into a war and because that war had been conducted in such a fashion that there was no political way out. Hitler had exchanged politics for war. The Allied proclamation of 'unconditional surrender' was the logical outcome, and one which Hitler understood most literally.[38]

Nor was it the case, as post-war apologists would have it, that Hitler's strategic blunders were tyrannically imposed upon a reluctant military leadership which could otherwise have carried Germany to final victory. Hitler's decisions in the military arena were by no means all as absurd as they were sometimes retrospectively painted.[39] Moreover, his regular circle of military advisers usually pandered to his known wishes, supported his suggestions and withheld criticism. And the advice received from front commanders was at times contradictory or based upon false intelligence, and frequently played to Hitler's own over-optimistic assessment of Germany's prospects.

The powerlessness of the generals did not reside in an individual incapacity to stand up to Hitler. Halder, Jodl, Guderian and von Manstein were among those who not infrequently brazened it out with Hitler. Other generals, too, had their run-ins with their commander-in-chief. Few of the top brass were outrightly Nazi. But the problem was that they had collectively backed the regime as long as it was winning. And they had no escape route once it was losing. They had flourished with Hitler. Now they had to perish with him. As Hitler repeatedly stated in the briefing conferences, there was no retreat; the generals had burnt their boats along with his own.[40]

It was in this context that Hitler's characteristic reaction – attack to regain the initiative – was turned by his generals into the last two major German military offensives of the war, 'Operation Citadel' in July 1943 and the assault through the Ardennes in December 1944. Both were bold strategic moves. They were conceived and initiated by Hitler himself. But his commanders not only willingly carried out the orders; they engaged in the shaping of them. Neither operation had a great chance of success. Each was a desperation move from weakness. With their failure, Germany's military effort, along with its political leadership, was bankrupt.

Meanwhile, all boats had been burnt in another fundamental sense. As military victory was revealed as an increasingly vain illusion, the fight to destroy Germany's racial enemies could, it was believed, still be won. The urgency to complete the physical liquidation of European Jewry as defeat was staring Germany in the face was the most evident manifestation of this. But compared with his active presence in the shaping of armaments policy and military strategy, Hitler's participation in the latter stages of Nazi genocidal policy is less plainly visible.

In March 1943, Hitler gave Goebbels permission to complete the removal of Jews from Berlin.[41] In April he attempted – though without success – to persuade Admiral Horthy to deport Hungarian Jews to concentration camps.[42] After a lengthy conferral with Himmler in mid June, he fully backed the SS leader's request to sustain radical measures in the deportation of the Jews.[43] In October, following the suggestion of Werner Best, his plenipotentiary in Denmark, he ordered the deportation of the Danish Jews, and around the same time, in order to avoid undue provocation of the Papacy, he accepted Foreign Office advice not to dispatch Rome's 8,000 Jews for immediate liquidation but to send them 'as hostages' to Mauthausen concentration camp in Austria (though, in fact, most were taken nonetheless direct to Auschwitz).[44]

These blanket orders sufficed. Everything else could be left to the SS, and to the unflagging organisational drive of Himmler's chief 'manager' of the 'Final Solution', Adolf Eichmann. Hitler saw Himmler several times a week. Often no one else was present, and no minutes were kept. It would have been extraordinary if the progress of the 'solution' to the 'Jewish Question' had never been mentioned. Hitler was undoubtedly kept broadly informed. It seems, though, unlikely that he enquired in great detail. He had spoken about the fate of the Jews, even in his close entourage, only in generalities – barbarous in their sentiments, but lacking the outright bluntness of Himmler's statements. He was, it appears, content in the knowledge that his prophecy of 1939 was being fulfilled – a claim he made for the last time on 26 May 1944 in a speech to his generals, who warmly applauded his comments.[45]

Until the last weeks of the Third Reich, Hitler's 'orders' – often vague expressions of whim, sometimes contradictory, frequently brutal, in many instances arbitrary or downright eccentric – never ceased to find willing agents who attempted to interpret them and put them into practice. Whatever Hitler's own paranoia, his wishes, down to the final stages of the Third Reich, were not being countermanded, disobeyed or sabotaged by his general staff, or by any other sector of the Nazi regime.

The undoubted strength of Hitler's personality, however much it continued to impress itself upon those in his immediate vicinity, can hardly in itself suffice to explain this unbroken mastery. The reasons for the continued subservience have to be sought outside Hitler himself, in the command structures of the Nazi state, in the vested interests which still interlocked with the dying regime, in the reserves of loyalty which were still not exhausted, and in the level of repression which left little alternative for most ordinary Germans.

Hitler's power remained, in the first instance, unbroken because of the very lack of governmental system in the Nazi regime. Hitler, as we have seen throughout, had been extremely alert to any conceivable restriction upon his powers, unwilling to be constrained by any formal structures or constitutional norms, and uninterested in preserving clear channels of control. The deposition of Mussolini by the Fascist Grand Council in July 1943 confirmed Hitler's fear of any institutional framework of control. The mooted Nazi senate which would elect the next leader after Hitler was, therefore, never called into being. The consequent dissolution of the state as a *system* of government meant that the position of the Führer remained indispensable to the functioning of the regime as a whole. Policy-making was utterly fragmented. Even in the different component parts, decisions were reached through Hitler dealing with specific individuals or groups, but not with a stable, collective body representing central government. This meant that particularist interests within the regime could be served only through retention of their bonds with the Führer. He was the 'enabler' whose authority was necessary for success in the competitive jungle of the Third Reich, the legitimator whose sanction was needed to accord priority to policy initiatives. The weakness of each of the individual parts within the 'system' was, in this way, the strength of Hitler's own authority.

The non-Nazi elites had backed Hitler and profited from his successes down to the middle of the war. The most important of these were the leadership of the Wehrmacht and industry. They had often only partly 'engaged' in the Nazi system, and had for the most part retained some reservations. But their partial enthusiasm had been acceptable as long as their collaboration had been total. And by the time they realised that Hitler was leading them inexorably to ruination, they could do

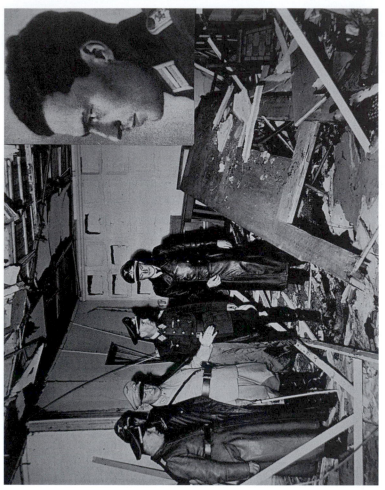

Figure 7.4 Göring (centre) points out the damage caused by the bomb placed in the briefing room of Hitler's headquarters by Colonel Claus Schenk Graf von Stauffenberg (inset) on 20 July 1944. Bormann is on the left of the picture.

no more than partially 'disengage' from the Nazi regime. Naturally, the 'disengagement' was greatest where vested interests were concerned. But until the final stages of the war, some significant affinities with the Nazi leadership still existed.

In the face of inevitable defeat, German industry was in the last phase of the war above all concerned to save what it could from destruction and to look to survival in a non-Nazi future. Nevertheless, there was scarcely a major German firm which had not been deeply implicated in the plunder of Europe, had not profited from its involvement in the war effort. Not a single leading industrialist or top-ranking manager was to be found among the disparate circles which made up the conspiracy against Hitler of July 1944. Happy though many of them would have been by this time to see the end of Hitler and his regime, they were unprepared to do anything active towards achieving that aim. The break with Nazism, when it came, was from the point of view of industrialists to be accomplished with as little disruption as possible, and with the retention of the author- itarian structures of industrial relations which the Nazis had reaffirmed.

Of the military leadership, those sufficiently concerned – for whatever motives – to take the risk of plotting to remove Hitler formed a cour- ageous, but unrepresentative, minority. Most leading generals – even such as Guderian, von Manstein and von Rundstedt, who were prepared at times openly to challenge Hitler's judgement – remained loyal to the end. Others, such as von Kluge, whose enthusiasm had waned, wavered but refrained from direct opposition. The leadership of the Luftwaffe and navy, from the outset more enthusiastic than that of the army for the Nazi regime, stayed for the most part loyal and warm in its support. Requested in February 1944 to sign a personal declaration of loyalty to Hitler, Field Marshal Weichs thought the reaffirmation of his soldierly oath 'unmil- itary', that the loyalty of the officer had to be taken for granted.[46] Even as late as March 1945, Field Marshal Kesselring saw it as his soldierly duty to carry out Hitler's orders without question.[47] Field Marshal Busch, indeed, allegedly went so far as to accuse Dönitz of failing to act in Hitler's spirit by refusing to fight on at the beginning of May 1945.[48]

The fervent patriotism which pushed the heroic few who joined the conspiracy to the belief that only Hitler's death could save Germany continued for the majority of military leaders – and their men – to provide some sort of bond with Hitler. Detestation of Bolshevism and fears of the consequences of defeat reinforced such bonds, even where the hopelessness of the military situation seemed self-evident. Moreover, the oath of allegiance which the army had sworn to Hitler personally presented again a most solemn tie which few could contemplate breaking. But the bonds between the military and Hitler went beyond the conventional soldierly allegiance to the head of state. The Wehrmacht had been a willing and active agent in the crusade against Bolshevism. It had played its part in the atrocities and barbarities in the eastern territories. Its complicity in genocide had not been coerced. The applause which the unambiguous comments of both Hitler and Himmler about the 'Final Solution' in May 1944 drew from the generals[49] indicates that there had been some affinity between Wehrmacht and Nazi leadership even on the most terrible outcome of racial policy.

The recognition by the leaders of the conspiracy to assassinate Hitler on 20 July 1944 of the unpopularity of their attempted coup, even should it prove successful – that it indeed amounted to 'resistance without the people'[50] – was testimony to the continued reserves of popular support on which the regime, and Hitler personally, could draw, even in mounting adversity. Hitler's popularity among the German people, greatly reduced though it was since the heyday of 1940, was, given the conditions of the last war years, remarkable. Not least, ordinary soldiers captured at the front revealed a high level of admiration for the person of the Führer into the last weeks of the Reich. Hitler's popular backing had still not completely dissolved.

The major upholders of the nimbus of the Führer were, naturally, the committed functionaries and activists of the Nazi Party and its manifold affiliations. There remained a hard core of fanatical believers whose faith, even *in extremis*, did not waver. Nor was it simply a matter of affective bonds with the regime. In material terms, an army of *apparatchiks* stood to lose by Hitler's downfall.

Above all this was the case for the Nazi leadership itself. The war had greatly extended the number of those who benefited materially from the Third Reich – those who had gained status and power, and with that profits from the regime's booty, plunder and corruption. Generous 'gifts' by Hitler helped to sweeten any souring loyalties, not only of his Party satraps, but also of field marshals in the Wehrmacht. Hitler had spoken in 1940 of a prudent policy of rewarding his military leaders not only with promotions to the position of field marshal and colonel-general but also with a tax-free bonus to remind them of their oath of loyalty.[51] Later in the war, Sperrle, Keitel, Guderian, von Leeb and von Reichenau were among those favoured by substantial 'donations'.[52]

In another important way, too, the Nazi elite and also significant sections of the non-Nazi elites remained bound to Hitler. The war – especially the barbarous, genocidal war in the east – greatly magnified the number of those who had 'burnt their boats' with the Nazi regime, who were bound to Hitler through their complicity in mass murder. For them, as for Hitler – who spoke of the need to 'burn boats' to achieve great deeds[53] – there was no way out. The reminder that they were 'all in it together' may, indeed, have been a conscious motive on Himmler's part in speaking openly and explicitly about the killing of the Jews to his SS leaders and then to the Party Gauleiter in his notorious Posen speeches in October 1943 (when he noted the names of those who had *not* heard his speech).[54] The same motive conceivably lay behind Hitler's unmistakable allusions to the 'Final Solution' and Himmler's categorical statements about the genocide against the Jews in their speeches to the generals in May 1944.

Naturally, the war itself – in some respects still more in its defensive phase, with 'backs to the wall', than during the earlier triumphs – provided a certain binding force, at the level both of the elites and of the people. Though most ordinary Germans yearned for nothing more than the end to the war, the patriotic defence against invading forces, especially in the east where it was bolstered by deep sentiments of anti-Bolshevism, blended into the racial ideologies of the desperadoes who were ruling Germany. The prospects of destruction and fears of revenge by the 'red hordes' – clear signs of the success of Nazi propaganda in this respect – formed an even more powerful negative bond, as did the simple lack of alternative which had arisen from the Allied demand of unconditional surrender.

Last, but certainly not least, terror – from beginning to end a central prop of Hitler's power – escalated wildly in the death throes of the regime as the positive binding elements lost much of their former force. In these last months, if not before, this was the most crucial foundation of all of Hitler's unbroken power. The apparatus of coercion remained loyal to Hitler until the last days of the Reich and in the hands of the most fanatical and ruthless section of the Nazi Movement, the SS, who were prepared to resort to any lengths in their defence of power. The web of Nazi organisations, staffed by loyal functionaries, ensured that even the most trivial expressions of defeatism and disloyalty met with draconian retaliation. On 20 July 1944 the one organisation with the capacity to remove Hitler, the army, had failed in its attempted coup. With the blood-letting and ferocious tightening of security which followed, and with the writing so obviously on the wall for the regime, it is scarcely surprising that the conclusion was almost universally drawn: any further challenge to the dying dictatorship was futile lunacy.

Figure 7.5 Men of the German 5th Parachute Division during the Ardennes Offensive, December 1944. The offensive was Hitler's final, desperate attempt to turn the tide of the war.

Only in the very last days of the Third Reich, with the Russians at the gates of Berlin, was Hitler's authority challenged even by the top Nazi leaders.[55] With Hitler holed up in the bunker and determined to stay there, Göring not unreasonably invoked the decree of June 1941 nominating him to the succession and requested permission to take over the leadership of the Reich if, within a few hours, he had not received a reply to his telegram presuming Hitler's incapacitation. This, it was claimed by Bormann, the Reich Marshal's arch-enemy, amounted to outright treason. Göring was promptly dismissed from all offices, and from the succession. Meanwhile Himmler, too, whose fantasy world was no smaller than Hitler's own, was imagining that with Hitler's death he could head a new German government which would do a deal with the western Allies in order to fight on against Bolshevism. He even had a new party in mind – the Party of National Union (*Nationale Sammlungspartei*). When news of Himmler's treachery seeped into the bunker, it was the last straw for Hitler. But before he made the preparations to end his life, he saw to it, in a mood of white-hot indignation, that Himmler too was stripped of office, honour and his place in the succession. The removal of both Göring and Himmler from the succession was duly affirmed in Hitler's testament, which conveyed the shreds of lingering authority to Admiral Dönitz.

As long as Hitler was alive, there was no question of replacing him by another leader. His actual power had, nevertheless, been in visible dissolution for months before the final drama in the bunker.

Already as early as September 1944, Hitler's authority was losing its grip. When his backing was sought to bring the Gauleiter under Speer's control in armaments matters, Hitler typically avoided committing himself, before offering Speer a lukewarm form of endorsement. It counted for nothing. The Gauleiter merely ignored it and continued their own interference in the economy where it suited them. Hitler's inability to come down unequivocally on one side or the other – less a simple personal foible than a product of his helpless dependence upon conflicting forces – was now beginning to find reflection in signs of waning authority.[56]

A little while later, Speer himself openly disobeyed an absurd Hitler order issued in a towering rage (and subsequently amended) to end all aircraft production.[57] Then, in early 1945, the Chief of Staff Guderian confronted Hitler more vehemently than had ever been done before in public about a tactical retreat in the east. And, astonishingly, Hitler gave way. It was a further indication that Hitler's authority, though still intact, was under pressure.[58]

Above all, Hitler's 'Nero order' for a 'scorched earth' policy to leave the enemy only ruins by destroying all industrial plant and infrastructural installations, which in the last weeks of a patently lost war amounted to no less than a damnation of his own people for their own 'weakness' in the struggle with the 'stronger eastern people', was consistently sabotaged by Speer.[59] Even after his authority had been suspended, Speer continued to dispatch orders through a variety of channels to prevent the implementation by still eager Gauleiter and other Party fanatics of the renewed destruction directives (with draconian threats, in some cases carried out, for non-compliance). It was a sign not simply of Speer's own belief in the senselessness of the directives, but also of the unwillingness of industrial leadership to see their own future capital destroyed along with the Nazi regime. When he confronted Speer with his disobedience, Hitler characteristically rejected the resignation of his Armaments Minister on prestige grounds. But his demand for Speer's compliance ended with no more than a feeble acceptance of the latter's bland expression of loyalty.[60]

In the last weeks, in the Berlin bunker, Hitler's mental state was more unstable and volatile than ever. His mood ricocheted between moments of euphoria – as when he heard of the death of Roosevelt and took it to be a sign of 'Providence' that events would now turn in Germany's favour – and the deepest depression, recognising at last that defeat was inevitable. He was a burnt-out shell of a man. But calm, detached, apathetic resignation could be instantaneously replaced by uncontrollable outbursts of wild rage at the failure of army divisions which in reality no longer even existed. Even at the last, loyal generals in his entourage were awaiting commands.[61] But Hitler had none now to give. Until the moment he killed himself, Hitler's orders remained unquestioned by his 'court' in the unreal world of the bunker. But in the real world outside the bunker, Hitler's power was at an end.

Notes and references

1. Albert Speer, *Erinnerungen*, Frankfurt am Main/Berlin, 1969, p. 315.

2. David Irving, *Die geheimen Tagebücher des Dr. Morell, Leibarzt Adolf Hitlers*, Munich, 1983, pp. 69, 293–303.

3. *Die Tagebücher von Joseph Goebbels*, pt II, vol. 7, p. 454.

4. See *Tagebücher des Dr. Morell*, pp. 193–202 for what follows.

5. *Tagebücher des Dr. Morell*, pp. 201–2.

6. Percy Ernst Schramm (ed.), *Kriegstagebuch des Oberkommandos der Wehrmacht*, 4 vols, Frankfurt am Main, 1961–5, iv, pt 2, pp. 1701–2.

7. *Lagebesprechungen*, p. 32.

8. Helmut Heiber's phrase in *Lagebesprechungen*, p. 32.

9. *Die Tagebücher von Joseph Goebbels*, pt II, vol. 7, pp. 452, 454, 561; vol. 8, p. 98.

10. Speer, p. 271.

11. *Die Tagebücher von Joseph Goebbels*, pt II, vol. 7, p. 452.

12. The following passages rely on Rebentisch, pp. 490–2.

13. Jochen von Lang, *Der Sekretär*, Stuttgart, 1977, p. 304.

14. Rebentisch, pp. 516–17.

15. Rebentisch, pp. 520–1.

16. See Speer, p. 272.

17. See Speer, pp. 221–2, 306, 360.

18. Speer, pp. 210–17.

19. According to Speer, p. 228.

20. Willi A. Boelcke (ed.), *Deutschlands Rüstung im Zweiten Weltkrieg. Hitlers Konferenzen mit Albert Speer 1942–1945*, Frankfurt am Main, 1969, p. 27.

21. *Deutschlands Rüstung*, pp. 32 ff., 37.

22. Rebentisch, p. 403.

23. Speer, pp. 550–1.

24. Speer, p. 249.

25. *Deutschlands Rüstung*, pp. 37–9. See Speer, p. 248.

26. See *Deutschlands Rüstung*, pp. 416–18, for completely misguided information on the state of fighter production given to Hitler on 12 Oct. 1944. Either Speer was deliberately misleading Hitler, or – which is probably more likely – he was himself ignorant of the production figures.

27. See Speer, pp. 246–8.

28. Wolfgang Schumann *et al.* (eds.), *Deutschland im Zweiten Weltkrieg*, 6 vols, East Berlin 1974–85, v, 477–8.

29. See Speer, pp. 372–4.

30. David Irving, *Führer und Reichskanzler. Adolf Hitler 1933–45*, Munich/Berlin, 1989, p. 573.

31. William Carr, *Hitler. A Study in Personality and Politics*, London, 1978, p. 80.

32. Speer, p. 451.

33. See Speer, pp. 374–8.

34. Speer, p. 572, n. 9.

35. *Deutschland im Zweiten Weltkrieg*, v, 486–95.

36. Speer, p. 375.

37. *Die Tagebücher von Joseph Goebbels*, pt II, vol. 7, p. 503.

38. Speer, p. 305.

39. See *Lagebesprechungen*, p. 31.

40. Speer, p. 306.

41. *Die Tagebücher von Joseph Goebbels*, pt II, vol. 7, p. 515.

42. Peter Longerich (ed.), *Die Ermordung der europäischen Juden. Eine umfassende Dokumentation des Holocaust 1941–1945*, Munich, 1989, pp. 321–2.

43. Irving, p. 571.

44. Raul Hilberg, *Die Vernichtung der europäischen Juden*, Berlin, 1982, pp. 392, 463; see also Meir Michaelis, *Mussolini and the Jews. German–Italian Relations and the Jewish Question in Italy, 1933–1945*, Oxford, 1978, pp. 362–9.

45. Hans-Heinrich Wilhelm, 'Hitlers Ansprache vor Generalen und Offizieren am 26 Mai 1944', *Militärgeschichtliche Mitteilungen*, 20 (1976), p. 156, and see p. 168, n. 77.

46. Irving, p. 631.

47. Speer, p. 446.

48. Speer, p. 495.

49. See note 45 above, and Bradley F. Smith and Agnes F. Peterson (eds.), *Heinrich Himmler. Geheimreden 1933 bis 1945 und andere Ansprachen*, Frankfurt am Main, 1974, p. 203.

50. Hans Mommsen, 'Gesellschaftsbild und Verfassungspläne des deutschen Widerstandes', in Walter Schmitthenner and Hans Buchheim (eds.), *Der deutsche Widerstand gegen Hitler*, Köln/Berlin, 1966, pp. 75–6.

51. *Heeresadjutant bei Hitler*, pp. 85–6.

52. BAK, R43II/1087a; for Sperrle, Nicolaus von Below, *Als Hitlers Adjutant 1937–45*, Mainz, 1980, p. 341. See also *Lagebesprechungen*, p. 618 and note 4.

53. *Monologe*, p. 406.

54. Irving, pp. 603–4.

55. For the following, see H. R. Trevor-Roper, *The Last Days of Hitler*, 3rd edn, London, 1962, pp. 144–57, 182–91, 227–33; and Speer, pp. 485–90.

56. Speer, pp. 405–7.

57. Speer, pp. 415–17.

58. Speer, pp. 428–9.

59. Speer, pp. 409–13, 434, 442–6, 448, 450, 452–62; see also Trevor-Roper, pp. 92–3.

60. Speer, pp. 457–61.

61. Trevor-Roper, p. 135.

✠

Hitler's power and destruction

The hallmark of Hitler's power was destruction. His political 'career' began out of the destruction of the Germany he had until then identified with, 'destroyed' in his mind by the 'Marxist' revolution of 1918. It ended in the far more comprehensive destruction of 'his' Germany through total defeat and devastation in 1945. Twelve years of his rule destroyed 'old' Germany, both territorially and in terms of its social order. They also destroyed 'old' Europe, both physically and in terms of its political order.

From the beginning, Hitler's most powerful driving force was a destructive one. The word 'annihilation' (*Vernichtung*) was seldom far from his lips, from his earliest speeches in Munich beerhalls down to his apocalyptic visions in the East Prussian Führer Headquarters and in the Berlin bunker.

From his employment as a Reichswehr agent down to the writing of his political testament on 29 April 1945, the destruction of the Jews remained a centrepiece of Hitler's thinking. The destruction of 'parasitic' capitalists, 'decadent' liberal democracy, and of 'subversive' Marxists belonged to his demagogic armoury from the earliest days of his political activity. And the destruction of 'Jewish Bolshevism' soon became the keystone of his entire 'world-view'.

The drive to destruction never left him, even in the years after 1933 when circumstances compelled him to play the role of the peace-seeking politician and statesman. In late summer 1938 he was disappointed not to

Figure C.1   The destruction of German cities: tens of thousands die in the firestorms of Hamburg after the bombing of the city by the RAF in 'Operation Gomorrah', July 1943.

be able to destroy the Czechs. In summer 1939 he was determined that no one should hinder him from destroying the Poles. His guidelines for policy in Poland were principled on the destruction of not only the Polish state, but also of the Polish people. Meanwhile, within Germany itself, Hitler had personally sanctioned a programme of action, dated to the day of the outbreak of war, to destroy the 'useless life' of the mentally sick and physically handicapped.

In 1941 the generals were told that the showdown with Bolshevism was to be entirely different to the war in the west: it was to be all-out 'war of annihilation'. Either total destruction of the enemy or total destruction of Germany would be the outcome. The untold slaughter of Soviet Jews, and the systematic massacres of captured Soviet prisoners of war followed. The genocidal character of the conflict was not only taken on board by Hitler: it was the very premiss of the war. It ruled out compromise. Final victory – not achieved despite the astonishing triumphs in 1940 – or total destruction were the only options. From late 1941, defeat and destruction were the only possible outcome.

Hitler's destructive drive did not spare his own army. The staggering losses at the front left him totally unmoved. The only time he was accidentally confronted with wounded soldiers in a train standing next to the Führer train, he had the curtains of his carriage drawn.[1] When his own strategic decisions left the German Sixth Army encircled at Stalingrad, he refused to consider a break-out and condemned them to their destruction. His reaction to the catastrophe was incomprehension at Field Marshal Paulus's choice of surrender rather than death.[2]

In 1944 Hitler rested his hope not on building a fighter defence formation capable of heading off enemy bombers, but on reducing English cities to rubble through the V-weapons. If the atom bomb had been available, there is no doubt whatsoever that he would have used it against London. As it was, German cities were increasingly reduced to ashes. Hitler never visited a single one, never showed signs of sympathy for the bombed-out populations, never revealed any remorse for the suffering inflicted upon German families.[3] His reactions were invariably paroxysms of fury at the ineptitude of the Luftwaffe to defend Germany, and vows to avenge the destruction by wreaking even greater destruction on British cities.

In the end, true to his own principles, Hitler tried to destroy Germany's chances of surviving him, through his 'Nero order' and scorched-earth commands of 1945. The German people had, in his eyes, deserved their own destruction since they had not proved strong enough to destroy the arch-enemy of Bolshevism.[4]

Figure C.2 The destruction of German cities: more tens of thousands are killed in the devastation of Dresden, February 1945.

In this catalogue of destruction, there is nothing which stands as a positive legacy of the years of Hitler's power. In art, architecture, music and literature, the Hitler regime stifled innovation and originality. Creative art, writing and thinking largely went into exile along with the representatives of 'decadent' art or forbidden literature. The loss to German culture through the forced emigration of writers of the calibre of Thomas and Heinrich Mann, Arnold and Stefan Zweig, Alfred Döblin and Bertold Brecht, the artists Wassily Kandinsky, Paul Klee and Oskar Kokoschka, and the architects Walter Gropius and Ludwig Mies van der Rohe was incalculable. Artists like Emil Nolde and writers like Gottfried Benn, who began with high hopes of the Third Reich, found themselves rapidly disillusioned and entered a form of 'inner emigration', their works banned or their creativity ended for the duration of Nazi rule. In the field of music, the late compositions of Richard Strauss, the *Carmina Burana* of Carl Orff, and the continued presence of the leading conductor Wilhelm Furtwängler formed only partial compensation for the loss of Schönberg and Hindemith, and the banning of the music of Mendelssohn and Mahler. Nazism was incapable of filling the vacuum left by its cultural blood-letting. Culturally, the Third Reich amounted to twelve sterile years.

Nor in the spheres of politics and economics did the Hitler era produce anything of lasting value. No governmental form or system which could serve as a possible model emerged. Lack of system, and lack of structure, in fact, were the characteristics of the Hitler state. Destruction of coherent channels of governmental authority rather than the erection of a definable 'system' of authoritarian administration was the prevailing feature. In economics, too, Hitler's regime left only negative lessons for the future. 'Nazi economics' were utterly predatory in nature, devoid of potential as a durable 'system'. They were based upon the idea of a modern form of slavery within state-directed capitalism – symbolised above all by the huge industrial complex at Auschwitz, in which the slave labour of major German firms was worked to death or liquidated when no longer capable of work. The inbuilt contradictions scarcely provided a recipe for a lasting economic 'new order'. It is hardly any wonder that already by the middle of the war, conceptions of a more rational economic order in which Nazi ideals played no part were being confidentially discussed in business circles.

Is the negative legacy of Nazism, its lack of constructive capacity, simply a consequence of Germany's total defeat? Have we underrated the capability of the Hitler regime to develop into a lasting system of power had the war been won? Clearly, all Nazi plans for the future were

Figure C.3 Soviet troops raise the Red Flag on the ruins of the Reichstag in Berlin on 30 April 1945, the day of Hitler's suicide.

predicated upon final victory being achieved. Grandiose architectural plans, in which Hitler took the keenest interest – he was still working on the plan for remodelling Linz with the Red Army at the gates of Berlin – were elaborated for the rebuilding of German cities on a monumental scale.[5] Hitler also had visions – different from the neo-agrarian dreams of Darré and Himmler – of a future highly advanced industrialised and technologically developed society, for which the conquered areas would provide raw materials and suppressed racial inferiors the labour. Capitalist industry would fall in line, or be taken over by the state if it could thereby be run more effectively. German workers would replace an effete bourgeoisie as a politically qualified elite. The vision was that of a revolutionary transformation of German society.[6] Meanwhile, Robert Ley – Labour Front boss and from 1941 Housing Commissar – was masterminding future schemes for the wholesale reconstruction of social insurance provision (on lines – leaving aside their racist premises – not too different in some respects from those in the British Beveridge Plan) and for huge housing programmes.[7] None of this came remotely near to fruition. More dwellings disappeared under the hail of bombs than could possibly have been built under Ley's ambitious housing programme. And the post-war West German social insurance programme drew on antecedents in imperial and Weimar Germany, but not on the model of the Third Reich.

Only a successful outcome to the war could have enabled the Nazi vision of a new society to be realised. Hitler is reported as having said, in the last weeks of the Third Reich, that he needed twenty years to produce an elite which had drunk his ideals like milk from the mother's breast. But, he added, the problem had been that time had always been against Germany.[8]

Indeed, the Hitlerian gamble had been flawed from the outset. The Nazi regime had been incapable of fighting the war it wanted at the time and on the terms it preferred. Once in a major war, which it had not wanted in 1939 but had been prepared to risk, a quick exit or limited peace was attainable only through western capitulation. The thrust for continental hegemony ruled out a German compromise settlement – increasingly so with every barbarous step the expansionist route took. And with Britain still unconquered, the dynamic of the German expansionist drive demanded an assault on the Soviet Union. The attempt to destroy the Soviet Union within a matter of months was not simply a matter of ideological will and racialist lunacy. Given the premiss of a war for supreme power on the European continent, it was a desperate move to bring Britain to

Figure C.4 German troops march into captivity in Berlin on the surrender of the city to the Soviets on 2 May 1945.

the conference table, to head off the increasingly certain entry into the conflict of the USA, and to secure indispensable raw materials.

It is sometimes alleged that Germany was on the verge of winning the war in late 1941, and would have done so had the German troops been allowed to press on to take Moscow instead of, on Hitler's orders, switching to the south. The argument seems misplaced. Strategically and economically, the sweep through the Ukraine with the intention of taking the Caucasus was probably the correct decision.[9] The taking of Moscow would have been a prestige defeat for the Soviet Union. But it would not have ended the war. The bulk of the Soviet industrial potential needed for continuing the struggle would have remained untouched. The over-extended German communications lines would have been highly exposed to counter-attacks from the flanks. More importantly, it is unlikely even then that the gamble of forcing Britain to the conference table and keeping America out of the war would have worked. Even with the resources of the western parts of the USSR at its disposal, Germany – with an inefficiently run armaments economy, with an ill-organised political structure, with its military strength still committed on all fronts, and with an unending conflict in prospect with partisan resistance directly fostered by Nazi barbarity – would still have had no answer in prospect to the material might of the USA. And in the development of the atom bomb, Germany lagged several years behind the USA, and could not have had a weapon ready before 1947 at the earliest.[10]

The Nazi regime would, in fact, even had it taken Moscow, have been incapable of drawing a line under victories achieved and settling down to consolidate existing gains. Already Hitler and the military leadership were talking of expansion into the Middle East. The 'system' could simply not 'come to rest'. Continuing, limitless expansion was in the very essence of Nazism. The likeliest prognosis in the counter-factual guessing game is, therefore, that the war would have continued, and that the outcome would – if somewhat delayed – have been not too dissimilar to what did in the event occur.

The least likely scenario is that Europe would have settled down to a lengthy peace under the heel of the jackboot, and that the Hitler regime would have taken shape as a well-coordinated, stable form of government. The 'new order' as witnessed in Poland and Russia amounted to anything but a coherent structure of rule. Instead, it reflected on a highly intens-ified scale the uncoordinated power-grabbing, rapaciousness and con-tinued warring of private fiefdoms which had already been the leading characteristic of the Hitler regime in the Reich itself.

Figure C.5 Hitler's legacy: the ruins of Berlin, 1945.

Moreover, the most obvious question for the continuation of Nazi rule – the question of a successor to Hitler, and even how to choose, elect, select or appoint such a successor – was left completely open. The nomination of Göring as successor acquired, the longer the war proceeded, increasingly nominal character. Hitler refused to introduce the Nazi senate which, it was envisaged, would determine the person to be the second Führer. And the bitter enmities among the leading Nazis make it difficult to imagine that Himmler, Bormann, Goebbels or Speer would have managed to secure the necessary legitimation within the Nazi ranks to win power and consolidate a prolonged period of rule, or that they could feasibly have turned Nazism into a systematic form of government.

All this is to suggest that not only destruction, but also self-destruction, was innate to the Nazi form of rule. Nazism was capable of destruction on a massive scale. But it was not capable of creating a lasting system of rule, of perpetuating and reproducing its own 'Behemoth' of monstrous and untrammelled plunder and exploitation. Of course, it took the combined might of the USA, the USSR and Great Britain to bring the Third Reich to its knees. But that is only to note the strength of brute force and destructive potential remaining in a system with its back to the wall facing complete obliteration, and how tenaciously the German armed forces and civilian population fought for what was, at the latest by Christmas 1941, a lost cause.

These comments point, then, unmistakably to the conclusion, which the preceding chapters have attempted to suggest, that the destructive – and self-destructive – nature of Nazism cannot be reduced to Hitler's own personal drive to destruction. The destruction which Hitler's very name symbolises was not the product of a single man's imagination, will and ruthlessness. It was immanent to the 'system' of Nazism itself. Concern with Hitler's 'psycho-history' can offer few clues as to why a complex, modern society was prepared to follow Hitler to the abyss. Without a readiness widespread even among many who were by no means convinced or avid Nazis to 'work' – directly or indirectly – 'towards the Führer', the peculiar form of personalised power exercised by Hitler would have been devoid of social and political foundations.

Popular support for Hitler's form of power was indispensable to the effective exercise of that power. Hitler was not a tyrant imposed upon Germany. He was in many respects, until well into the war, a highly popular national leader. The extent of his popularity was a major condition for the expansion of his personalised power. The destructive dynamic embodied in the person of Hitler is not comprehensible outside the social and political motivations which were embedded in the acceptance of an unrestrained form of personal rule.

A key to the extraordinary character of Hitler's power lies, as was suggested at the outset of our analysis, in the notion (derived from Max Weber) of 'charismatic rule'. This notion provides the crucial link between the social motivations which forged the bonds with Hitler, the peculiar expression of personalised power that was a chief characteristic of the form of political domination in the Third Reich, and the destructive dynamic of Nazism.

We outlined the features of 'charismatic rule' in the Introduction. We have used the concept in a specific sense to depict a form of personalised rule based upon perceptions of 'heroic' leadership among the 'following' of a leader – a form of rule which, arising out of systemic crisis, is scarcely possible to reconcile with systematised government; inherently unstable therefore, immanently destructive of regulated structures, and, dependent upon continued successes and the avoidance of subsiding into 'routinised' government, ultimately also self-destructive.

This model has clear application to many of the issues raised in the preceding chapters. It relates firstly to the quasi-messianic attractiveness of Hitler even before 1933 to millions of Germans, as the collapse in legitimation of the Weimar state promoted a readiness to accept a radically different form of government based upon personal rule, implying personal responsibility. The model also fits both the constancy of Hitler's 'missionary' vision and his incapacity to engage in the rational formulation of 'mid-range' government policy or the establishment of clear, operable priorities. It corresponds to Hitler's prepossession with questions of his own prestige, with his penchant for the theatrical effect and propaganda impact of the major coup, with his fears about a possible loss of popularity, his reluctance to face the German people when reverses were mounting in the last war years. It matches Hitler's inability – also for prestige reasons and because his position demanded that he remain aloof from political in-fighting and retain the loyalty of all his paladins – to take sides and reach clear decisions on personnel matters affecting rival claimants among the Gauleiter or other loyal chieftains. It further corresponds to a type of political domination in which personal loyalties of a neo-feudal kind gained primacy over bureaucratic structures of government, where formalised status was replaced by personal standing in the supreme leader's retinue, where public property could be dispensed into private domains, and where economic exploitation, in compliance with the visionary aims of the leader, was conceived in terms of a modernised form of slave production. Not least, the model of 'charismatic rule' accords with the erosion of the apparatus of governmental administration and the undermining of anything resembling an ordered or rational *system* of government. Finally, it indicates a form of rule whose dynamic cannot be allowed to subside, in which Hitler's own predilection for the 'all or nothing' gamble was not simply a personal choice, but was structurally conditioned by the need to avoid stagnation and to sustain the successes on which, ultimately, the continuation of 'charismatic rule' must rest.

The two last points seem vital ones. The erosion of 'rational' government by personalised rule offered a framework for the growing autonomy of the 'charismatic' leader, providing also for the 'self-selection' (without a stream of clear orders from on high) of the 'guidelines for action'[11] which the leader's ideological 'vision' established as the implied main goals to be worked towards by the whole society. Hence, the ideological objectives most closely identified with the leader came gradually into sharper focus, without the leader necessarily having to offer clear directives for their implementation.

The dynamism at the heart of 'charismatic rule' is, however, unending. There can by the very notion of 'charismatic rule' be no sagging into 'normality' or 'routine', no final drawing of the line on the attainment of goals. The 'vision' of the leader has to remain a vision, whatever parts of it are ultimately implemented. The longer Hitler's rule continued, the less likely it ever seemed to lapse into a 'system', and the more it destroyed all patterns of organised governmental structures. The longer it continued, the more extensive, rather than more narrow, became the visionary expansionist goals. 'Utopianism' and 'charismatic rule' go hand in hand. But since the stability of a 'normal' governmental system can never be attained, the immanent instability of 'charismatic rule', given the type of 'utopia' envisaged by Hitler, is bound, ultimately, to be not simply destructive but self-destructive. Hitler's personal suicidal tendencies – registered, for example, at the time of the 1923 Putsch, the death of his niece Geli Raubal in 1931, the Strasser crisis in 1932, and in a number of black moments in autumn 1944[12] – blended into the incapacity of his form of authoritarian rule to reproduce itself and survive.

Devoid of constructive, creative energy, articulating only ever wilder urges to destroy, the likeliest end to Hitler's power was, then, the end which did eventually take place: a bullet in the head, leaving the German people to pay the price for their readiness to be taken in by a leader offering not limited policy options, but a tempting, though illusory and empty, chiliastic vision of political redemption.

Notes and references

1. Speer, p. 259.

2. *Lagebesprechungen*, pp. 125–30.

3. See Speer, pp. 311–12, 560, n. 6, and for his callousness towards the German people in the last weeks of the war, pp. 444–6.

4. Speer, p. 446

5. See Jochen Thies, *Architekt der Weltherrschaft. Die 'Endziele' Hitlers*, Düsseldorf, 1979.

6. See Rainer Zitelmann, *Hitler. Selbstverständnis eines Revolutionärs*, Stuttgart, 1987.

7. See Marie-Louise Recker, *Nationalsozialistische Sozialpolitik im Zweiten Weltkrieg*, Munich, 1985.

8. François Genoud (ed.), *The Testament of Adolf Hitler*, London, 1961, pp. 58–9.

9. Carr, p. 95.

10. Speer, pp. 242–3. And see now Mark Walker, *German National Socialism and the Quest for Nuclear Power, 1939–1949*, Cambridge, 1990, pp. 155 ff.

11. See Martin Broszat, 'Soziale Motivation und Führer-Bindung des Nationalsozialismus', *Vierteljahreshefte für Zeitgeschichte*, 18 (1970), pp. 392–409.

12. See Carr, pp. 109–11.

✠

Trends in recent research on Hitler

There are no signs, since this book was initially published in 1991, of interest in Hitler and the Third Reich diminishing. Books, scholarly essays, newspaper articles, television documentaries and other mass-media productions of widely varying quality continue to pour out. Only a few can be mentioned here.

Where for many years, in fact since Karl Dietrich Bracher's work of the 1960s,[1] there had been no attempt at a comprehensive history of the Third Reich, the last fifteen years or so have seen the appearance of several such studies – notably those by Hans-Ulrich Thamer, Norbert Frei, Jost Dülffer, Ludolf Herbst, Klaus Fischer, and most recently Michael Burleigh – differently accented but each contributing significantly to a deepened understanding of Nazism.[2]

Directly relating to Hitler, Alan Bullock's massive parallel study of Hitler and Stalin was followed by two extensive biographies of the German Dictator published in France, the first (resting on extensive acquaintance with recent literature and later translated into German) by Marlis Steinert, the second (contrasting with my own in its strong emphasis on Hitler's 'precise design' for power and the coherence of his 'project' from 1919 onwards) by François Delpla.[3] A further lengthy biography of Hitler – the first from historians formerly of the German Democratic Republic, Manfred Weißbecker and Kurt Pätzold – placed particular emphasis on the strength of Hitler's support from the German elites, and ended with a warning of the potential in society for a future revival of fascism.[4]

The ceaseless speculation about Hitler's psychological problem, which had led especially in the 1970s to some highly imaginative 'psycho-history', prompted an interesting new approach – a combined effort by Paul and Peter Matussek and Jan Marbach (a psychiatrist, a historian and a sociologist) – to see Hitler as a 'pathological case', a type of schizophrenic whose outward projection of his inward feelings of shame and inadequacy happened to find a society ready to receive him with open arms.[5] Though the authors do their best to avoid it, the danger of attributing the horrors that took place to someone who was mentally sick and a society deluded enough to follow him cannot even so be fully excluded. Beyond that, it seems likely that the authors are operating with a definition of schizophrenia which is too open and imprecise for medical diagnosis. A more conventional usage would not apply the term 'schizophrenic' to Hitler.

The question of evil lay at the centre of Ron Rosenbaum's attempt to explain Hitler.[6] Ultimately, Rosenbaum himself had to admit that the search for the moment when the innocent child became the evil monster is unfruitful, and contented himself with an interesting confrontation with different historiographical interpretations of Hitler. Historiography is also the basis of John Lukacs's assessment of varying approaches to Hitler – liberally interspersed with his own interpretation, seeing Hitler, among other things, as a much underrated statesman.[7]

It is exceedingly unlikely that any sensational new primary sources directly relating to Hitler will be found. Even so, since the writing of this book was completed in 1990 the source-base relating to Hitler has been amplified in important ways. Research on Hitler prior to the takeover of power in 1933 has been enriched through scholarly editions of his early speeches and writings together with the full publication of his trial for high treason in 1924 and a new scholarly edition of his 'Second Book' of 1928 (not published, for political reasons related to the sensitivies about the 'South Tyrolean Question', at the time).[8] Still needed, in my view, is a full scholarly edition of *Mein Kampf*. This remains blocked by the Bavarian state, which controls the rights, mainly out of concern about the possible abuse of the text by neo-Nazis and, presumably, because even now Hitler's book is believed to have a potentially seductive force. (Arguably, the censorship helps to retain a certain mystique around a largely indigestible racist diatribe – if one of historical importance. Since all of Hitler's known writings, speeches and other public statements between 1919 and 1945 are available in scholarly editions, and since *Mein Kampf* itself is widely accessible in translation to those anxious to read this dire tract, the objections to a *scholarly* edition of this key historical text do not appear altogether rational, although it is easy to understand the German sensitivities, and for now the prohibition remains in place.) For the later years, there is now also available a valuable edition of Hitler's wartime decrees to complement the old – and imperfect – edition of his speeches and proclamations between 1932 and 1945, and the classic Hitlerian texts of the 'Table Talk' and the '*Lagebesprechungen*' (military briefings).[9] A further text of significance, if not emanating from Hitler himself, is the superb edition, by Peter Witte and others, of Himmler's desk-diary, discovered a few years ago in Moscow.[10]

Probably the single most valuable new source to cast light on Hitler that has become available in the last decade or so, since it was found in the former Soviet archives, is the *complete* diary of Reich Propaganda Minister Joseph Goebbels, now available in the fine multi-volume edition of Elke Fröhlich, from the renowned Institut für Zeitgeschichte in Munich.[11] (Parts of the diary had long been known, although they had left crucial gaps in the evidence, which have now been closed.) Despite, of course, the diaries being heavily coloured both through Goebbels's own adulation for Hitler and by the obvious self-glorification in entries intended for later publication, they remain an indispensable source – effectively a running commentary on Hitler's thoughts and actions from someone in his company on an almost daily basis before the war and frequently during the war years themselves.

A key question, but one which can never be answered beyond the last shadow of doubt, is this: why and when did Hitler become a pathological antisemite? In his early biography – a masterpiece for its time – Alan Bullock had portrayed Hitler as an 'opportunist entirely without principle', and without genuine ideological conviction, who 'exalted force over the power of ideas' and stood for nothing more than 'domination, dressed up as the doctrine of race'. Hitler's antisemitism, in this reading, was, therefore, little more than a vehicle for obtaining, then using, power.[12] Hugh Trevor-Roper had already in the early 1950s reached a wholly different conclusion, regarding Hitler as a man of ideas, however repulsive.[13] And once Eberhard Jäckel had published his penetrating analysis of *Mein Kampf* in 1969, the view that Hitler was no more than a ruthless and unscrupulous opportunist could no longer be sustained.[14] Alan Bullock himself had given up such a notion by the time he published his dual biography of Hitler and Stalin in 1991.[15] But if Hitler could now generally be accepted as *both* an ideologue of deeply held dogmatic convictions *and* as a propagandist of brilliance, with no contradiction between the two,[16] just when and why he became a paranoid antisemite remains less than wholly clear.

Most historians have in some measure followed Hitler's own account, touched on in Chapter 1, and interpreted his antisemitism as a product of his time in Vienna, when, sinking almost literally into the gutter and landing for a time in a doss-house, he was searching for scapegoats. Joachim Fest, in his acclaimed biography of 1973, took this line.[17] Others have, however, pointed to the fact that those who knew Hitler before 1919 made no mention of his antisemitism, which was among the most strikingly unmissable and omnipresent features of his public persona in the years thereafter.[18] In his detailed study of Hitler in the immediate post-war era, Anton Joachimsthaler joins those who have dated the emergence of his pathological antisemitism, therefore, to the period embracing the last phase of the First World War and the revolutionary months that followed, which the future dictator experienced from the vantage point of his barracks in Munich.[19] In her splendid study of Hitler's Vienna, Brigitte Hamann forcefully argued that Hitler's anti-semitism did not date from the Vienna period, pointing out that some of his associates, even friends, at that time were Jewish.[20] (Whether Hitler had genuine friends, then or later, might seriously be doubted, though this is here a tangential point.)

In my biography I also dated the full emergence of Hitler's manic hatred of Jews to 1918–19 but, unlike Brigitte Hamann, saw this as a final stage, under the traumatic impact of the lost war and revolution, of a process that stretched back at least to the Vienna time, if not earlier.[21] To conclude from the Vienna years that *this* man in *this* city at *this* time was not antisemitic stretches credulity. Even in Linz, before going to Vienna, Hitler had been a supporter of Georg Schönerer, a vehement racist anti-semite as well as an extreme pan-Germanist. In Vienna, Hitler admired the well-liked mayor of the city, the populist antisemite Karl Lueger. That Hitler had Jewish associates does not mean he was not antisemitic. He needed his Jewish associates to help sell his paintings and eke out a living; his dealings with them, as I saw it, were pragmatic business arrangments unhindered by, perhaps even fostering, his underlying hostility to Jews. But his antisemitism, so I suggested, was 'normal' anti-semitism for the time, not especially noticeable in the rabidly antisemitic climate of Vienna in those years. He certainly went into the First World War with a strong dislike of what he called 'alien influence' and 'inner internationalism', as a letter of 1915 demonstrates.[22] Though the Jews were not specifically mentioned in the letter, it would have been odd had they, of all groups, given Hitler's known feelings only four years later, been excluded from such sentiments. But the indications are that it took the declining fortunes of war and the trauma of revolution to convert this 'normal' antisemitism into the pathological antisemitism that, once established, never left him down to his suicide in the bunker.

Germany's ignominious capitulation, as Hitler saw it, in November 1918 is almost certainly the key. His entire 'career', once he entered politics in 1919, was devoted to overcoming the shame of this capitulation. Who, in his perverted and paranoid vision, were those responsible for this ignominy? Who, in their quest for world domination, were the internationally based enemies of Germany, the wire-pullers of capitalism in Wall Street and the City of London at the same time as they were the exponents of Bolshevism in Moscow? Who threatened at every turn the 'redemption' of Germany that Hitler saw as his life's mission? It was consistent with this new 'rationalisation' of his long-existent phobias that, in his first written political statement, dating from September 1919, Hitler ended by seeing 'the removal of the Jews altogether' as the aim of a future nationalist government in Germany.[23] His earlier antipathy had been turned, under the impact of the lost war and socialist revolution, into the pivot of a pathological, potentially genocidal, ideology.

This ideology amounted to a small number of deeply-held and self-reinforcing convictions: making Germany the dominant power on the continent of Europe, and eventually in the world; winning 'living space' at the expense of the Soviet Union to obtain and secure that dominance; and destroying the Jews, seen as the most powerful international enemy and threat to Germany's future. These limited *idées fixes* were underpinned by the crude social Darwinism of unending struggle as the very basis of human existence and the right of the strongest in that struggle to survive, whatever means were necessary to secure that survival. The interlocking ideas, however repellent, were internally coherent (given the irrational premises), even if they never amounted to an intellectualised doctrine as was the case with Marxism. But recent research has reinforced the view that I advanced in Chapter 2 (and in other writings, including my biography of Hitler) that the central tenets of Hitler's personal *Weltanschauung* were not decisive in the mobilisation of the masses on the way to the acquisition of power in 1933.[24] Millions of Germans voted for Hitler in the full knowledge, of course, that he and his Movement were rabidly antisemitic. But, as Peter Fritzsche has underlined, 'most voters did not back Hitler mainly because they shared his hatred of the Jews'.[25] Hitler was able to rise to power because, in a crisis-ridden society with a totally discredited political system, he was successful in mobilising discontented masses in new ways behind slogans of national renewal, and behind the intention to bring about a ruthless showdown with all enemies of that renewal.

The evident, increasingly widespread readiness before 1933 to accept the necessity of not just the defeat but the violent destruction of political enemies, and the need for rebuilding a society based upon racial purity (demanding the exclusion of those who did not 'belong'), provided the platform for the subsequent acceptance, even approval, of the repression of 'outsiders' to the 'national community', which Eric Johnson and Robert Gellately have emphasised.[26] As I remarked a decade ago in Chapter 4 of this book, 'the coercive force which lay behind Hitler's power is inseparable from the consensus in broad swathes of German society with much of what was happening in Hitler's name. Coercion and consent were two sides of the same coin – twin props of Hitler's power'. This verdict is now reinforced by Pierre Ayçoberry's excellent study of the social bases of Nazi power, while a good deal of research has elucidated the structure and personnel of the main agency of repression, the Gestapo, and shown how deeply its coercion depended upon collaboration from ordinary Germans.[27]

Nowhere has research on Nazi Germany made greater headway in the past ten years than in examination of the processes of persecution and extermination of the Jews. In the first of two planned volumes, Saul Friedländer skilfully synthesised extensive earlier research and, with an emphasis upon the centrality of Hitler and ideology, showed how ever wider sections of regime and society became complicitous in policies that ended in genocide.[28] David Bankier's valuable collection of essays on German society and the persecution of the Jews down to their deportation in 1941 does much to deepen understanding of the social and organisational mechanisms at work in the radicalisation of anti-Jewish policy.[29] And a detailed study (with attached documentary sources) by Michael Wildt provides clear insights into the mentalities of those, including Adolf Eichmann, in the Jewish office of the SD (*Sicherheitsdienst*, or Security Service), as ideas on how to 'solve the Jewish Question' took increasingly radical shape in the later 1930s.[30]

Above all, research on the emergence of the 'Final Solution' – the steps to full-scale genocide taken in 1941–2 – has been intensified and deepened since the opening of the archives of the Soviet Union and other parts of eastern European at the beginning of the 1990s. The popular best-seller by Daniel Goldhagen, *Hitler's Willing Executioners*, is something of a distraction here.[31] Its undifferentiated picture of a society of 'elimina-tionist antisemites', thirsting since the nineteenth century to be rid of the Jews and finding, finally, under Hitler the chance to achieve this goal, has been widely criticised by experts in the field.[32] Goldhagen's claim that the perpetrators of the Holocaust were 'ordinary Germans' thirsting to 'eliminate' the Jews was set against the implication of Christopher Brown-ing's classic analysis of a killing-squad in Poland in 1942.[33] Browning argued that those pulling the trigger on Jewish women and children were, far from being ideological zealots or anti-Jewish fanatics, 'ordinary men' caught up in murderous action. As so often in historical explanation, though in this instance in a particularly highly-charged context of genocide, historians were polarising 'intent' and 'situation' in an attempt to comprehend how human beings thought and acted. But no one had apparently thought of empirically investigating the sociology of the killers on the basis of a statistical analysis until it was recently attempted by Michael Mann, who concluded that the majority of the killers were neither 'ordinary Germans', nor 'ordinary men', but for the most part diehard Nazis who had long been socialised in repressive violence.[34]

The most important breakthroughs in research on the emergence of the 'Final Solution' have been achieved by German scholars, systemat-ically exploring the newly available records in East European archival repositories for the first time. The work of Götz Aly helped to pave the way. His analysis of the links between Nazi plans for the resettlement of ethnic Germans and the piecemeal steps culminating in a comprehensive genocidal programme marked an important beginning.[35] Ulrich Herbert has been the central figure in steering research into the personnel of the chief agency of genocide, the Reich Security Head Office, and their motives.[36] Knowledge of the group around Eichmann in the organisation of the 'Final Solution' was greatly furthered through the meticulously researched study by the Austrian historian Hans Safrian.[37] Among those carrying out path-breaking work into the emergence of genocide in differ-ent parts of eastern Europe have been Dieter Pohl, Thomas Sandkühler, Christoph Dieckmann and Christian Gerlach.[38] Another German scholar (based in England), Peter Longerich, has provided the invaluable service of linking the findings of such research to an excellent general synthesis of the 'policy of annihilation'.[39]

The general pattern arising from such research, and drawn together by Longerich, accords well with the interpretation offered in this book of the relationship between Hitler's power and genocide. Longerich sees no single order by Hitler unleashing genocide, but rather a series of escalatory phases, eventually culminating by spring 1942 in an all-out genocidal programme. Key steps in this development were the invasion of the Soviet Union in June 1941, accompanied by the killing, in the initial phase, of thousands of male Jews in the Soviet Union by the German Security Police *Einsatzgruppen* (and their sub-units); the extension of the murderous onslaught to women and children in mid-summer 1941; the deportation of German, Austrian and Czech Jews in the autumn; the confirmation, around the time of the German declaration of war on the United States in December 1941, that the Jews would have to pay for the world war for which, in Nazi eyes, they were responsible; and, following the Wannsee Conference in January 1942, the widening of a by now coordinated programme of deportation and extermination to western Europe by the spring and summer.

Other historians have nevertheless continued to try to pinpoint a 'fundamental' decision to launch the 'Final Solution' by Hitler to a particular date. In his fine study of Himmler and genocidal policy, Richard Breitman argued – though, to my knowledge, he has not been followed in this by other experts in the field – that Hitler gave the general order for the extermination of the Jews as early as January 1941.[40] Tobias Jersak favoured August 1941, in the immediate wake of the Atlantic Charter in which Roosevelt and Churchill put forward a programme for the future world order after the defeat of the Axis powers, though the argument remains, in my view, less than compelling, not least in that no obvious change of direction in genocidal policy seems datable to August 1941.[41] Christian Gerlach argued instead for the declaration of war on the United States as the crucial moment, and saw Hitler's meeting with his Party leaders the next day, 12 December, as the occasion when he imparted his 'fundamental decision' to exterminate Europe's Jews.[42]

Hitler was keen to retain a veil of secrecy over the murder of the Jews, and the 'Final Solution' was a taboo subject even among his close entourage in the Führer Headquarters during the war. Not least for this reason, his own role is often hidden in the shadows. His imprint is nonetheless unmistakable, his intervention at critical junctures decisive: Hitler authorised the killing plans that were part of 'Operation Barbarossa' – what Christopher Browning long ago called the 'quantum jump' into genocide;[43] the massive expansion of the slaughter in the summer of 1941 that followed *tête-à-tête* talks with Heinrich Himmler, head of the SS, in July;[44] Hitler's authorisation was needed in September for the deportation of Reich Jews that autummn;[45] and in December his speech to the Party chiefs prompted swift escalation of the killing that, by then, had already long since reached genocidal proportions.[46] It seems, nevertheless, highly unlikely that Hitler, who refrained from discussing the 'Final Solution' in explicit terms even in his closest entourage, would have announced a 'fundamental decision' on extermination to the gathering of some fifty Party bosses. Much more probable is that his repetition – in terms which even for him were extraordinarily vehement – of his 'prophecy' of 30 January 1939, that the Jews would be destroyed in the event of another world war, was now interpreted by those who heard his speech as a signal for a total onslaught on Europe's Jews. My own interpretation, advanced here and at greater length in my biography of Hitler, largely accords, therefore, with Longerich's notion of a series of escalatory steps in which a genocidal drive gathers momentum on the basis of a combination of central directives and local initiatives, at each critical juncture with Hitler's express approval, knowledge and authorisation, but without a single, explicit 'Führer order', even verbal, to unleash the 'Final Solution'.

Among studies relating to Hitler's last years, dealt with in Chapter 7 of this book, as the Dictator attempted to hold out, Canute-style, until the tide of war eventually engulfed him, are Gitta Sereny's penetrating psychological insights into Albert Speer's relationship with the Dictator and Joachim C. Fest's biography of Speer.[47] The self-reflections of the Nazi leaders captured at the end of the war, revealing in the way they account for their actions under Hitler and their dealings with him, are skilfully presented and analysed by Richard Overy.[48] The state of Hitler's mental and physical health in these years, which has given rise to unending speculation and much misconception, has been exhaustively analysed in recent years by Ernst Günther Schenck (a doctor who fleetingly came into contact with Hitler in April 1945), Ellen Gibbels (who first showed, beyond reasonable doubt, that Hitler suffered from Parkinson's Disease) and, most extensively, by Fritz Redlich (himself a former psychiatrist).[49] Redlich concluded, sensibly in my opinion, that Hitler's health problems 'did not have any decisive impact on his political or military actions' (though he thought that they 'accelerated his operations due to his fear that he would run out of time'), and diagnosed Hitler's mental state as one of 'political paranoia'. When his wife asked him if that diagnosis meant simply that Hitler was 'an evil person', Redlich agreed.[50]

The opening of the Soviet archives has led to further speculation about the precise nature of Hitler's demise in the bunker. The Soviet files pertaining to Hitler's death and the remains allegedly discovered in the garden of the Reich Chancellery by Soviet troops are assessed by Ada Petrova and Peter Watson.[51] The most detailed analysis of the documentary evidence surrounding the last days of Hitler, his death and the disposal of the corpse is by Anton Joachimsthaler, who is dismissive of claims that the Soviets found any more than scattered remains of Hitler's body, and dispels many of the false stories put about in the immediate aftermath of the war, some of which continue to linger even today.[52] Of course, there remain those who continue to believe that Hitler, (and perhaps Eva Braun, too) was spirited out of Berlin at the end of the war, with a double taking his place in the bunker as the Wagnerian finale approached.

There is as yet no foreseeable end to the preoccupation with Hitler and his regime. It is still too early for the Nazi era to be regarded as mere history. The moral scars are too deep. The trauma, for the millions of victims of Hitler and their descendants, and in quite different fashion for the German people who have had to live with his legacy, continues. New works on the Third Reich will appear, new approaches will be tried. But the sense of morbid wonder at the rapidity with which a modern democracy could succumb to the politics of national salvation and undergo such a steep and calamitous collapse of civilised values and descent into genocidal war on an unprecedented scale will remain.

Notes and references

1. Karl Dietrich Bracher, *The German Dictatorship*, Harmondsworth, 1973 (original German publication, 1969).

2. Hans-Ulrich Thamer, *Verführung und Gewalt. Deutschland 1933–1945*, Berlin, 1986; Norbert Frei, *Der Führerstaat. Nationalsozialistische Herrschaft 1933 bis 1945*, Munich 1987 (6th revised edn, 2001; trans. *National Socialist Rule in Germany: the Führer State 1933–1945*, Oxford/Cambridge, Mass., 1993); Jost Dülffer, *Deutsche Geschichte 1933–1945. Führerglaube und Vernichtungskrieg*, Stuttgart/Berlin/Cologne, 1992 (trans. *Nazi Germany 1933–1945. Faith and Annihilation*, London, 1996); Ludolf Herbst, *Das nationalsozialistische Deutschland 1933–1945*, Frankfurt am Main, 1996; Klaus P. Fischer, *Nazi Germany. A New History*, London, 1995; Michael Burleigh, *The Third Reich. A New History*, London, 2000.

3. Alan Bullock, *Hitler and Stalin. Parallel Lives*, London, 1991; Marlis Steinert, *Hitler*, Paris, 1991 (German: Munich, 1994); François Delpla, *Hitler*, Paris, 1999.

4. Manfred Weißbecker and Kurt Pätzold, *Adolf Hitler. Eine politische Biographie*, Leipzig, 1995.

5. Paul Matussek, Peter Matussek and Jan Marbach, *Hitler. Karriere eines Wahns*, Munich, 2000.

6. Ron Rosenbaum, *Explaining Hitler. The Search for the Origins of his Evil*, New York, 1998.

7. John Lukacs, *The Hitler of History*, New York, 1998. The same author also wrote a thoughtful, personalised account of the critical phase of the war in the summer of 1940: John Lukacs, *The Duel. Hitler vs. Churchill, 10 May–31 July 1940*, Oxford, 1992.

8. *Hitler. Reden, Schriften, Anordnungen: Februar 1925 bis Januar 1933*, ed. Institut für Zeitgeschichte, 5 vols in 12 parts, Munich etc., 1992–8; Gerhard L. Weinberg (ed.), *Hitlers Zweites Buch. Ein Dokument aus dem Jahre 1928,* Stuttgart*,* 1961 (new edn, printed as Vol. 2A of *Hitler. Reden, Schriften, Anordnungen*, with the title *Außenpolitische Standortbestimmung nach der Reichstagswahl Juni–Juli 1928*, Munich etc., 1995; *Der Hitler-Prozeß 1924. Wortlaut der Hauptverhandlung vor dem Volksgericht München*, 4 vols, ed. Lothar Gruchmann, Reinhard Weber and Otto Gritschneder, Munich, 1997–9.

9. Martin Moll (ed.), *'Führer-Erlasse' 1939–1945*, Stuttgart, 1997; Max Domarus (ed.), *Hitler. Reden und Proklamationen 1932–1945*, 2 vols in 4 parts, Wiesbaden, 1973; Henry Picker, *Hitlers Tischgespräche im Führerhauptquartier 1941–1942*, ed. Percy Ernst Schramm, Stuttgart, 1963; Werner Jochmann (ed.), *Adolf Hitler. Monologe im Führerhauptquartier 1941–1944. Die Aufzeichnungen Heinrich Heims*, Hamburg, 1980; *Hitlers Lagebesprechungen – Die Protokollfragmente seiner militärischen Konferenzen 1942–1945*, ed. Helmut Heiber, Stuttgart, 1962. (The English translation of *Hitler's Table Talk 1941–44*, Oxford, 1953, is not always reliable. No authentic German text has ever come to light of the supposed final 'table talks', published as *The Testament of Adolf Hitler. The Hitler–Bormann Documents, February–April 1945*, London, 1961. See Kershaw, *Hitler: Nemesis*, pp. 1024–5, note 121.)

10. Peter Witte *et al.* (eds.), *Der Dienstkalender Heinrich Himmlers 1941/42*, Hamburg, 1999.

11. *Die Tagebücher von Joseph Goebbels. Teil I, Aufzeichnungen 1923–1941*, 9 vols (vols 3–9 so far published), *Teil II, Diktate 1941–1945*, 15 vols, ed. Elke Fröhlich, Munich etc., 1993– . An abridged version was made available by Ralf Georg Reuth, *Joseph Goebbels. Tagebücher 1924–1945*, 5 vols., Munich/Zurich, 1992.

12. Alan Bullock, *Hitler. A Study in Tyranny*, (1952), 2nd edn, Harmondsworth, 1962, p. 804.

13. H. R. Trevor-Roper, 'The Mind of Adolf Hitler', in *Hitler's Table Talk*, pp. vii–xxxv.

14. Eberhard Jäckel, *Hitlers Weltanschauung. Entwurf einer Herrschaft*, Tübingen, 1969.

15. See Rosenhaum, p. 89.

16. This was the line I advanced in Ian Kershaw, 'Ideologue and Propagandist: Hitler in Light of his Speeches, Writings, and Orders, 1925–1928', *Yad Vashem Studies*, 23 (1993), pp. 321–4.

17. Joachim C. Fest, *Hitler. Eine Biographie*, (1973) paperback edn, Frankfurt am Main/Berlin/Vienna, 1976, p. 63.

18. Notably Rudolf Binion, *Hitler among the Germans*, New York, 1976, pp. 2–3.

19. Anton Joachimsthaler, *Korrektur einer Biographie. Adolf Hitler, 1908–1920*, Munich, 1989, pp. 44–5 (new extended edn, with the title *Hitlers Weg begann in München, 1913–1923*, Munich, 2000, p. 10).

20. Brigitte Hamann, *Hitlers Wien. Lehrjahre eines Diktators*, Munich/Zurich, 1996, pp. 496–503; and see Brigitte Hamann, 'Hitler and Vienna: the Truth about his Formative Years', in Hans Mommsen (ed.), *The Third Reich between Vision and Reality. New Perspectives on German History 1918–1945*, Oxford/New York, 2001, pp. 23–37, esp. pp. 33–6.

21. Kershaw, *Hitler: Hubris*, pp. 60–7, 94–5, 104–5.

22. Eberhard Jäckel and Axel Kuhn (eds.), *Hitler. Sämtliche Aufzeichnungen 1905–1924*, Stuttgart, 1980, p. 69; and see Kershaw, *Hitler: Hubris*, pp. 94–5.

23. Jäckel and Kuhn, pp. 88–90.

24. This view was first put forward in a brilliant essay by Martin Broszat, 'Soziale Motivation und Führer-Bindung im Nationalsozialismus', *Vierteljahreshefte für Zeitgeschichte*, 18 (1970), pp. 392–409.

25. Peter Fritzsche, *Germans into Nazis*, Cambridge, Mass./London, 1998, p. 8 (and see pp. 159–60, and 208–9).

26. Eric A. Johnson, *Nazi Terror: the Gestapo, Jews, and Ordinary Germans*, New York, 1999; Robert Gellately, *Backing Hitler. Consent and Coercion in Nazi Germany*, Oxford, 2001.

27. Pierre Ayçoberry, *The Social History of the Third Reich, 1933–1945*, New York, 1999. For the role of the Gestapo, see Robert Gellately, *The Gestapo and German Society. Enforcing Racial Policy, 1933–1945*, Oxford, 1990; and Gerbard Paul and Klaus-Michael Mallmann (eds.), *Die Gestapo. Mythos und Realität*, Darmstadt, 1995.

28. Saul Friedländer, *Nazi Germany and the Jews. The Years of Persecution, 1933–39*, London, 1997.

29. David Bankier (ed.), *Probing the Depths of German Antisemitism. German Society and the Persecution of the Jews, 1933–1941*, New York/Oxford/Jerusalem, 2000.

30. Michael Wildt, *Die Judenpolitik des SD 1935 bis 1938. Eine Dokumentation*, Munich, 1995.

31. Daniel J. Goldhagen, *Hitler's Willing Executioners. Ordinary Germans and the Holocaust*, New York, 1997.

32. See Julius H. Schoeps (ed.), *Ein Volk von Mördern? Die Dokumentation zur Goldhagen-Kontroverse um die Rolle der Deutschen im Holocaust*, Hamburg, 1996; Edouard Husson, *Une culpabilité ordinaire? Hitler, les allemands et la Shoah*, Paris, 1997; Dieter Pohl, 'Die Holocaust-Forschung und Goldhagens Thesen', *Vierteljahreshefte für Zeitgeschichte*, 45 (1997), pp. 1–48; and Johannes Heil and Rainer Erb (eds.), *Geschichtswissenschaft und Öffentlichkeit. Der Streit um Daniel J. Goldhagen*, Frankfurt am Main, 1999.

33. Christopher R. Browning, *Ordinary Men. Reserve Police Battalion 101 and the Final Solution in Poland*, New York, 1992.

34. Michael Mann, 'Were the perpetrators of genocide "Ordinary Men" or "Real Nazis"? Results from fifteen hundred biographies', *Holocaust and Genocide Studies*, 14 (2000), pp. 331–66.

35. Götz Aly, *'Endlosung'. Völkerverschiebung und der Mord an den europäischen Juden*, Frankfurt am Main, 1995 (trans. *'Final Solution'. Nazi Population Policy and the Murder of the European Jews*, London, 1999).

36. See esp. Ulrich Herbert, *Best. Biographische Studien über Radikalismus, Weltanschauung und Vernunft 1903–1989*, Bonn, 1996; and Ulrich Herbert (ed.), *Nationalsozialistische Vernichtungspolitik 1939–1945. Neue Forschungen und Kontroversen*, Frankfurt am Main, 1998.

37. Hans Safrian, *Eichmann und seine Gehilfen*, (1993) Frankfurt am Main, 1995.

38. Dieter Pohl, *Von der 'Judenpolitik' zum Judenmord. Der Distrikt Lublin des Generalgouvernements 1939–1944*, Frankfurt am Main, 1993; Dieter Pohl, *Nationalsozialistische Judenverfolgung in Ostgalizien. Organisation und Durchführung eines staatlichen Massenverbrechens*, Munich, 1996; Thomas Sandkühler, *'Endlösung' in Galizien. Der Judenmord in Ostpolen und die Rettungsinitiativen von Berthold Beitz*, Bonn, 1996; Christoph Dieckman, 'Der Krieg und die Ermordung der litauischen Juden', in Herbert, *Vernichtungspolitik*, pp. 292–329 (a preview of Dieckmann's forthcoming major study of the killing of the Jews of Lithuania); Christian Gerlach, 'Die Wannsee-Konferenz, das Schicksal der deutschen Juden und Hitlers politische Grundsatzentscheidung, alle Juden Europas zu ermorden', *Werkstattgeschichte*, 18 (1997), pp. 7–44; Christian Gerlach, *Krieg, Ernährung, Völkermord. Forschungen zur deutschen Vernichtungspolitik im Zweiten Weltkrieg*, Hamburg, 1998; and Christian Gerlach, *Kalkulierte Morde. Die deutsche Wirtschafts- und Vernichtungspolitik in Weißrußland 1941 bis 1944*, Hamburg, 2000.

39. Peter Longerich, *Politik der Vernichtung. Eine Gesamtdarstellung der nationalsozialistischen Judenverfolgung*, Munich/Zurich, 1998.

40. Richard Breitman, *The Architect of Genocide. Himmler and the Final Solution*, London, 1991, pp. 153–4.

41. Tobias Jersak, 'Die Interaktion von Kriegsverlauf und Judenvernichtung', *Historische Zeitschrift*, 268 (1999), pp. 311–49.

42. Gerlach, 'Die Wannsee-Konferenz' (see n. 38 for full reference).

43. Christopher R. Browning, *The Final Solution and the German Foreign Office. A Study of Referat DIII of Abteilung Deutschland 1940–43*, New York/London, 1978, p. 8.

44. Christopher R. Browning, *The Path to Genocide. Essays on Launching the Final Solution*, Cambridge, 1992, pp. 100–6; also Christopher R. Browning, 'Hitler and the euphoria of victory. The path to the Final Solution' in David Cesarani (ed.), *The Final Solution. Origins and Implementation*, London/New York, (1994) paperback edn, 1996, pp. 137–47, here p. 138.

45. See Longerich, pp. 429ff; Kershaw, *Hitler: Nemesis*, pp. 477ff.

46. See Kershaw, *Hitler: Nemesis*, pp. 490–1.

47. Gitta Sereny, *Albert Speer: His Battle with the Truth*, London, 1995; Joachim C. Fest, *Speer. Eine Biographie*, Berlin, 1999.

48. Richard Overy, *Interrogations. The Nazi Elite in Allied Hands, 1945*, London, 2001.

49. Ernst Günther Schenck, *Patient Hitler. Eine medizinische Biographie*, Düsseldorf, 1989; Ellen Gibbels, *Hitlers Parkinsonkrankheit: Zur Frage eines hirnorganischen Psychosyndroms*, Berlin, 1990; Ellen Gibbels, 'Hitlers Nervenkrankheit. Eine neurologisch-psychiatrische Studie', *Vierteljahreshefte für Zeitgeschichte*, 42 (1994), pp. 155–220; Fritz Redlich, *Hitler. Diagnosis of a Destructive Prophet*, New York/Oxford, 1999.

50. Redlich, p. 341.

51. Ada Petrova and Peter Watson, *The Death of Hitler: the Final Words from Russia's Secret Archives*, London, 1995.

52. Anton Joachimsthaler, *Hitlers Ende. Legenden und Dokumente* (1994), Augsburg, 1999 (abridged Engl. version: *The Last Days of Hitler. The Legends, the Evidence, the Truth*, London, 1996).

Further reading

Introduction

Binion, Rudolf, *Hitler among the Germans*. New York, 1976.

Bracher, Karl Dietrich, *The German Dictatorship*. Harmondsworth, 1973.

Bracher, Karl Dietrich, *Zeitgeschichtliche Kontroversen um Faschismus, Totalitarismus, Demokratie*. Munich, 1976.

Broszat, Martin, *The Hitler State: the Foundation and Development of the Internal Structure*. London, 1981.

Bullock, Alan, *Hitler. A Study in Tyranny*, rev. edn, London, 1964.

Burleigh, Michael, *The Third Reich. A New History*. London, 2000.

Carr, William, *Hitler: a study in Personality and Politics*. London, 1978.

Deuerlein, Ernst, *Hitler. Eine politische Biographie*. Munich, 1969.

Eichholtz, Dietrich and Kurt Gossweiler, *Faschismusforschung. Positionen, Probleme, Polemik*. Berlin (-Ost), 1980.

Elias, Norbert, *Studien über die Deutschen*. Frankfurt am Main, 1989.

Fest, Joachim C., *Hitler*. London, 1974.

Funke, Manfred, *Starker oder schwacher Diktator? Hitlers Herrschaft und die Deutschen*. Düsseldorf, 1989.

Graml, Hermann, 'Probleme einer Hitler-Biographie. Kritische Bemerkungen zu Joachim C. Fest', in *Vierteljahreshefte für Zeitgeschichte* 22 (1974), 76–92.

Haffner, Sebastian, *The Meaning of Hitler*. London, 1979.

Hamann, Brigitte, *Hitler's Vienna: a Dictator's Apprenticeship*. Oxford, 1999.

Jäckel, Eberhard, *Hitlers Herrschaft*. Stuttgart, 1986.

Kershaw, Ian, *The Nazi Dictatorship. Problems and Perspectives of Interpretation*. 4th edn London, 2000.

Kershaw, Ian, *Hitler, 1889–1936: Hubris*. London, 1998.

Kershaw, Ian, *Hitler, 1936–1945: Nemesis*. London, 2000.

Laqueur, Walter (ed.), *Fascism. A Reader's Guide*. Harmondsworth, 1979.

Lepsius, M. Rainer, 'Charismatic leadership. Max Weber's model and its applicability to the rule of Hitler', in Carl Friedrich Graumann and Serge Moscovici (eds.), *Changing Conceptions of Leadership*. New York, 1986.

Lukacs, John, *The Hitler of History*. New York, 1998.

Pätzold, Kurt and Manfred Weißbecker, *Adolf Hitler. Eine politische Biographie*. Leipzig, 1995.

Mason, Timothy W., 'Intention and explanation. A current controversy about the interpretation of National Socialism', in Gerhard Hirschfeld and Lothar Kettenacker (eds.), *Der 'Führerstaat': Mythos und Realität*. Stuttgart, 1981.

Mason, Timothy W., 'Open questions on Nazism', in Raphael Samuel (ed.), *People's History and Socialist Theory*. London, 1981, pp. 205–10.

Matussek, Paul, Peter Matussek and Jan Marbach, *Hitler. Karriere eines Wahns*. Munich, 2000.

Mommsen, Hans, *Adolf Hitler als 'Führer' der Nation*. (Deutsches Institut für Fernstudien an der Universität Tübingen) Tübingen, 1984.

Mommsen, Hans, *Der Nationalsozialismus und die deutsche Gesellschaft*. Reinbek, 1991.

Rosenbaum, Ron, *Explaining Hitler. The Search for the Origins of his Evil*. New York, 1998.

Schreiber, Gerhard, *Hitler-Interpretationen*. Darmstadt, 1984.

Steinert, Marlis, *Hitler*. Munich, 1994.

Thamer, Hans-Ulrich, *Verführung und Gewalt. Deutschland 1933–1945*. Berlin, 1986.

Toland, John, *Adolf Hitler*. London, 1977.

Waite, Robert O., *Adolf Hitler. The Psychopathic God*. New York, 1977.

Wippermann, Wolfgang (ed.), *Kontroversen um Hitler*. Frankfurt am Main, 1986.

Zitelmann, Rainer, *Adolf Hitler. Eine politische Biographie*. Göttingen/Zurich, 1989.

Chapter 1

Fest, Joachim C., *The Face of the Third Reich*, Harmondsworth, 1972.

Heiber, Helmut (ed.), *Das Tagebuch von Joseph Goebbels 1925/26*. Stuttgart, 1960.

Hitler, Adolf, *Mein Kampf*. edn Munich, 1934.

Hitler, Adolf, *Reden, Schriften, Anordnungen. Februar 1925 bis Januar 1933*, edn Institut für Zeitgeschichte, 5 vols in 12 parts, Munich, 1992–1998.

Jäckel, Eberhard, *Hitler's Weltanschauung. A Blueprint for Power*. Middletown, Conn., 1972.

Jäckel, Eberhard and Axel Kuhn (eds.), *Hitler. Sämtliche Aufzeichnungen 1905–1924*. Stuttgart, 1980.

Joachimsthaler, Anton, *Korrektur einer Biographie. Adolf Hitler 1908–1920*. Munich, 1989.

Jochmann, Werner (ed.), *Adolf Hitler. Monologe im Führerhauptquartier 1941–1944*. Hamburg 1980.

Kotze, Hildegard von and Helmut Krausnick (eds.), *Es spricht der Führer. 7 exemplarische Hitler-Reden*. Gütersloh, 1966.

Kuhn, Axel, *Hitlers außenpolitisches Programm. Entstehung und Entwicklung 1919–1939*. Stuttgart, 1970.

Maser, Werner, *Adolf Hitler. Legende, Mythos, Wirklichkeit*. 3rd edn Munich, 1976.

Maser, Werner, *Hitlers Briefe und Notizen*. 2nd edn Düsseldorf, 1988.

Phelps, Reginald, 'Hitlers "grundlegende" Rede über den Antisemitismus', *Vierteljahreshefte für Zeitgeschichte* 16 (1968), pp. 390–420.

Picker, Henry, *Hitlers Tischgespräche im Führerhauptquartier*. 2nd edn Stuttgart-Degerloch, 1963.

Stoakes, Geoffrey, *Hitler and the Quest for World Dominion. Nazi Ideology and Foreign Policy in the 1920s*. Leamington Spa, 1987.

The Testament of Adolf Hitler. The Hitler–Bormann Documents, February–April 1945, with an Introduction by H. R. Trevor-Roper. London, 1961.

Thies, Jochen, *Architekt der Weltherrschaft. Die 'Endziele' Hitlers*. Düsseldorf, 1979.

Tyrell, Albrecht, *Vom 'Trommler' zum 'Führer'. Der Wandel von Hitlers Selbstverständnis zwischen 1919 und 1924 und die Entwicklung der NSDAP*. Munich, 1975.

Wagener, Otto, *Hitler aus nächster Nähe. Aufzeichnungen eines Vertrauten 1929–1932*, ed. Henry A. Turner. Frankfurt am Main, 1987.

Weinberg, Gerhard L., *Hitlers Zweites Buch*. Stuttgart 1961.

Wippermann, Wolfgang, *Der konsequente Wahn. Ideologie und Politik Adolf Hitlers*. Munich, 1989.

Zitelmann, Rainer, *Hitler. The Politics of Seduction*. London, 1999.

Chapter 2

Allen, William Sheridan, *The Nazi Seizure of Power*. 2nd edn New York, 1984.

Auerbach, Hellmuth, 'Hitlers politische Lehrjahre und die Münchener Gesellschaft', *Vierteljahreshefte für Zeitgeschichte* 25 (1977), 1–45.

Bessel, Richard, 'The rise of the NSDAP and the myth of Nazi propaganda', *Wiener Library Bulletin*, 33 (1980), 20–29.

Bessel, Richard, *Political Violence and the Rise of Nazism*. New Haven, London, 1984.

Bessel, Richard and Edgar Feuchtwanger (eds.), *Social Change and Political Development in Weimar Germany*. London, 1981.

Böhnke, *Die NSDAP im Ruhrgebiet 1920–1933*. Bonn, 1974.

Bracher, Karl Dietrich, *Die Auflösung der Weimarer Republik*. Stuttgart, 1955.

Broszat, Martin, *German National Socialism 1919–1945*. Santa Barbara, 1966.

Broszat, Martin, 'Zur Struktur der NS-Massenbewegung', *Vierteljahreshefte für Zeitgeschichte* 31 (1983), pp. 52–76.

Broszat, Martin, *Hitler and the Collapse of Weimar Germany*. Leamington Spa, 1987.

Childers, Thomas, *The Nazi Voter. The Social Foundations of Fascism in Germany, 1933–1939*. Chapel Hill, London, 1983.

Childers, Thomas (ed.), *The Formation of the Nazi Constituency 1919–1933*. London, Sydney, 1986.

Deuerlein, Ernst, 'Hitlers Eintritt in die Politik und die Reichswehr', *Vierteljahreshefte für Zeitgeschichte* 7 (1959), 177–227.

Deuerlein, Ernst (ed.), *Der Hitler-Putsch. Bayerische Dokumente zum 8./9. November 1923*. Stuttgart, 1962.

Deuerlein, Ernst, *Der Aufstieg der NSDAP in Augenzeugenberichten*. Munich, 1974.

Falter, Jürgen W., *Hitlers Wähler*. Munich, 1991.

Fischer, Conan, *Stormtroopers. A Social, Economic and Ideological Analysis*. London, 1983.

Fritzsche, Peter, *Germans into Nazis*. Cambridge, Mass., 1998.

Gordon, Harold J., *Hitler and the Beer Hall Putsch*. Princeton, 1972.

Gossweiler, Kurt, *Kapital, Reichswehr und NSDAP 1919–1924*. Berlin (East), 1982.

Gritschneder, Otto, *Bewährungsfrist für den Terroristen Adolf H. Der Hitler-Putsch und die bayerische Justiz*. Munich, 1990.

Hambrecht, Rainer, *Der Aufstieg der NSDAP in Mittel- und Oberfranken (1925–1933)*. Nuremberg, 1976.

Hamilton, Richard F., *Who voted for Hitler?* Princeton, 1982.

Horn, Wolfgang, *Der Marsch zur Machtergreifung. Die NSDAP bis 1933*. Düsseldorf, 1980.

Jablonsky, David, *The Nazi Party in Dissolution. Hitler and the Verbotzeit, 1923–1925*. London, 1989.

Jäckel, Eberhard, 'Wie kam Hitler an die Macht?', in Karl Dietrich Erdmann and Hagen Schulze (eds.), *Weimar. Selbstpreisgabe einer Demokratie. Eine Bilanz heute*. Düsseldorf, 1980.

James, Harold, *The German Slump. Politics and Economics, 1924–1936*. Oxford, 1986.

Jamin, Mathilde, *Zwischen den Klassen. Zur Sozialstruktur der SA-Führerschaft*. Wuppertal, 1984.

Kissenkoeter, Udo, *Gregor Strasser und die NSDAP*. Stuttgart, 1978.

Koshar, Rudy, *Social Life, Local Politics and Nazism. Marburg 1880–1935*. Chapel Hill, London, 1986.

Krebs, Albert, *Tendenzen und Gestalten der NSDAP. Erinnerung an die Frühzeit der Partei*. Stuttgart, 1959.

Large, David Clay, *Munich's Road to the Third Reich*. New York, 1997.

Longerich, Peter, *Die braunen Bataillone. Geschichte der SA*. Munich, 1989.

Merkl, Peter, *Political Violence under the Swastika*. Princeton, 1975.

Neebe, Reinhard, *Großindustrie, Staat und NSDAP*. Göttingen, 1981.

Noakes, Jeremy, *The Nazi Party in Lower Saxony*. Oxford, 1971.

Nyomarkay, Joseph, *Charisma and Factionalism in the Nazi Party*. Minneapolis, 1967.

Orlow, Dietrich, *The History of the Nazi Party 1919–1933*, Pittsburgh, 1969.

Pätzold, Kurt and Michael Weißbecker, *Geschichte der NSDAP 1920–1945*. Cologne, 1981.

Paul, Gerhard, *Aufstand der Bilder. Die NS-Propaganda vor 1933*. Bonn, 1990.

Petzold, Joachim, *Die Demagogie des Hitlerfaschismus*. Berlin (East), 1982.

Phelps, Reginald, 'Hitler als Parteiredner 1920', *Vierteljahreshefte für Zeitgeschichte* 11 (1963), pp. 274–330.

Pridham, Geoffrey, *Hitler's Rise to Power. The Nazi Movement in Bavaria*. London, 1973.

Stachura, Peter D., *Gregor Strasser and the Rise of Nazism*. London, 1983.

Stachura, Peter D. (ed.), *The Nazi Machtergreifung*. London, 1983.

Turner, Henry, *Hitler's Thirty Days to Power: January 1933*. London, 1996.

Turner, Henry A., *German Big Business and the Rise of Hitler*. New York/Oxford, 1985.

Tyrell, Albrecht (ed.), *Führer befiehl . . . Selbstzeugnisse aus der 'Kampfzeit' der NSDAP. Dokumentation und Analyse*. Düsseldorf, 1969.

Chapter 3

Angermund, Ralph, *Deutsche Richterschaft 1919–1945*. Frankfurt am Main, 1990.

Arendt, Hannah, *The Origins of Totalitarianism*. 3rd edn London, 1967.

Aronson, Shlomo, *Reinhard Heydrich und die Frühgeschichte von Gestapo und SD*. Stuttgart, 1971.

Backes, Uwe *et al.*, *Reichstagsbrand. Aufklärung einer historischen Legende*. Munich/Zurich, 1986.

Bessel, Richard, '1933: A failed Counter-Revolution', in E. E. Rice (ed.), *Revolution and Counter-Revolution*. Oxford, 1991, pp. 109–27.

Bracher, Karl Dietrich, Wolfgang Sauer and Gerhard Schulz, *Die nationalsozialistische Machtergreifung. Studien zur Errichtung des totalitären Herrschaftssystems in Deutschland 1933/34*. Cologne/Opladen, 1960.

Broszat, Martin, 'Politische Denunziationen in der NS-Zeit: Aus Forschungserfahrungen im Staatsarchiv München', *Archivalische Zeitschrift* 73 (1977), 209–38.

Broszat, Martin *et al.* (eds.), *Deutschlands Weg in die Diktatur*. Berlin, 1983.

Broszat, Martin and Horst Möller, *Das Dritte Reich. Herrschaftsstruktur und Geschichte*. Munich, 1983.

Buchheim, Hans *et al.*, *Anatomy of the SS State*. London, 1968.

Fraenkel, Ernst, *The Dual State*. New York, 194.

Gellately, Robert, 'The Gestapo and German society. Political denunciation in the Gestapo case files', *Journal of Modern History* 60 (1988), 655–94.

Gellately, Robert, *Backing Hitler. Consent and Coercion in Nazi Germany*. Oxford, 2001.

Gellately, Robert, *The Gestapo and German Society. Enforcing Racial Policy 1933–1945*. Oxford, 1990.

Gruchmann, Lothar, *Justiz im Dritten Reich. Anpassung und Unterwerfung in der Ära Gürtner*. Munich, 1988.

Höhne, Heinz, *The Order of the Death's Head*. London, 1969.

Höhne, Heinz, *Mordsache Röhm. Hitlers Durchbruch zur Alleinherrschaft 1933/34*. Reinbek, 1984.

Johnson, Eric A., *Nazi Terror. The Gestapo, Jews, and Ordinary Germans*. New York, 1999.

Koehl, Robert, *The Black Corps. The Structure and Power Struggles of the Nazi SS*. Madison, Wisc., 1983.

Löwenthal, Richard and Patrik von zur Mühlen (eds.), *Widerstand und Verweigerung in Deutschland 1933 bis 1945*. Berlin, Bonn, 1984.

Mann, Reinhard, *Protest und Kontrolle im Dritten Reich. Nationalsozialistische Herrschaft im Alltag einer rheinischen Großstadt*. Frankfurt am Main, New York, 1987.

Matthias, Erich and Rudolf Morsey (eds.), *Das Ende der Parteien 1933*. Düsseldorf, 1960.

Michalka, Wolfgang (ed.), *Die nationalsozialistische Machtergreifung*, Paderborn, 1984.

Mommsen, Hans, 'Der Reichstagsbrand und seine politischen Folgen', *Vierteljahreshefte für Zeitgeschichte* 12 (1964), 351–413.

Paul, Gerhard and Klaus-Michael Mallmann (eds.), *Die Gestapo. Mythos und Realität*. Darmstadt, 1995.

Studien zur Geschichte der Konzentrationslager. Stuttgart, 1970.

Tuchel, Johannes and Reinold Schattenfroh, *Zentrale des Terrors. Prinz-Albrecht-Straße 8: Das Hauptquartier der Gestapo*. Berlin, 1987.

Chapter 4

✝

Ayçoberry, Pierre, *The Social History of the Third Reich, 1933–1945*. New York, 1999.

Bock, Gisela, *Zwangssterilisation im Nationalsozialismus*. Opladen, 1986.

Bramsted, Ernest K., *Goebbels and National Socialist Propaganda 1925–1945*. Michigan, 1965.

Broszat, Martin *et al.* (eds.), *Bayern in der NS-Zeit*. 6 vols, Munich, 1977–1983.

Bull, Hedley (ed.), *The Challenge of the Third Reich*. Oxford, 1986.

Burleigh, Michael and Wolfgang Wippermann, *The Racial State. Germany 1933–1945*. Cambridge, 1991.

Conway, John S., *The Nazi Persecution of the Churches, 1933–1945*. London, 1970.

Frei, Norbert, *National Socialist Rule in Germany: the Führer State 1933–1975*. Oxford/ Cambridge, Mass., 1993.

Frei, Norbert (ed.), *Medizin und Gesundheitspolitik in der NS-Zeit*. Munich, 1991.

Höhne, Heinz, *Die Zeit der Illusionen. Hitler und die Anfänge des 3. Reiches 1933–1936*. Düsseldorf, 1991.

Kater, Michael, 'Hitler in a Social Context', *Central European History* 14 (1981), 243–72.

Kater, Michael, 'Sozialer Wandel in der NSDAP im Zuge der nationalsozialistischen Machtergreifung', in Wolfgang Schieder (ed.), *Faschismus als soziale Bewegung*. 2nd edn Göttingen, 1983, pp. 25–67.

Kater, Michael, *The Nazi Party. A Social Profile of Members and Leaders 1919–1945*. Oxford, 1983.

Kater, Michael, *Doctors under Hitler*. Chapel Hill, London, 1989.

Kershaw, Ian, *Popular Opinion and Political Dissent in the Third Reich. Bavaria 1933–1945*. Oxford, 1983.

Kershaw, Ian, *The 'Hitler-Myth'. Image and Reality in the Third Reich*. Oxford, 1987.

Kleßmann, Christoph and Falk Pingel (eds.), *Gegner des Nationalsozialismus*, Frankfurt am Main, New York, 1980.

Klönne, Arno, *Jugend im Dritten Reich. Die Hitler-Jugend und ihre Gegner*. Cologne 1982 and Munich, 1990.

Koonz, Claudia, *Mothers in the Fatherland: Women, the Family and Nazi Politics*. London, 1987.

Mason, Timothy W., *Arbeiterklasse und Volksgemeinschaft*. Opladen, 1975.

Merson, Allan, *Communist Resistance in Nazi Germany*. London, 1985.

Mommsen, Hans and Susanne Willems (eds.), *Herrschaftsalltag im Dritten Reich. Studien und Texte*. Düsseldorf, 1988.

Noakes, Jeremy, 'The Oldenburg Crucifix struggle of November 1936. A case study of opposition in the Third Reich', in Peter D. Stachura (ed.), *The Shaping of the Nazi State*. London, 1978.

Orlow, Dietrich, *The History of the Nazi Party, 1933–1945*. Pittsburgh, 1973.

Peukert, Detlev, *Die KPD im Widerstand*. Wuppertal, 1980.

Peukert, Detlev, *Inside Nazi Germany: Conformity, Opposition and Racism in Everyday Life*. London, 1987.

Peukert, Detlev and Jürgen Reulecke (eds.), *Die Reihen fest geschlossen. Beiträge zur Geschichte des Alltags unter dem Nationalsozialismus*. Wuppertal, 1981.

Prinz, Michael, *Vom neuen Mittelstand zum Volksgenossen*. Munich, 1986.

Reichel, Peter, *Der schöne Schein des Dritten Reiches. Faszination und Gewalt des Faschismus*. Frankfurt am Main, 1993.

Sachse, Carola *et al.*, *Angst, Belohnung, Zucht und Ordnung. Herrschaftsmechanismen im Nationalsozialismus*. Opladen, 1982.

Saldern, Adelheid von, *Mittelstand im 'Dritten Reich'*. Frankfurt am Main, 1979.

Schoenbaum, David, *Hitler's Social Revolution: Class and Status in Nazi Germany 1933–1939*. Garden City, New York, 1967.

Scholder, Klaus, *Die Kirchen und das Dritte Reich*. 2 vols, Berlin 1977 and 1985.

Stephenson, Jill, *The Nazi Organisation of Women*. London, 1981.

Stern, J. P., *Hitler: the Führer and the People*. London, 1975.

Sywottek, Jutta, *Mobilmachung für den Krieg. Die propagandistische Vorbereitung der deutschen Bevölkerung auf den Zweiten Weltkrieg*. Opladen, 1976.

Unger, Aryeh H., *The Totalitarian Party*. Cambridge, 1974.

Welch, David, *Propaganda and the German Cinema 1933–1945*. Oxford, 1983.

Welch, David (ed.), *Nazi Propaganda. The Power and the Limitations*. London, 1983.

Welch, David, 'Propaganda and indoctrination in the Third Reich. Success or failure?' *European History Quarterly* 17 (1987), 403–22.

Welch, David, *The Third Reich. Politics and Propaganda*. London/New York, 1993.

Chapter 5

Bankier, David, 'Hitler and the policy-making process on the Jewish Question', *Holocaust and Genocide Studies* 3 (1988), 1–20.

Bankier, David (ed.), *Probing the Depths of German Antisemitism. German Society and the Persecution of the Jews, 1933–1941*. New York/Oxford/Jerusalem, 2000.

Barkai, Avraham, *Das Wirtschaftssystem des Nationalsozialismus*. Cologne, 1977.

Barkai, Avraham, *Vom Boykott zur 'Entjudung'*. Frankfurt am Main, 1988.

Benz, Wolfgang, *Herrschaft und Gesellschaft im nationalsozialistischen Staat*. Frankfurt am Main, 1990.

Botz, Gerhard, *Wohnungspolitik und Judendeportation in Wien 1938 bis 1945*. Vienna, 1975.

Botz, Gerhard, *Nationalsozialismus in Wien. Machtübernahme und Herrschaftssicherung 1938/39*. 3rd edn Buchloe, 1988.

Caplan, Jane, *Government without Administration. State and Civil Service in Weimar and Nazi Germany*. Oxford, 1988.

Carr, William, *Arms, Autarky and Aggression. A Study in German Foreign Policy, 1933–1939*. London, 1972.

Carroll, Berenice, *Total War. Arms and Economics in the Third Reich*. The Hague, Paris, 1968.

Deutsch, Harold C., *Das Komplott oder die Entmachtung der Generale*. Eichstätt, 1974.

Diehl-Thiele, Peter, *Partei und Staat im Dritten Reich*. Munich, 1969.

Döscher, Hans-Jürgen, *Das Auswärtige Amt im Dritten Reich*. Berlin, 1987.

Dülffer, Jost, 'Der Beginn des Krieges 1939. Hitler, die innere Krise und das Mächtesystem', *Geschichte und Gesellschaft* 2 (1976), 443–70.

Forndran, Eberhard (ed.), *Innen- und Außenpolitik unter nationalsozialistischer Bedrohung*. Opladen, 1977.

Forstmeier, Friedrich and Hans-Erich Volkmann (eds.), *Wirtschaft und Rüstung am Vorabend des Zweiten Weltkrieges*. Düsseldorf, 1975.

Friedländer, Saul, *Nazi Germany and the Jews. The Years of Persecution*. London, 1997.

Fröhlich, Elke (ed.), *Die Tagebücher von Joseph Goebbels. Teil I: Aufzeichnungen 1923 bis 1941*. 9 vols, Munich, 1997–; *Teil II: Diktate 1941–1945*. 15 vols, Munich, 1993–8.

Funke, Manfred (ed.), *Hitler, Deutschland und die Mächte*. Düsseldorf, 1978.

Gordon, Sarah, *Hitler, Germans, and the 'Jewish Question'*. Princeton, 1984.

Graml, Hermann, *Antisemitism in the Third Reich*. Oxford, 1992.

Gruchmann, Lothar, 'Die "Reichsregierung" im Führerstaat', in Günther Doecker and Winfried Steffani (eds.), *Klassenjustiz und Pluralismus*. Hamburg, 1973, pp. 187–223.

Hayes, Peter, *Industry and Ideology. IG Farben in the Nazi Era*. Cambridge, 1987.

Hildebrand, Klaus, *The Foreign Policy of the Third Reich*. Berkeley, 1973.

Hüttenberger, Peter, *Die Gauleiter. Studie zum Wandel des Machtgefüges in der NSDAP*. Stuttgart, 1969.

Hüttenberger, Peter, 'Nationalsozialistische Polykratie', *Geschichte und Gesellschaft* 2 (1976), 417–42.

Jacobsen, Hans-Adolf, *Nationalsozialistische Außenpolitik*. Frankfurt am Main, 1968.

Janßen, Karl-Heinz and Fritz Tobias, *Der Sturz der Generäle. Die Blomberg-Fritsch-Krise 1938*. Munich, 1994.

Koehl, Robert, 'Feudal Aspects of National Socialism', *American Political Science Review* 54 (1960), 921–33.

Messerschmidt, Manfred, *Die Wehrmacht im NS-Staat. Zeit der Indoktrination*. Hamburg, 1969.

Michalka, Wolfgang (ed.), *Nationalsozialistische Außenpolitik*. Darmstadt, 1978.

Militärgeschichtliches Forschungsamt (ed.), *Das Deutsche Reich und der Zweite Weltkrieg*, vol. 1, Stuttgart 1979.

Mommsen, Hans, *Beamtentum im Dritten Reich*. Stuttgart, 1966.

Mommsen, Wolfgang J. and Lothar Kettenacker (eds.), *The Fascist Challenge and the Policy of Appeasement*. London, 1983.

Müller, Klaus-Jürgen, *Das Heer und Hitler. Armee und nationalsozialistisches Regime 1933–1940*. 2nd edn Munich, 1988.

Müller, Klaus-Jürgen, *Armee, Politik und Gesellschaft in Deutschland 1933–1945*. Paderborn 1979.

Müller, Klaus-Jürgen, *General Ludwig Beck*. Boppard am Rhein, 1980.

Müller, Klaus-Jürgen, *Armee und Drittes Reich 1933–1939. Darstellung und Dokumentation*. Paderborn, 1987.

Nicosia, Francis R. and Lawrence D. Stokes, *Germans against Nazism. Nonconformity, Opposition, and Resistance in the Third Reich*. New York, Oxford, 1990.

Pehle, Walter H. (ed.), *Der Judenpogrom 1938. Von der 'Reichskristallnacht' zum Völkermord*. Frankfurt am Main, 1988.

Petzina, Dieter, *Autarkiepolitik im Dritten Reich. Der nationalsozialistische Vierjahresplan*. Stuttgart, 1968.

Peterson, Edward N., *The Limits of Hitler's Power*. Princeton, 1969.

241

Rebentisch, Dieter and Karl Teppe (eds.), *Verwaltung contra Menschenführung im Staat Hitlers*. Göttingen, 1986.

Rees, Laurence, *The Nazis. A Warning from History*. London, 1997.

Schleunes, Karl A., *The Twisted Road to Auschwitz. Nazi Policy towards German Jews 1933–1939*. Urbana, 1970.

Smelser, Ronald M., *The Sudeten Problem 1933–1938: Volkstumspolitik and the Formulation of Nazi Foreign Policy*. Folkestone, 1975.

Smelser, Ronald M., *Robert Ley. Hitler's Labor Front Leader*. Oxford, 1988.

Weinberg, Gerhard L., *The Foreign Policy of Hitler's Germany. Diplomatic Revolution in Europe 1933–1936*. Chicago, London, 1970.

Wendt, Bernd-Jürgen, *Großdeutschland. Außenpolitik und Kriegsvorbereitung des Hitler-Regimes*. 2nd edn Munich, 1993.

Chapter 6

✠

Adam, Uwe Dietrich, *Judenpolitik im Dritten Reich*. Düsseldorf, 1972.

Aly, Götz, *'Final Solution'. Nazi Population Policy and the Murder of the European Jews*. London, 1999.

Bankier, David, *The Germans and the Final Solution. Public Opinion under Nazism*. Oxford, 1992.

Bartov, Omer, *The Eastern Front 1941–1945. German Troops and the Barbarisation of Warfare*. London, 1985.

Bartov, Omer, *Hitler's Army. Soldiers, Nazis and War in the Third Reich*. New York/Oxford, 1991.

Birn, Ruth Bettina, *Die Höheren SS- und Polizeiführer*. Düsseldorf, 1986.

Bloch, Michael, *Ribbentrop*. London, 1994.

Breitman, Richard, *The Architect of Genocide. Himmler and the Final Solution*. London, 1991.

Broszat, Martin, *Nationalsozialistische Polenpolitik 1939–1945*. Stuttgart, 1961.

Broszat, Martin, 'Hitler und die Genesis der "Endlösung". Aus Anlaß der Thesen von David Irving', *Vierteljahreshefte für Zeitgeschichte* 25 (1977), 737–75; reprinted in Broszat, Martin, *Nach Hitler. Der schwierige Umgang mit unserer Geschichte*. Munich, 1988, pp. 45–92.

Broszat, Martin and Klaus Schwabe (eds.), *Die deutschen Eliten und der Weg in den Zweiten Weltkrieg*. Munich, 1989.

Browning, Christopher R., *The Final Solution and the German Foreign Office*. New York, 1978.

Browning, Christopher R., 'Zur Genesis der "Endlösung". Eine Antwort an Martin Broszat', *Vierteljahreshefte für Zeitgeschichte* 29 (1981), 97–109.

Browning, Christopher R., *Fateful Months. Essays on the Emergence of the Final Solution*. New York, London, 1985.

Browning, Christopher R., *Ordinary Men. Reserve Police Battalion 101 and the Final Solution in Poland*. New York, 1992.

Burrin, Philippe, *Hitler and the Jews. The Genesis of the Holocaust*. London, 1994.

Carr, William, *Poland to Pearl Harbor. The Making of the Second World War*. London, 1985.

Creveld, Martin van, *Hitler's Strategy 1940–1941. The Balkan Clue*. Cambridge, 1973.

Dallin, Alexander, *German Rule in Russia 1941–1945. A Study of Occupation Policies*. 2nd edn Basingstoke/London, 1981.

Eichholtz, Dietrich, *Geschichte der deutschen Kriegswirtschaft*. 2 vols, Berlin (East), 1984/85.

Fleming, Gerald, *Hitler and the Final Solution*. Oxford, 1986.

Frei, Norbert and Hermann Kling (eds.), *Der nationalsozialistische Krieg*. Frankfurt am Main, New York, 1990.

Friedlander, Henry, *From Euthanasia to the Final Solution*. Chapel Hill, London, 1995.

Gerlach, Christian, *Krieg, Ernährung, Völkermord. Forschungen zur deutschen Vernichtungspolitik im Zweiten Weltkrieg*. Hamburg, 1998.

Goldhagen, Daniel, *Hitler's Willing Executioners. Ordinary Germans and the Holocaust*. New York, 1996.

Gruchmann, Lothar, 'Euthanasie und Justiz im Dritten Reich', *Vierteljahreshefte für Zeitgeschichte* 20 (1972), 235–79.

Herbert, Ulrich, *Best. Biographische Studien über Radikalismus, Weltanschauung und Vernunft 1903–1989*. Bonn, 1996.

Herbert, Ulrich (ed.), *Nationalsozialistische Vernichtungspolitik 1939–1945. Neue Forschungen und Kontroversen*. Frankfurt am Main, 1998.

Hilberg, Raul, *The Destruction of the European Jews*. New York, 1961.

Hillgruber, Andreas, *Hitlers Strategie, Politik und Kriegsführung 1940–1941*. Frankfurt am Main, 1965.

Jäckel, Eberhard and Jürgen Rohwer (eds.), *Der Mord an der Juden im Zweiten Weltkrieg*. Stuttgart, 1985.

Klee, Ernst, *'Euthanasie' im NS-Staat. Die 'Vernichtung lebensunwerten Lebens'*. Frankfurt am Main, 1983.

Knipping, Franz and Klaus-Jürgen Müller (eds.), *Machtbewußtsein in Deutschland am Vorabend des Zweiten Weltkrieges*. Paderborn, 1984.

Knopp, Guido, *Hitler's Henchmen*. Stroud, 2000.

Knopp, Guido, *Holokaust*. Stroud, 2001.

Koehl, Robert, *RKFDV: German Resettlement and Population Policy, 1939–1945*. Cambridge, Mass., 1957.

Krausnick, Helmut and Hans-Heinrich Wilhelm, *Die Truppe des Weltanschauungskrieges*. Stuttgart, 1981.

Kube, Alfred, *Pour le mérite und Hakenkreuz. Hermann Göring im Dritten Reich*. Munich, 1986.

Longerich, Peter, *Politik der Vernichtung. Eine Gesamtdarstellung der nationalsozialistischen Judenverfolgung*. Munich, 1998.

Madajczyk, Czeslaw, *Die Okkupationspolitik Nazideutschlands in Polen 1939–1945*. Berlin, 1987.

Mann, Michael, 'Were the perpetrators of genocide "Ordinary Men" or "Real Nazis"? Results from fifteen hundred biographies', *Holocaust and Genocide Studies* 14 (2000), pp. 331–66.

Marrus, Michael R., *The Holocaust in History*. London, 1988.

Martens, Stefan, *Hermann Göring. 'Erster Paladin des Führers' und 'Zweiter Mann im Reich'*. Paderborn, 1985.

Mayer, Arno, *Why did the Heavens not Darken? The 'Final Solution' in History*. New York, 1988.

Michalka, Wolfgang, *Ribbentrop und die deutsche Weltpolitik 1933–1940. Außenpolitische Konzeptionen und Entscheidungsprozesse im Dritten Reich*. Munich, 1980.

Milward, Alan S., *The German Economy at War*. London, 1965.

Militärgeschichtliches Forschungsamt (ed.), *Das Deutsche Reich und der Zweite Weltkrieg*. vols 2–6, Stuttgart, 1979–1990.

Militärgeschichtliches Forschungsamt (ed.), *Der Zweite Weltkrieg. Analyse, Grundzüge, Forschungsbilanz*. Munich, 1989.

Mommsen, Hans, 'Die Realisierung des Utopischen. Die "Endlösung" der "Judenfrage" im "Dritten Reich" ', in *Geschichte und Gesellschaft* 9 (1983), 381–420.

Overy, Richard J., 'Hitler's war and the German economy: A reinterpretation', *Economic History Review* 35 (1982), 272–91.

Rebentisch, Dieter, *Führerstaat und Verwaltung im Zweiten Weltkrieg*. Stuttgart, 1989.

Recker, Marie-Louise, *Nationalsozialistische Sozialpolitik im Zweiten Weltkrieg*. Munich, 1985.

Rees, Laurence, *War of the Century. When Hitler fought Stalin*. London, 1999.

Rich, Norman, *Hitler's War Aims*. 2 vols, London, 1973/74.

Saffrian, Hans, *Eichmann und seine Gehilfen*. Frankfurt am Main, 1995.

Schieder, Wolfgang (ed.), *'Vernichtungspolitik'*. Hamburg, 1991.

Schmuhl, Hans-Walter, *Rassenhygiene, Nationalsozialismus, Euthanasie*. Göttingen, 1987.

Streim, Alfred, *Die Behandlung sowjetischer Kriegsgefangener im 'Fall Barbarossa'*. Heidelberg/Karlsruhe, 1981.

Streit, Christian, *Keine Kameraden. Die Wehrmacht und die sowjetischen Kriegsgefangenen 1941–1945*. Stuttgart, 1978.

Wegner, Bernd, *Hitlers Politische Soldaten. Die Waffen-SS 1933–1945*. Paderborn, 1982.

Weinberg, Gerhard L., *The Foreign Policy of Hitler's Germany. Starting World War II*. Chicago, London, 1980.

Chapter 7

Boelcke, Willi A. (ed.), *Deutschlands Rüstung im Zweiten Weltkrieg. Hitlers Konferenzen mit Albert Speer 1942–1945*. Frankfurt am Main, 1969.

Borsdorf, Ulrich and Mathilde Jamin (eds.), *Über Leben im Krieg. Kriegserfahrungen in einer Industrieregion 1939–1945*. Reinbek, 1989.

Broszat, Martin, Klaus-Dietmar Henke and Hans Woller (eds.), *Von Stalingrad zur Währungsreform*. Munich, 1988.

Fest, Joachim, *Plotting Hitler's Death: the German Resistance to Hitler 1933–1945*. London, 1997.

Fest, Joachim, *Speer. Eine Biographie*. Berlin, 1999.

Goebbels, Joseph, *Tagebücher 1945. Die letzten Aufzeichnungen*. Hamburg, 1977.

Graml, Hermann (ed.), *Widerstand im Dritten Reich, Probleme, Ereignisse, Gestalten*. Frankfurt am Main, 1984.

Hancock, Eleanor, *National Socialist Leadership and Total War 1941–45*. New York, 1991.

Heiber, Helmut (ed.), *Hitlers Lagebesprechungen. Die Protokollfragmente seiner militärischen Konferenzen 1942–1945*. Stuttgart, 1962.

Herbert, Ulrich, *Hitler's Foreign Workers: Enforced Foreign Labor in Germany under the Third Reich*. Cambridge, 1997.

Herbst, Ludolf, *Der Totale Krieg und die Ordnung der Wirtschaft*. Stuttgart, 1982.

Hoffmann, Peter, *The History of the German Resistance 1933–1945*. London, 1977.

Hoffmann, Peter, *Stauffenberg. A Family History, 1905–1944*. Cambridge, 1995.

Irving, David, *The Secret Diaries of Hitler's Doctor*. London, 1990.

Irving, David, *Führer und Reichskanzler. Adolf Hitler 1933–1945*. Munich/Berlin, 1989.

Joachimsthaler, Anton, *Hitlers Ende. Legenden und Dokumente*. Munich, 1995.

Lang, Jochen von, *Der Sekretär. Martin Bormann. Der Mann, der Hitler beherrschte*. Frankfurt am Main, 1980.

Lochner, Louis (ed.), *Goebbels Tagebücher aus den Jahren 1942/43*. Zurich, 1948.

Müller, Klaus Jürgen (ed.), *Der deutsche Widerstand 1933–1945*. Paderborn, 1986.

Mehringer, Hartmut, *Widerstand und Emigration. Das NS-Regime und seine Gegner*. Munich, 1997.

Redlich, Fritz, *Hitler: Diagnosis of a Destructive Prophet*. New York, Oxford, 1999.

Schenck, Ernst Günther, *Patient Hitler. Eine medizinische Biographie*. Düsseldorf, 1989.

Schmädeke, Jürgen and Peter Steinbach (eds.), *Der Widerstand gegen den Nationalsozialismus*. Munich/Zurich, 1985.

Schmidt, Matthias, *Albert Speer. Das Ende eines Mythos*. Bonn/Munich, 1982.

Schmitthenner, Walter and Hans Buchheim (eds.), *Der deutsche Widerstand gegen Hitler*. Cologne/Berlin 1966.

Schramm, Percy Ernst (ed.), *Kriegstagebuch des Oberkommandos der Wehrmacht*. 4 vols, Frankfurt am Main, 1961–65.

Schumann, Wolfgang *et al.* (eds.), *Deutschland im Zweiten Weltkrieg*. 6 vols, Berlin (East), 1974–85.

Sereny, Gitta, *Albert Speer: His Battle with the Truth*. London, 1995.

Speer, Albert, *Inside the Third Reich*. London, 1970.

Steinert, Marlis, *Hitlers Krieg und die Deutschen*. Düsseldorf 1970.

Trevor-Roper, Hugh, *The Last Days of Hitler*. Pan Books edn London, 1973.

Walker, Mark, *German National Socialism and the Quest for Nuclear Power 1939–1949*. Cambridge, 1989.

Conclusion

Broszat, Martin, 'Soziale Motivation und Führer-Bindung des Nationalsozialismus', *Vierteljahreshefte für Zeitgeschichte* 18 (1970), 392–409.

Dahrendorf, Ralf, *Society and Democracy in Germany*. London, 1968.

Mommsen, Hans, 'Der Nationalsozialismus. Kumulative Radikalisierung und Selbstzerstörung des Regimes', *Meyers Enzyklopadisches Lexikon*, vol. 16 (1976), pp. 785–90.

Mommsen, Hans, 'Nationalsozialismus als vorgetäuschte Modernisierung', in Walter H. Pehle (ed.), *Der historische Ort des Nationalsozialismus*. Frankfurt am Main, 1990.

Mommsen, Hans, 'Cumulative radicalisation and progressive self-destruction as structural determinants of the Nazi dictatorship', in Ian Kershaw and Moshe Lewin (eds.), *Stalinism and Nazism. Dictatorships in Comparison*. Cambridge, 1997, pp. 75–87.

Neumann, Franz, *Behemoth: the Structure and Practice of National Socialism*. London, 1942.

Noakes, Jeremy, 'Nazism and Revolution', in Noel O'Sullivan (ed.), *Revolutionary Theory and Political Reality*. London, 1983, pp. 73–100.

Rauschning, Hermann, *Die Revolution des Nihilismus*. Zurich/New York, 1938.

Chronology*

1889

20 April   Adolf Hitler born in Braunau am Inn.

1907–1913   Hitler lives in Vienna.

1913

24 May   Moves to Munich.

1914

16 Aug.   Joins the 'List Regiment' (Reserve Infantry Regiment 16).
2 Dec.   Awarded Iron Cross 2nd Class.

1918

4 Aug.   Awarded Iron Cross 1st Class.
23 Oct.   Temporarily blinded through gas, enters military hospital in Stettin, and
                moved from there to Pasewalk (Pomerania), where he hears of the revolu-
                tion of 9 Nov. 1918 before being released on 19 Nov. and returning to
                Munich.
7–8 Nov.   Revolution in Munich.
9 Nov.   Proclamation of German Republic in Berlin; abdication of Kaiser Wilhelm II.

1919

5 Jan.   Foundation in Munich by Anton Drexler and Karl Harrer of German
                Workers' Party, with initially 20–40 members.
6–7 April   'Councils Republic' (*Räterepublik*) proclaimed in Munich; bloodily sup-
                pressed on 1–2 May.
5–12 June   Hitler attends Reichswehr 'political education' course at Munich University;
                subsequently deployed by Reichswehr at Lechfeld Camp to indoctrinate
                soldiers waiting for demobilisation.
28 June   Signing of Versailles Treaty.
12 Sept.   As Reichswehr informant, Hitler attends meeting of German Workers' Party
                in Munich; joins shortly afterwards.

---

* This chronology is based partly on the excellent and much fuller Chronology in Martin
Broszat and Norbert Frei (eds.), *Das Dritte Reich im Überblick*, Munich, 1989, pp. 177–289.

1920

24 Feb.	Proclamation of programme of German Workers' Party (a week later renamed National Socialist German Workers' Party).
31 March	Hitler leaves the Reichswehr.
17 Dec.	NSDAP purchases *Münchener Beobachter*, renamed as *Völkischer Beobachter* (from 8 Feb. 1923, the Party's daily newspaper).

1921

11 July	Hitler quits the NSDAP because of policy differences with the leadership and offers ultimatum on conditions for his rejoining.
29 July	Extraordinary Party Members' Meeting elects Hitler as Party Chairman with dictatorial powers.
3 Aug.	Foundation of what soon became the NSDAP's paramilitary organisation, the SA (stormtroopers).

1922

24–7 July	Hitler in prison in Munich following disturbances at an opposition meeting the previous September.
10 Oct.	Julius Streicher, racist–nationalist leader in Nuremberg, merges his *völkisch* faction into the NSDAP and accepts Hitler's leadership.

1923

11 Jan.	Beginning of Ruhr occupation through French and Belgian troops to enforce reparations payments; the Reich government proclaims 'passive resistance'.
27–9 Jan.	First 'Reich Party Rally' of the NSDAP takes place in Munich.
Feb.	Beginning of the month, uniting of SA with other Bavarian paramilitary groups as potential for a possible putsch grows.
1 March	Hermann Göring becomes commander of SA.
26 Sept.	State of emergency proclaimed in Bavaria.
8–9 Nov	Hitler Putsch: proclamation of national revolution and deposition of governments of Bavaria and the Reich; march through Munich ends when police open fire, killing sixteen; Hitler and others arrested.

1924

26 Feb.	Trial of Hitler (and other Putsch leaders) for high treason begins in Munich.
1 April	Hitler sentenced to five years in prison and a fine of 200 gold Marks.
20 Dec.	Released from his imprisonment in Landsberg am Lech.

1925

26 Feb.	Refoundation of NSDAP.
9 March	Hitler banned from speaking in Bavaria; ban lasts till 5 March 1927; other states follow suit; ban in Prussia only lifted in Sept. 1928.

| 26 April | Paul von Hindenburg elected as Reich President, following the death of Friedrich Ebert. |
| 18 July | First volume of *Mein Kampf* published. |

1926

14 Feb.	Meeting of Party leaders in Bamberg; Hitler quells hopes of Gregor Strasser and others of reforming Party programme.
3–4 July	Second Reich Party Rally, in Weimar.
10 Dec.	Second volume of *Mein Kampf* published.

1927

| 9 March | First public speech of Hitler in Munich following lifting of ban. |
| 19–21 Aug. | Third Reich Party Rally, in Nuremberg. |

1928

| 28 May | Reichstag elections: the NSDAP attains only 2.6 per cent of the vote, giving the Party twelve seats. |
| 16 Nov. | First public speech of Hitler in Berlin following lifting of speaking ban in state of Prussia. |

1929

23 June	Coburg becomes first German town to give the NSDAP a majority in local elections.
1–4 Aug.	Fourth Reich Party Rally, in Nuremberg.
22 Dec.	Plebiscite against the Young Plan (signed on 7 June and stipulating reparations payments over the following fifty-nine years) produces only 13.8 per cent support for the motion of rejection backed by the Nazis and other extreme nationalist groups.

1930

23 Jan.	Wilhelm Frick becomes first Nazi to take up a ministerial post in a state government, as Minister of the Interior in a coalition government in Thuringia.
30 March	Heinrich Brüning forms minority government after resignation (on 27 March) of SPD-led 'grand coalition'.
16–18 July	Nazi Party joins others in rejecting Brüning's deflationary proposals; Reichstag dissolved as a consequence.
14 Sept.	Reichstag elections: the NSDAP gains 18.3 per cent and becomes the second-largest party in the Reichstag with 107 seats.
25 Sept.	Hitler attests on oath before the Reich Court in Leipzig that the NSDAP will not attempt to gain power by illegal means.

1931

5 Jan.	Ernst Röhm becomes SA Chief of Staff.
13 July	Collapse of the Darmstädter und Nationalbank brings disastrous worsening of economic crisis.
18 Sept.	Hitler's niece Geli Raubal commits suicide in his Munich appartment.
11 Oct.	Rally of the 'National Opposition' (NSDAP, DNVP, Stahlhelm) in Bad Harzburg, though serious divisions prevail within 'Harzburger Front'.

1932

26 Jan.	Hitler speaks to the Industrieklub in Düsseldorf.
25 Feb.	Hitler offered nominal ministerial post by Nazi-run government in Braunschweig; takes oath of allegiance to state on following day and is able by this means to acquire German citizenship.
13 March	Hitler gains 30.1 per cent of the vote in the Reich presidential election; a second election is necessary because Hindenburg (with 49.6 per cent) just fails to attain the absolute majority needed for his re-election.
10 April	Second presidential election; Hitler's vote rises to 36.8 per cent, but Hindenburg is re-elected with 53.0 per cent.
13 April	SA and SS banned.
24 April	State elections in Prussia, Bavaria, Württemberg, Anhalt, Hamburg leave the NSDAP as the largest (in Bavaria second-largest) party.
30 May	Brüning resigns after losing Hindenburg's support.
1 June	Franz von Papen appointed Reich Chancellor.
16–19 June	Reparations conference in Lausanne agrees the end of German reparations payments (after payments to the USA had been frozen through the Hoover Moratorium of 24 July 1931).
16 June	Ban on SA lifted.
20 July	The 'Prussia Putsch': by emergency decree, the government of Prussia under the Social Democratic Minister President Otto Braun is deposed; Social Democrats in the civil service and police are removed from office; Reich Chancellor von Papen takes over responsibility for Prussia as Reich Commissar.
31 July	Reichstag election: the NSDAP gains 37.3 per cent of the vote, wins 230 seats, and becomes the largest party in the Reichstag.
13 Aug.	In an audience with Hindenburg, Hitler refuses offer of post of Vice Chancellor, and insists upon full responsibility for government, which Hindenburg rejects.
12 Sept.	von Papen dissolves Reichstag.
6 Nov.	Reichstag elections; the vote for the NSDAP falls to 33.1 per cent, but the Nazis remain, with 197 seats, the strongest in the Reichstag.
17 Nov.	von Papen resigns as Reich Chancellor.

19 Nov.	A number of businessmen, headed by Hjalmar Schacht, appeal to Hindenburg to make Hitler Reich Chancellor.
2 Dec.	Hindenburg appoints General von Schleicher as Reich Chancellor.
8 Dec.	Gregor Strasser resigns all his offices in the Nazi Party.

1933

4 Jan.	von Papen and Hitler discuss cooperation in government at meeting in the house of the Cologne banker Kurt von Schröder.
15 Jan.	Elections in the tiny state of Lippe bring a vote of 39.5 per cent for the NSDAP.
17–29 Jan.	Manoeuvring centred upon Hitler, von Papen and the circle around Reich President Hindenburg isolates Schleicher and leads to agreement on a Hitler Chancellorship (with von Papen as Vice Chancellor) in a cabinet comprised mainly of conservatives.
28 Jan.	Schleicher resigns.
30 Jan.	Hitler appointed Reich Chancellor by Reich President von Hindenburg. Only two other Nazis (Frick and Göring) besides Hitler in the 'national government'.
27 Feb.	The Reichstag building burnt down; interpreted by the Nazi leadership as the start of a communist uprising.
28 Feb.	'Reichstag Fire Decree' (For the Protection of People and State') suspends civil rights. Mass arrests of Communists and other left-wing opponents follow.
5 March	Reichstag election; the Nazi Party gains 43.9 per cent of the vote (and 288 seats), its coalition partners (the Nationalists) 8 per cent.
5–9 March	Seizure of power in *Länder* not previously under Nazi control.
20 March	Himmler announces the establishment of the first concentration camp at Dachau.
23 March	The Reichstag votes to accept an Enabling Act, giving the Hitler government comprehensive legislative powers.
1 April	Nationwide boycott of Jewish shops.
1 May	End to recruitment to the NSDAP; 1.6 million new members since 30 Jan. 1933 had taken the total membership to 2.5 million.
2 May	Forcible dissolution of the trades unions.
10 May	Burning of the books of 'un-German' authors in university cities.
22 June	SPD banned; the other parties dissolve themselves during the following weeks.
14 July	Law to prevent the formation of parties other than the NSDAP establishes the one-party state.
20 July	Conclusion of Reich Concordat with the Papacy.

| 14 Oct. | Germany leaves the League of Nations and the Geneva Disarmament Conference. |
| 12 Nov. | New 'election' to the Reichstag: the NSDAP attains 92.2 per cent of the vote; in an accompanying plebiscite, 95.1 per cent support the decision to leave the League of Nations. |

1934

20 Jan.	'Law for the Ordering of National Labour' weights industrial relations heavily against the work-force and in favour of management.
26 Jan.	Non-aggression treaty between Germany and Poland.
30 Jan.	'Law on the Reconstruction of the Reich' abolishes the sovereignty of the Länder.
24 April	People's Court established to deal with treasonable offences.
30 June	'Night of the Long Knives': Ernst Röhm and other SA leaders arrested and shot without trial; the end of the SA as a political force.
2 Aug.	Death of Reich President von Hindenburg: the offices of President and Chancellor amalgamated; the Reichswehr swears a personal oath of allegiance to Hitler as 'Führer and Reich Chancellor'.
19 Aug.	Plebiscite produces result of 89.9 per cent support for uniting of offices of head of state and head of government in Hitler's person.

1935

13 Jan.	Saar Plebiscite (in accordance with the Versailles Treaty): 90.8 per cent support for incorporation in the German Reich.
1 March	The Saar returns to Germany.
16 March	Introduction of conscription, with the aim of building an army of thirty-six divisions.
11–14 April	Creation of 'Stresa Front' by the governments of France, Italy and Great Britain in attempt to bind Germany to its treaty obligations.
18 June	German–British Naval Treaty: strength of German navy set at 35 per cent of that of the British navy.
15 Sept.	Promulgation of the 'Nuremberg Laws', denying Reich citizenship to Jews, banning marriage and sexual relations between Jews and non-Jews, and forming the basis of wide-ranging discriminatory measures during the next years.
3 Oct.	Italian attack on Abyssinia.

1936

| 6 Jan. | Italy leaves the 'Stresa Front' and takes back its guarantee of Austrian independence in return for German support of policy towards Abyssinia. |
| 7 March | Germany reoccupies the demilitarised Rhineland in direct breach of the Locarno Treaty of 1925. |

29 March	'Reichstag election' brings 99 per cent support for Hitler.
17–18 July	Beginning of Spanish Civil War.
1 Aug.	Hitler opens the Olympic Games in Berlin.
9 Sept.	Announcement of the 'Four-Year Plan', placing the German economy as far as possible on an autarkic basis and laying the preparations for a war economy.
1 Nov.	Mussolini announces the 'Berlin–Rome Axis'.
25 Nov.	Anti-Comintern pact between Germany and Japan.
1 Dec.	The Hitler Youth, a Party affiliation, declared to be the state youth organisation; membership of 5,437,601 by end of year.

1937

30 Jan.	The Enabling Act extended by the Reichstag for a further four years.
14 March	Pope Pius XI condemns Nazi church policy and criticises racial policy in the Encyclical 'Mit brennender Sorge'.
1 May	Temporary lifting of ban (permanently lifted on 1 May 1939) on new membership of NSDAP (which had been imposed in May 1933). Membership rises to 5.3 million by 1939, and to 8.5 million by 1945.
24 June	Secret directive of War Minister Blomberg indicates Czechoslovakia as a possible target.
15 July	Foundation of the 'Reichswerke Hermann Göring' steel production works in Salzgitter.
25–9 Sept.	State visit of Mussolini.
5 Nov.	'Hossbach meeting' in Reich Chancellory: Hitler addresses leaders of the armed forces and Foreign Minister von Neurath about the need to solve the 'problem of living space' by force by 1943 at the latest, with Austria and Czechoslovakia as targets in the near future.
6 Nov.	Italy joins the Anti-Comintern pact of Germany and Japan and leaves the League of Nations on 11 Dec.

1938

4 Feb.	'Blomberg–Fritsch Crisis': War Minister Blomberg (following his marriage to a former prostitute) and head of the army Werner Fritsch (wrongly accused of homosexuality as a result of a plot by Himmler and Göring to remove him) dismissed; Hitler takes the opportunity to replace the conservative von Neurath by Ribbentrop as Foreign Minister, and to take over himself the supreme command over the Wehrmacht.
12 March	German troops march into Austria following an ultimatum and forced resignation of Chancellor Schuschnigg the previous day.
13 March	Law to incorporate Austria in the German Reich.

10 April	Over 99 per cent support for Hitler in the plebiscite and 'election' to the 'Greater German Reichstag'.
20 May	Czechoslovakia mobilises its troops.
30 May	Hitler's directive to the Wehrmacht declares the intention to destroy Czechoslovakia at the earliest opportunity.
June	Start of the building of the 'Westwall' fortification along the German western border.
9 June	Demolition of the synagogue in Munich.
25 July	Ban on practising by Jewish doctors.
10 Aug.	Synagogue in Nuremberg demolished.
17 Aug.	Jews compelled to add to existing names the forename of 'Sara' or 'Israel'.
18 Aug.	Chief of Staff Ludwig Beck submits his resignation because of Hitler's intention to wage war against Czechoslovakia.
Sept.	Sudeten crisis.
27 Sept.	Jewish lawyers banned from practising.
29–30 Sept.	Munich Conference determines that the Sudetenland should belong to Germany after 1 Oct.
21 Oct.	Hitler gives secret directive to prepare for the destruction of the remainder of the Czechoslovakian state.
28 Oct.	17,000 Jews of Polish statehood deported to Polish territory.
7 Nov.	An official of the German embassy in Paris, Ernst vom Rath, shot by a young Jew, Herschel Grynszpan, and dies two days later.
9–10 Nov.	'Reichskristallnacht': nationwide pogroms result in the murder of 91 Jews, the injuring and maltreatment of countless others, the burning of 191 synagogues, the wild destruction and looting of 7,500 Jewish shops and other property, and the arrest and incarceration in concentration camps of around 30,000 male Jews. Legislation during the following few days forces Jews out of the economy and on to the fringes of society. Almost 80,000 Jews are driven to leave Germany in 1939, compared with around 40,000 in 1938 and 23,000 in 1937.

1939

30 Jan.	Hitler 'prophesises' in a speech to the Reichstag the destruction of the Jews in the event of another war.
14–15 March	German troops march into Czechoslovakia. A 'Reich Protectorate of Bohemia and Moravia' is set up on 16 March, while Slovakia declares its independence and concludes a friendship treaty with Germany.
21 March	Hitler demands the return of Danzig and the Corridor from Poland.
23 March	German annexation of the Memel territory in Lithuania.

31 March	Britain and France guarantee support for Poland; German demands rejected by Poland.
3 April	Hitler gives directive for preparation of attack on Poland.
22 May	Germany and Italy agree to form a military alliance (the 'Pact of Steel').
23 Aug.	Germany and the Soviet Union sign a non-aggression treaty (the 'Hitler–Stalin Pact'), with a secret clause about the division of Poland.
1 Sept.	Germany attacks Poland.
3 Sept.	Great Britain and France declare war on Germany.
6 Oct.	German conquest of Poland completed.
9 Oct.	Hitler wishes to attack in the west at the earliest opportunity; an offensive initially set for 12 Nov. is, however, repeatedly postponed.
12–17 Oct.	First deportation to Poland of Jews from Austria and Czechoslovakia.
8 Nov.	Failed attempt on Hitler's life by the Swabian joiner Georg Elser, who had planted a bomb in the Bürgerbräukeller in Munich.

1940

9 April	German invasion of Denmark and Norway.
10 May	German western offensive begins; breach of neutrality of the Netherlands, Belgium and Luxemburg.
4 June	Evacuation of British troops from Dunkirk.
22 June	French armistice signed in Forest of Compiègne in same railway carriage in which Marshal Foch had received the German capitulation on 11 Nov. 1918.
16 July	Preparations laid for the invasion of Britain ('Operation Sealion'); eventually, on 17 Sept., postponed indefinitely.
31 July	Hitler notifies military leaders of decision to attack the Soviet Union ('Operation Barbarossa').
27 Sept.	Conclusion of tripartite pact between Germany, Italy and Japan.
23 Oct.	Hitler meets Franco, but is unable to persuade him to bring Spain into the war.
18 Dec.	Hitler's directive for 'Case Barbarossa' envisages attack on Soviet Union before the end of the war with Great Britain.

1941

17–30 March	Hitler expounds principles of the eastern war to military leaders; the Russian campaign to be a 'war of annihilation'.
6 April	German invasion of Yugoslavia and Greece.
10 May	Rudolf Hess, Deputy to the Führer in charge of the Nazi Party, flies to Britain and is imprisoned there; declared mentally ill by Hitler and replaced by Martin Bormann, with the title 'Head of the Party Chancellory'.

6 June	The *'Kommissarbefehl'* ('Commissar Order') of the Supreme Command of the Wehrmacht provides instructions for the liquidation of Soviet Political Commissars.
22 June	German invasion of the Soviet Union.
17 July	Alfred Rosenberg appointed 'Reich Minister for the Occupied Eastern Territories'.
1 Sept.	German Jews compelled to wear the Yellow Star of David (which Polish Jews had been forced to wear since 23 Nov. 1939).
2 Oct.–5 Dec.	The battle for Moscow brings the failure of the German Blitzkrieg in the east and leads to a crisis in the army leadership which is unprepared for a winter war in the Soviet Union.
14 Oct.	Order to deport Jews from Reich territory to eastern ghettos.
Early Dec.	Mass killing of Jews through use of 'gas vans' begins in Chelmno, Poland.
11 Dec.	German declaration of war on the USA following Japanese attack (7 Dec.) on Pearl Harbor.
16 Dec.	Hitler refuses to allow further German retreat in face of Soviet counter-offensive; army head Walther von Brauchitsch dismissed (19 Dec.); Hitler himself takes over as head of the army.

1942

20 Jan.	'Wannsee Conference' in Berlin to coordinate measures for the 'Final Solution of the Jewish Question'.
8 Feb.	Albert Speer, Hitler's architect, appointed Reich Minister for Armaments and Munition, replacing Fritz Todt, who had been killed in an air crash. German armaments production sharply increases under Speer's direction.
17 March	First mass killings of Jews from ghettos in southern Poland take place in Belzec, marking the beginning of 'Aktion Reinhard': the systematic killing in the extermination camps of Belzec, Sobibor and Treblinka of, especially, Polish Jews, organised by Odilo Globocnik, SS and Police Chief in the Lublin District.
End of March	First transports of Jews from western Europe and from Germany to Auschwitz.
26 April	Hitler obtains approval from Reichstag for supreme judicial powers to override formal law where necessary.
27 May	Assassination attempt on Reinhard Heydrich, head of the Reich Security Head Office, in Prague; he subsequently died on 4 June. On 10 June the German police raze the village of Lidice to the ground as retaliation.
June	Beginning of systematic mass gassings of Jews in Auschwitz-Birkenau.
28 June	German offensive begins in Soviet Union.
July–Aug.	German army advances towards Stalingrad.

24 Sept.	Army Chief of Staff Franz Halder replaced by General Kurt Zeitzler following bitter dispute between Hitler and general staff over army strategy and tactics.
5 Oct.	Himmler orders deportation of all Jews from concentration camps in the Reich to Auschwitz.
23 Oct.	British counter-offensive begins in north Africa.
22 Nov.	German 6th Army of around 250,000 men encircled in the area of Stalingrad.

1943

14–26 Jan.	Roosevelt and Churchill, at Casablanca Conference, demand Germany's 'unconditional surrender'.
31 Jan–2 Feb.	Capitulation of 6th Army in Stalingrad.
18 Feb.	Goebbels' Sportpalast speech proclaims 'total war', in extensive propaganda campaign following the defeat at Stalingrad.
March	Closing of numerous ghettos in the east; survivors taken to the extermination camps; deportations of Dutch Jews to Sobibor.
13 April	Mass graves of thousands of murdered Polish officers discovered at Katyn, near Smolensk.
19 April	Rising in the Warsaw ghetto of the remaining 60,000 Jews after some 300,000 had been taken to the extermination camp at Treblinka; ruthlessly put down by SS and police units, but lasts until 16 May.
13 May	German capitulation in Tunisia.
10 July	Allied landing in Sicily.
5–13 July	German offensive 'Citadel' fails after major tank battles at Kursk, opening way for Soviet advances and recapture of Kiev on 6 Nov.
25 July	Mussolini ousted from power in Italy.
24 Aug.	Reichsführer SS Heinrich Himmler replaces Wilhelm Frick as Reich Minister of the Interior.
10 Sept.	German troops occupy northern Italy after announcement (8 Sept.) of Badoglio government's armistice with the Allies.
15 Sept.	Mussolini freed from his internment by German paratroopers and on 26 Sept. founds 'Fascist Republic' with its capital in Salo but effectively under German military control.
28 Nov.–1 Dec.	Allied Conference in Teheran: agreement in principle of Roosevelt, Churchill and Stalin on a post-war division of Germany.

1944

19 March	German occupation of Hungary.
April–June	Mass deportations of Greek and Hungarian Jews to Auschwitz.
6 June	Allied landing on Normandy coast.

10 June	Units of SS-Panzerdivision 'Das Reich' burn French village of Oradour-sur-Glane to ground, killing 600 inhabitants (including women and children) as retaliation for increased activity of French Résistance.
12 June	First VI missiles fired on British targets.
22 June	Beginning of major Soviet offensive against central German front leads to catastrophic defeats for Wehrmacht.
20 July	Attempted coup d'état fails when Hitler is injured, but not killed, by a bomb in his East Prussian headquarters planted by Oberst Claus Graf Schenk von Stauffenberg. A number of army officers implicated, including Stauffenberg himself, shot on same evening. Widespread arrests and subsequent trials and executions of those involved in the plot follow.
24 July	Majdanek extermination camp liberated by the Red Army.
25 July	Goebbels given sweeping powers to mobilise remaining resources for total war.
31 July	Americans break through near Avranches, leading to rapid reconquest of France.
1 Aug.	Rising of Polish Home Army in Warsaw; forced to surrender on 2 Oct. after Stalin refuses any help.
19 Aug.	Rising of Résistance in Paris leads to armistice in city concluded by German commander, General Dietrich von Choltitz.
25 Aug.	American and French troops (under de Gaulle) enter Paris.
8 Sept.	First V2 rockets launched to bomb London and Antwerp.
25 Sept.	All able-bodied German men between sixteen and sixty years old called to serve in the *Volkssturm*, an ill-equipped and untrained 'people's army'.
16 Oct.	Hungary's ruler Admiral Horthy forced to revoke armistice with Soviet Union and hand over power to leader of fascist Arrow Cross movement Férencz Szálasi.
21 Oct.	Aachen first major German town to be occupied by allied troops.
1 Nov.	Himmler orders ending of gassings in Auschwitz and removal of any traces of killings.
16 Dec.	Hitler begins Ardennes offensive, which enjoys initial successes but then rapidly fails.

1945

12 Jan.	Beginning of major Soviet offensive against German eastern front.
27 Jan.	Remaining 5,000 inmates in Auschwitz liberated by Red Army.
30 Jan.	Last broadcast speech by Hitler.
4–11 Feb.	Yalta Conference of allied leaders; deliberations on post-war settlement; as regards Germany, Stalin, Churchill and Roosevelt agree to inclusion of France as fourth occupying power.

7 March	American troops cross the Rhine at Remagen.
19 March	Hitler's 'Nero order' to destroy all industrial plant to prevent it falling into enemy hands; Speer contrives in the following weeks to block, for the most part, the implementation of the order.
11 April	Buchenwald concentration camp (outside Weimar) handed over by remaining prisoners to American troops after guards had fled.
13 April	Red Army takes Vienna.
15 April	British troops liberate Bergen-Belsen concentration camp.
16 April	Beginning of battle for Berlin.
25 April	American and Soviet troops meet up at Torgau on the Elbe.
28 April	Mussolini captured by Italian partisans and shot.
29 April	Hitler's will stipulates Admiral Dönitz as his successor as head of state and exhorts the German people to continued 'merciless opposition' to 'international Jewry'.
30 April	Hitler commits suicide in the bunker of the Reich Chancellory in Berlin.
2 May	The Red Army takes Berlin.
7–9 May	German capitulation in the US headquarters in Reims, repeated in the Soviet headquarters in Berlin.

Abbreviations

BAK   Bundesarchiv Koblenz.

BVP   Bayerische Volkspartei (Bavarian People's Party).

DBS   *Deutschland-Berichte der Sozialdemokratischen Partei Deutschlands, 1934–1940*, 7 vols, Frankfurt am Main, 1980.

DDP   Deutsche Demokratische Partei (German Democratic Party).

DNVP   Deutschnationale Volkspartei (German National People's Party).

DVP   Deutsche Volkspartei (German People's Party).

Gestapo   Geheime Staatspolizei (Secret State Police).

IMG   *Der Prozeß gegen die Hauptkriegsverbrecher vor dem Internationalen Militärgerichtshof*, 42 vols, Nuremberg, 1947–9.

JK   Eberhard Jäckel and Axel Kuhn (eds.), *Hitler. Sämtliche Aufzeichnungen 1905–1924*, Stuttgart, 1980.

KPD   Kommunistische Partei Deutschlands (Communist Party of Germany).

MK   Adolf Hitler, *Mein Kampf*, 85–94th edn, Munich, 1934.

MK Watt   Adolf Hitler, *Mein Kampf*, London, 1969, trans. by Ralph Mannheim, with an introduction by D. C. Watt.

N&P   Jeremy Noakes and Geoffrey Pridham (eds.), *Nazism 1919–1945: A Documentary Reader*, 4 vols, Exeter, 1983–98.

NSDAP   Nationalsozialistische Deutsche Arbeiterpartei (National Socialist German Workers' Party).

SA   Sturmabteilung (Storm Troop).

SD   Sicherheitsdienst (Security Service).

SPD   Sozialdemokratische Partei Deutschlands (Social Democratic Party of Germany).

SS   Schutzstaffeln (Protection Squads).

Index

Page numbers in italics denote illustration/caption